A critical introduction to phonology

Of sound, mind, and body

Continuum Critical Introductions to Linguistics

Series Editor: Ken Lodge, University of East Anglia

Continuum Critical Introductions to Linguistics are comprehensive introductions to core areas in linguistics. The introductions are original and approach the subject from unique and different perspectives. Using contemporary examples and analogies, these books seek to explain complicated issues in an accessible way. The books prompt critical thinking about each core area, and are a radical departure from traditional, staid introductions to the subject. Written by key academics in each field who are not afraid to be controversial, each book will be essential reading for undergraduate students.

Titles in the series:

A Critical Introduction to Phonology
Of Sound, Mind, and Body
Daniel Silverman

A Critical Introduction to Phonetics
Ken Lodge

A critical introduction to phonology

Of sound, mind, and body

Daniel Silverman

continuum
LONDON • NEW YORK

Continuum
The Tower Building
11 York Road
London SE1 7NX

15 East 26th Street
New York
NY10010

British Library Cataloguing-in-Publication Data
A catalogue record for this book is available from the British Library.

ISBN: HB: 0-8264-8660-6
PB: 0-8264-8661-4

Library of Congress Cataloging-in-Publication Data

Typeset by Fakenham Photosetting Limited, Fakenham, Norfolk

Contents

Dedication		vi
Acknowledgments		vii
Preface	I speak from my heart	viii
Part One	I speak with my mouth	1
Chapter One	Three types of sound substitution	3
Chapter Two	Contrastive sound substitution	31
Part Two	I speak my mind	59
Chapter Three	Neutralizing sound substitution	61
Chapter Four	Allophonic sound substitution	87
Chapter Five	Variation and probability	114
Chapter Six	The pull of phonetics; the push of phonology	158
Part Three	I speak therefore you are	189
Chapter Seven	*Parlo ergo es*	191
Appendix	Primer of phonetic rudiments	222
Glossary		255
Index		259

Dedication

To my mom

Here's one of the many reasons why:

The scene: our living room, early evening in Chautauqua, summer 2000. My mom is sitting on the couch reading the *Times*.

Me (entering from outside):
Ok Mom, I have a pronouncement:
Religion is for children!
Philosophy is for adolescents!
But *science* is for *adults*!

My mom (looking up from the paper):

Dan, *pronouncements* are for *children*.

Acknowledgments

Large portions of this work were conceived and written in 2002, while I was a Fellow at Edinburgh University's Institute for Advanced Studies in the Humanities. In Edinburgh, I am very grateful to Anthea Taylor, Donald Ferguson and John Frow at the Institute, to my good friend and colleague Mircea Itu for great times at restaurants and the pub, to Russell Stewart Fountain who lived across the Crescent, to Michael Conway who took me up the hill, and especially to lifelong friends Gary, Karen and Rosie (and now Duncan) Biggar who were always there for me. Thanks also to Arpad Hornyak, Bob Ladd, Benjamin Platts-Mills, Jim Scobbie and Ivan Yuen, and to Viktor Tron for his astonishingly careful reading of an early draft of this book, and for all the great discussions at the Blind Poet and elsewhere. I am very much indebted to you, Viktor.

The remainder of this work was written in New York in the latter half of 2004 and into 2005, where I was a fellow of the more mundane variety. Back in the states, Naomi Gurevich, Gary Linebaugh and Margaret Russell provided me with invaluable assistance and genuine friendship. Special thanks to Devin Casenhiser, whose big brain is matched by his big heart.

For additional comments on portions large and small, and/or for general support, I am grateful to Ree Adler, Phil Carr, Dan Everett, Dong-Bo Hsu, Keith Johnson, Peter Ladefoged, Jerry Levinson, Ken Lodge, Jenny Lovel, Paul Mathews, John Ohala, Kevin Ryan, Michal Schnaider Beeri, Steve Scher, Helaine Silverman, Paul Silverman and Richard Wright.

Endless thanks to my way cool bro, Jeremy Silverman, who provided me with two – count them, two – toothcomb edits of this work. Jer, you're an honorary linguist in my book (is that a compliment?).

Of course, thanks to Jie Zhang and Lois Leardi.

There are many other individuals who have influenced my thinking, helped me maintain my enthusiasm, or otherwise aided, abetted and inspired from afar. Among them are Neil Babitch, Ian Buruma, Frederick C. Crews, Terrence Rafferty, Ira Robbins, Tim Smith, Jeff Starrs and Hans Vandenburg.

And if anyone wants to know what my life was like after leaving the wonderful Department of Linguistics at UCLA in 1997 until returning to wonderful New York in 2004, just ask Theodore Roszak!

Preface
I speak from my heart

This book on phonology can be read not only by linguists, but also by philosophers, anthropologists, psychologists, evolutionary biologists and computer scientists. It's been my experience that experts in these fields often harbour a passing interest in linguistics, but quickly hit a brick wall when trying to penetrate the theoretical intricacies of the discipline. This book is written with these scholars very much in mind, because the approach espoused herein does not call upon the reader to make any concessions to the particularism that dominates mainstream linguistic theory. My hope is to establish a dialogue with these scholars by levelling the playing field: phonology, when done right, is *not* the exclusive domain of linguists, but should be open to all who can make a contribution to our thinking. In turn, experts in other fields might find that we phonologists can make a contribution to theirs.

The book espouses a theory of phonology that is interdisciplinary in scope. Phonetic theory is featured quite prominently, but both evolutionary biology (as metaphor) and cognitive psychology make significant appearances as well. Phonology herein is viewed as a self-organized and self-sustaining system of social conventions that passively evolves as a consequence of language *use*. Due to the limited variation that is inherent in speech production, phonological systems are at once sufficiently stable to fulfil their communicative function and sufficiently variable to be under constant – if slow-going – modification. Systemic changes are often the consequence of the communicative success or failure of the word variants that we use. Successful speech propagates; today's spontaneous, unplanned innovation may become tomorrow's new norm. An indebtedness to Darwin's theory of evolution by natural selection should be apparent even to the most casual of readers.

As the book assumes no previous knowledge of either phonology or linguistics in general, it may even be of interest to the general reading public. If you can make it past Chapter Two – the most difficult chapter in the book – then the remainder may prove quite accessible and, dare I say, enjoyable.

For students of phonology, the content of this book may help to hone their analytical skills. It might help solidify their own inclinations on the subject, or better, it might instead help them 'liquefy' their thinking, giving them the impetus to ask their professors some challenging questions, or to rethink certain received notions as they embark on writing their dissertations.

For established scholars who teach phonology, this book may serve as a supplement or an alternative to mainstream books. Thinking positively, I envision much constructive class discussion emerging. Phonologists will be quick to note my indebtedness to a number of schools of linguistic thought. The Kazan School is featured quite prominently, but strong traces of both The Prague School and American Structuralism are present as well. The influence of the Generative School should be obvious, since rule-based and constraint-based analyses are featured, albeit reconceptualized as generalizations about sound change. Finally, the phonological theories of John Ohala served as a constant source of inspiration.

So if this book is for established experts, for students of phonology, for experts in other fields, and also for absolute beginners, then I guess this book is for *everybody*. Ah, would that it were true! Truth is, phonology isn't easy (and over the years, I've noticed that some people find it a tad esoteric...): it focuses on the most obscure minutiae of the most everyday and natural of topics, spoken language. It requires patience, concentration and, most importantly, an ability to wipe clean one's subjective feelings about the language that one uses, and to place in their stead a rigorous objectivity. But phonology is not the exclusive domain of linguists or academics. It *can* be understood and appreciated by anyone who is ready to expend a little effort.

New York
March, 2005

A note on fonts

All phonetic transcriptions are written in IPA, the International Phonetic Alphabet, and are enclosed in square brackets. As new symbols are introduced in the text, they are noted, and their basic articulatory and acoustic characteristics are usually discussed. Still, for beginners, there will be a lot to internalize. For readers unfamiliar with the IPA, it is discussed in some detail in the Appendix. I also provide the full IPA chart at the end of this section (Figure 1).*

* Unless otherwise noted, English transcriptions are intended to represent standard American pronunciation.

THE INTERNATIONAL PHONETIC ALPHABET (revised to 1993, corrected 1996)

CONSONANTS (PULMONIC)

	Bilabial	Labiodental	Dental	Alveolar	Postalveolar	Retroflex	Palatal	Velar	Uvular	Pharyngeal	Glottal
Plosive	p b			t d		ʈ ɖ	c ɟ	k g	q ɢ		ʔ
Nasal	m	ɱ		n		ɳ	ɲ	ŋ	ɴ		
Trill	ʙ			r					ʀ		
Tap or Flap				ɾ		ɽ					
Fricative	ɸ β	f v	θ ð	s z	ʃ ʒ	ʂ ʐ	ç ʝ	x ɣ	χ ʁ	ħ ʕ	h ɦ
Lateral fricative				ɬ ɮ							
Approximant		ʋ		ɹ		ɻ	j	ɰ			
Lateral approximant				l		ɭ	ʎ	ʟ			

Where symbols appear in pairs, the one to the right represents a voiced consonant. Shaded areas denote articulations judged impossible.

CONSONANTS (NON-PULMONIC)

Clicks	Voiced implosives	Ejectives
ʘ Bilabial	ɓ Bilabial	ʼ Examples:
ǀ Dental	ɗ Dental/alveolar	pʼ Bilabial
ǃ (Post)alveolar	ʄ Palatal	tʼ Dental/Alveolar
ǂ Palatoalveolar	ɠ Velar	kʼ Velar
ǁ Alveolar lateral	ʛ Uvular	sʼ Alveolar fricative

VOWELS

	Front	Central	Back
Close	i • y	ɨ • ʉ	ɯ • u
	ɪ ʏ		ʊ
Close-mid	e • ø	ɘ • ɵ	ɤ • o
		ə	
Open-mid	ɛ • œ	ɜ • ɞ	ʌ • ɔ
	æ	ɐ	
Open	a • ɶ		ɑ • ɒ

Where symbols appear in pairs, the one to the right represents a rounded vowel.

OTHER SYMBOLS

ʍ Voiceless labial-velar fricative

w Voiced labial-velar approximant

ɥ Voiced labial-palatal approximant

ʜ Voiceless epiglottal fricative

ʢ Voiced epiglottal fricative

ʡ Epiglottal plosive

ɕ ʑ Alveolo-palatal fricatives

ɺ Alveolar lateral flap

ɧ Simultaneous ʃ and x

Affricates and double articulations can be represented by two symbols joined by a tie bar if necessary. k͡p t͡s

SUPRASEGMENTALS

ˈ Primary stress

ˌ Secondary stress ˌfoʊnəˈtɪʃən

ː Long eː

ˑ Half-long eˑ

˘ Extra-short ĕ

| Minor (foot) group

‖ Major (intonation) group

. Syllable break ɹi.ækt

‿ Linking (absence of a break)

DIACRITICS Diacritics may be placed above a symbol with a descender, e. g. ŋ̊

˳ Voiceless n̥ d̥	¨ Breathy voiced b̤ a̤	̪ Dental t̪ d̪
ˬ Voiced s̬ t̬	˜ Creaky voiced b̰ a̰	̺ Apical t̺ d̺
ʰ Aspirated tʰ dʰ	̼ Linguolabial t̼ d̼	̻ Laminal t̻ d̻
̹ More rounded ɔ̹	ʷ Labialized tʷ dʷ	˜ Nasalized ẽ
̜ Less rounded ɔ̜	ʲ Palatalized tʲ dʲ	ⁿ Nasal release dⁿ
̟ Advanced u̟	ˠ Velarized tˠ dˠ	ˡ Lateral release dˡ
̠ Retracted e̠	ˤ Pharyngealized tˤ dˤ	̚ No audible release d̚
¨ Centralized ë	~ Velarized or Pharyngealized ɫ	
ˣ Mid-centralized e̽	˔ Raised e̝ (ɹ̝ = voiced alveolar fricative)	
̩ Syllabic n̩	˕ Lowered e̞ (β̞ = voiced bilabial approximant)	
̯ Non-syllabic e̯	̘ Advanced Tongue Root e̘	
˞ Rhoticity ə˞ a˞	̙ Retracted Tongue Root e̙	

TONES AND WORD ACCENTS

LEVEL	CONTOUR
e̋ or ˥ Extra high	ě or ˩˥ Rising
é ˦ High	ê ˥˩ Falling
ē ˧ Mid	e᷄ ˦˥ High rising
è ˨ Low	e᷅ ˩˨ Low rising
ȅ ˩ Extra low	e᷈ ˧˦˧ Rising-falling
ꜜ Downstep	↗ Global rise
ꜛ Upstep	↘ Global fall

Figure 1 The IPA chart

Important terms are usually written in italics when they are introduced. Most of these terms also have glossary entries. Experts will be very quick to notice that I occasionally modify standard definitions: I narrow the definition of *neutralization*; I broaden the definitions of *allophony, sound substitution* and *sound change*; I reconfigure the definition of *bi-uniqueness*, all in service to my approach to phonology. I also use italics for emphasis, to add some orthographic intonation to the text. Finally, conclusions or assertions that are especially pithy, pointed or provocative are written in italics as well.

Quotation marks are usually used for terms whose standard definitions or whose very value as theoretically relevant notions I call into question, for example 'phonologization'. I suppose these might be regarded as scare quotes. I also use quotation marks for the English translation of foreign languages.

Language occupies a completely isolated place in the realm of nature: it is a combination of physiological and acoustic phenomena governed by physical laws, and of unconscious and psychical phenomena governed by laws of an entirely different kind. This fact leads us to a most important question: what is the relation ... between the physical principle and the unconscious and psychical principle?

Mikołaj Kruszewski, 1881

Part 1
I speak with my mouth

1 Three types of sound substitution

Setting the scene

When I was little my father and I sometimes played a game called Jotto. To play Jotto, each of us would secretly write down a five-letter word, and then take turns guessing what the other person wrote. After each guess the other player would report the number of letters that appeared in his original word. For example, my father might write down 'sport', S-P-O-R-T. If I guessed 'brick', B-R-I-C-K, he'd say 'one', because only one of the letters in 'brick' – the 'R' – appears in his word 'sport'. Although my next guess could be a word with a whole new batch of letters, a conservative strategy was to find a word with only a single letter different from the previous guess. For example, if I next guessed 'trick', T-R-I-C-K, my father would have answered 'two', because two of the letters in this word, 'T' and 'R', appear in his word. At this point, I could safely conclude that 'T' is in his word, that 'B' is not in his word, and that one of the remaining four letters of 'R', 'I', 'C' and 'K' is also in his word. By systematically eliminating certain letters, and systematically determining the presence of others, the alphabet could eventually be whittled down to just a few letters out of which the right word could be spelled. The first person to guess the other's word would win.

This book is about phonology – the study of linguistic sound systems. Broadly speaking, whereas *phonetics* explores the *physical* aspects of speech, *phonology* explores its *functional* aspects. Both disciplines thus explore speech patterns, but to rather different – if highly interdependent – ends. Phonologists are primarily concerned with documenting *sound substitutions* – the replacement of one sound with another. In Jotto, you replace one letter with another letter to give you a new word. In spoken language, it is the replacement of one *sound* with another that serves this same function. While letters are intended to represent sounds, we all know that the English writing system is far from perfect in this respect. In fact, we'll soon see that the English writing system serves to confound our understanding of the true nature of the English sound system.

Investigating sound substitutions is one of the primary tasks of phonologists because of the functional consequences that these substitutions have for word meaning. As in the 'brick'–'trick' example, we see that sound substitutions can change the meaning of a word. Substituting one sound for another is a very efficient way to create many words from the sounds that we produce with our vocal tracts, and so it's no accident that phonological systems have evolved this property. But, as we'll soon see, some sound substitutions *eliminate* a distinction in word meaning that existed before the substitution, and other sound substitutions take place without changing a word's meaning.

In my childhood I also played a game that was quite similar to Jotto, called Mastermind. Instead of five-letter words, Mastermind uses pegs of six colours. Your secret code is any combination of four pegs, say, Yellow–Black–Red–Green (but you can use colours more than once if you want to). The logical strategy of Jotto applies in the same way with Mastermind: take an initial guess about the code of your opponent, get feedback, and modify your next guess accordingly. The feedback in Mastermind is a bit more detailed than it is in Jotto, because you're told how many pegs are positioned correctly in your row of four, in addition to how many are merely present. However, Mastermind is a much less interesting game conceptually, because there are no constraints on what sorts of colour sequences might be used. Every guess could minimally alter the previous one by replacing one colour with another, or by minimally altering the sequence: I could follow a guess Red–Blue–White–Green with *Black*–Blue–White–Green, or maybe *Blue–Red*–White–Green. By contrast, in Jotto you can't necessarily replace any one letter with another to directly test your hypothesis. Since your tests are constrained by English spelling, you can minimally alter your next guess only if the result is also a well-formed word. So sometimes circuitous trial-and-error routes are required to isolate the correct letters. For example, when I played Jotto, I could never change B-R-I-C-K to, say, B-N-I-C-K, to test for 'R' and 'N', because 'bnick' isn't a word of English; the language has no words that start with 'B-N'. In fact, you can't make any word out of those five letters, so you have to try a different strategy. This constraint on letter sequences and combinations adds a significant level of sophistication and challenge to Jotto, and makes it a much better game than Mastermind, which has no restrictions on sequences and combinations.

So, whereas Mastermind players are fully unconstrained, Jotto players must operate in accordance with letter-sequential or combinatorial constraints. But what might be the *origin* of these constraints in Jotto? Did I have unconscious knowledge of some sort of spelling constraint that prohibited words from starting with 'B-N', and is this constraint the reason why I would never even think to guess 'bnick'? I don't think so. A simpler and more straightforward reason for rejecting 'bnick' as a guess in Jotto is that I just didn't know any word spelled B-N-I-C-K. Since I didn't know such a word, it would never even occur to me to use it as my next guess. In Jotto, the constraint isn't a matter of 'B-N-I-C-K violates the spelling rules of English'. It's simply that 'there's no English word spelled that way'; good guesses in Jotto are constrained only by our experience and familiarity with reading and writing English. So there isn't a *structural* constraint on possible Jotto guesses. Rather, there's an *experiential* constraint based on my knowledge and use of actual English words. By contrast, sequences of coloured pegs are totally arbitrary to me. One sequence is as good or as bad as the next. Since sequences of coloured pegs serve no function in my life, I have no greater or lesser experience or familiarity with any particular combination of them.

Phonology is more like Jotto than like Mastermind, but not merely because Jotto deals with actual words of language while Mastermind doesn't. Rather, just as in Jotto, there's an experience-based constraint on what sounds can be substituted for what other sounds. In phonology, just as in Jotto, the constraint is very simple, almost trivial: the replacement of one sound with another always results in a sound sequence that can be paired with a particular *meaning* that is shared by speakers and their speech communities. For example, in English, the difference between, say, 'fit' and 'pit' resides in the first sound of each word. Both 'fit' and 'pit' are words of English; they mean different things for a speaker of English. Sound replacements that change meaning are known as *contrastive* sound substitutions. English speakers never engage in a sound substitution if the results aren't meaningful, that is, if the resulting form is not a word of English. The sound substitutions that we employ are strictly constrained, but – contrary to the beliefs of many linguists – I believe that sound substitutions are not governed by a system of rules or constraints on good form. We never substitute an 'n' for the 'r' in 'brick', but not because the result would violate English rules or constraints on sound sequences. Instead, we don't say 'bnick' simply because we never learned to pair that sound sequence with a particular meaning, and so it's not English – it serves no linguistic function.

Before continuing, let me clarify something. When I say that speakers engage in sound substitutions, I do not mean this in any *procedural* sense, like the way someone plays Jotto. Speakers don't start with one word, and then change that word into another by replacing – or adding and/or subtracting – sounds. Rather, when I use the term 'sound substitution' I am simply offering a helpful characterization of the patterns that phonologists take note of as they document speech. But these substitutions should not be regarded as a result of a *process*. Focusing on sound substitutions of the 'brick'–'trick' sort helps to reveal the remarkable systematicity that is present in linguistic sound systems, but this doesn't mean that this characterization genuinely reflects the cognitive organization of the sound system itself. Some linguists, including me, suspect that we should treat many of the individual sounds that we might extract from the speech signal as *convenient fictions*: they might lack genuine structural status as individual elements, but they make the job of discussing phonological patterns much easier.

Now, among non-existent sound sequences in English, some certainly sound better than others. For example, 'blick' sounds better than 'bnick', even though neither is a word. If some non-words *feel* better or worse than others, how can I say that the only relevant distinction to be made is whether the sound sequence is an actual word or not? Many phonologists – though not I – think that 'blick' is a *possible* word because it doesn't violate any sound-sequencing constraints of English, except that it just happens to be missing, and so it feels okay. These phonologists propose that 'bnick', by contrast, involves a genuine violation of an unconscious sound-sequencing constraint, and so it sounds awful to English ears. Such a constraint might strictly prohibit English words starting with the sound sequence 'bn'.

But such an approach, flawed when applied to Jotto, is just as flawed when applied to English. When I speak English, every sound substitution is always one word or another. There are no relevant *feelings* on my part about whether the sound substitution is good or not. They are all good, because they are all English. So if 'blick' feels good, and 'bnick' doesn't, parallel sorts of feelings are nowhere to be found when we compare real words. Does it even make sense to ask whether the word 'brick' feels better than the word 'trick'? Even if some people have an intuition on the matter, would their feelings somehow teach us anything about linguistic sound structure? I maintain that *we can't determine the structural properties of linguistic sound systems based on how people feel about the sounds they use.* This has been stated quite emphatically by the scholars Bernard Bloch and George L. Trager. Writing in 1942, they assert that 'The ordinary speaker of English, we are told ... "feels" or "conceives of" the two [l]s in "little" as "the same sound". This may or may not be true; if true, it is an interesting fact, but it can never be used by the linguist as a criterion for his classifications, or even as a proof that he has classified correctly'. Bloch and Trager continue: 'The native speaker's feeling about sounds or about anything else is inaccessible to investigation by the techniques of linguistic science, and any appeal to it is a plain evasion of the linguist's proper function. The linguist is concerned solely with the facts of speech. The psychological correlates of these facts are undoubtedly important; but the linguist has no means – as a linguist – of analyzing them'.

Just out of curiosity though, what can we say about the feelings engendered by 'blick' versus 'bnick'? Since we can't assign meanings to these two sound sequences when we speak them, we can only treat these spoken forms as non-linguistic sound signals. What we have to do, then, is compare the purely physical properties of 'blick', which we transcribe phonetically as [b̥lɪk], and those of 'bnick', which we transcribe [b̥nɪk], to the inventory of English words that we have in our heads. Let's be systematic about it. Let's take each major subpart of the speech signal of these two words – as represented by the phonetic symbols employed – and see if there are any English words that share these properties. The lists in Table 1.1 include every substring of the component sounds of 'blick' and 'bnick'. Beginnings and ends of words are indicated by cross-hatching, '#'. Sequences that are found in English words are accompanied by some examples.

For [b̥lɪk], there are many perfectly good English words that also have these sound sequences, and so every subpart of the form sounds familiar to an English speaker. The one exception, of course, is the complete form [b̥lɪk], which we already know isn't a word at all, although English speakers are indeed familiar with its occurrence as a possible sequence (if not a complete word) in other languages, for example Hans Blix ([b̥lɪks]).

The case of [b̥nɪk] is quite different. Look at the blanks in the list for [b̥nɪk]. These gaps have one thing in common: in English, there is an overall absence of words starting with [b̥n]. When I hear [b̥nɪk], I

Table 1.1 Subsequences of [b̥lɪk] and [b̥nɪk]

[b̥lɪk]	*Examples*	[b̥nɪk]	*Examples*
#[b̥...]	bean, birth	#[b̥...]	bean, birth
#[b̥l...]	blend, blue	#[b̥n...]	
#[b̥lɪ...]	blimp, blister	#[b̥nɪ...]	
#[b̥lɪk]#		#[b̥nɪk]#	
[...lɪ...]	clip, slit	[...nɪ...]	snicker, catnip
[...lɪk]#	slick, lick	[...nɪk]#	nick, picnic
[...ɪk]#	sick, kick	[...ɪk]#	sick, kick
[...k]#	folk, lock	[...k]#	folk, lock

can't think of any words that start with that sequence of sounds. So 'blick' feels okay, because every partial sequence of sounds is fine in English. But 'bnick' sounds terrible, because several of these sequences are never found in English ([b̥n], [b̥nɪ], [b̥nɪk]). Maybe, just maybe, some pronunciations of 'banana' or 'benevolence' begin with [b̥n] when speaking fast. If so, [b̥n] is not completely absent, but instead is just very rare indeed. But does this mean, again – and as many phonologists actually believe – that somewhere in my brain I have an inventory of sound-sequencing constraints, one of which forbids [b̥n] at the beginning of words? No, it doesn't. All it means is that there are no English words pronounced this way (bananas aside), just as in Jotto, where there are no words *spelled* that way.

So, any feelings we might have about what is a good word, a possible word, or an impossible word, merely reveal the limits of our linguistic experience, and nothing more. Tellingly, there might be a few words that really *do* feel funny. For example, every New Yorker knows that a knish [kʰnɪʃ] is a savoury potato or kasha pastry, but [kʰn] really does feel a bit off, even to us New Yorkers. Does English have a rule that says 'no [kʰn] at the beginning of words'? Obviously not, because we have 'knish', which is, albeit, a Yiddish loan. Rather, it's just that [kʰn]-initial words are very rarely encountered. In fact, English used to have sequences like [kʰn] and [g̥n], as indicated in the spelling of 'knee' [kʰni] and 'gnat' [g̥næt], but they fell out of the language about 300 years ago. So nowadays, since we have so little experience with such words, they sound funny.

Actually, there is another possible objection to my account for our different feelings for 'bnick' versus 'blick': maybe 'bnick' is more difficult to pronounce, and so it sounds strange to us. Well, this is simply not the case. I can very easily close my lips for the [b̥], and then lift my tongue tip while letting air flow out my nose for the [n]. Making these sounds in sequence is no problem at all, especially since the two sounds are made with parts of the mouth that function independently from each other: there's no reason that the transition from the [b̥] to the [n] should pose any articulatory difficulties whatsoever. I can even think of a few examples in English that have [b̥n] in the middle of the word: 'Abner', 'obnoxious', 'abnormal', 'hobnob'. So [b̥n] is not more difficult to say than [b̥l]. If you do think 'bnick' is difficult to pronounce, it's probably because you have practically no experience in making the [b̥n] sequence at the beginning of a word, and not because of any intrinsic difficulty.

As for sequences like [b̥n], [kʰn] and [g̥n] at the beginning of words, it turns out that it is hard to clearly *hear* sounds like [b̥], [k] or [g̥] in this context. Such *auditory* facts might explain why some sequences survive and flourish over generations of speakers, while others are extinguished or never arise. The rarity or absence of some sound sequences and the prevalence of others are important for phonologists to take note of, and have to do with a very complex interaction, over generations of speakers, between the physical properties of sound, sound perception, and, yes, speech production (hence the subtitle of this book). Indeed, much of the discussion that follows is devoted to motivating the prevalence of some sounds and sound sequences in comparison to others. But the important point for now is that *our effortless mastery of English sound substitutions derives from familiarity and experience with English words themselves, and not from a mentally-compiled list of sound-sequential rules or constraints on what constitutes a good word of English.*

Three types of sound substitution

If we think about the situation logically, the sound substitutions that we observe in English, or in any language, are limited to only three functional types. In *contrastive* sound substitution, word meaning is *changed* (as in the case of 'brick'–'trick'). There are, in addition, two types of *non*-contrastive sound substitution. In *neutralizing* sound substitution, the substitution of one sound with another results in two words sounding exactly the same, and so phonetic evidence for their distinction in meaning is eliminated. For example, as we discuss in the next section, when you say 'phone book', 'phone' often comes out sounding exactly like 'foam'. In *allophonic* sound substitution, the substitution of one sound with another does *not* change the meaning of the word: the meaning remains the same even after the sound substitution. For example, as discussed below in detail, the last sound of the word 'invite' is pronounced differently when you say 'invite someone' compared to when you say 'invite anyone', yet both pronunciations have the same meaning. (Recall that language is more like Jotto than like Mastermind; we only engage in sound substitutions that have functional relevance, and so logical possibilities that are not real words are not relevant to our discussion.)

These two additional types of sound substitution inevitably sabotage what we might call *bi-uniqueness* between sound and meaning. If phonological systems had the property of bi-uniqueness, then each sound sequence which makes up a word would uniquely match up with a single meaning, and each meaning would uniquely match up with a single sound sequence. But no language has this property. Instead, there is inevitably a one-to-many relation between sound and meaning (neutralization), and also a many-to-one relation between sound and meaning (allophony). (All languages also have homophones that are not a consequence of sound substitutions, but instead are words with different meanings that simply are pronounced the same way, like English 'dear' and 'deer', for example.) Non-bi-uniqueness due to sound substitution creates a remarkable complexity in sound–meaning relations that has often stymied linguists in their understanding of the relevant structural properties of language, but non-bi-uniqueness *never* stymies children as they are learning their language. So let's consider each of the three types of sound substitution in turn, to try to get a handle on their basic attributes.

1. Contrastive sound substitution

First, a sound substitution can change the meaning of a word. Our Jotto example has shown this quite clearly and intuitively. We can substitute the first sound in 'brick', which we transcribe [b̥ɹɪk], with the first sound in 'trick', which we transcribe [tʰɹ̥ɪk]. The result of this sound substitution is a change in word meaning. The specific change in meaning is not important for our purposes. The fact that [b̥ɹɪk] usually refers to a block of stone or concrete, and [tʰɹ̥ɪk] can be a prank or a ploy, is only incidental. The important point is that each form corresponds to a different meaning, regardless of the particular meanings involved. Given the words 'brick' and 'trick', we can conclude that [b̥] and [tʰ] are contrastive in the context [__ɹɪk]. That is, substituting [tʰ] for [b̥] in the context [__ɹɪk] results in a change of word meaning. But for now, that's all we can conclude about the relationship between [b̥] and [tʰ]. We can't yet conclude that [b̥] and [tʰ] are contrastive in any other context (although further investigation will very quickly show that they do indeed contrast in many other contexts as well, for example, 'back'–'tack', 'best'–'test'). In order to determine the extent to which [b̥] and [tʰ] can be substituted for each other, phonologists have to look at many other words, and other sound contexts. For example, in English [tʰ] is never substituted for [b̥] in 'block'. Indeed, further investigation would reveal that [tʰ] never precedes [l̥] at the beginning of an English word.

Interestingly, we can substitute one sound for another rather effortlessly on demand, by *consciously* manipulating our speech sounds. For example, if I ask you to take the word 'brick' and substitute a 't' for the 'b', you can perform the task effortlessly, and give me 'trick'. Some linguists argue that our ability to consciously manipulate speech sounds on demand opens a window onto the genuine structural properties of linguistic sound systems. That is, our intuitions about speech sounds, and our ability to consciously manipulate these speech sounds, provide evidence of these sounds' status as linguistically significant phonological entities. But just as *our feelings about language* are extremely unreliable with respect to offering insight into linguistic sound structure, *our ability to consciously manipulate speech sounds provides us with no insight whatsoever about linguistic sound structure*. When we play with our language, there is no reason to assume that the elements we are manipulating are the genuine building blocks of the sound system.

In fact, our ability to consciously manipulate speech sounds does not derive from our implicit knowledge of English phonology at all. Rather, it derives from our *explicit* knowledge of the orthographic (writing) system we use to visually (or tactually, in the case of Braille) represent language. English uses an alphabetic writing system in which each symbol loosely – though quite imperfectly – represents a contrastive sound of the language. As we master our writing system, we know that switching a letter typically results in a change of sound, and – most importantly – typically results in a change of word meaning: replacing the 'B' in B-R-I-C-K with a 'T' gives us another word, T-R-I-C-K. Remember that this is *explicit* knowledge, not implicit. We are *taught* the alphabet, and how we can use it as a tool to represent the sounds and words of English. As a consequence of this explicit learning, we can apply the alphabetic principle in order to understand how sound substitutions might change word meaning. The claim, then, is that our ability to substitute sounds on demand does not provide evidence for the cognitive organization of language, and so it does not establish a direct link between *our intuitions about sound structure* and *the genuine structural properties* of our phonological system.

How have researchers come to this conclusion? It turns out that illiterates do *not* have the same skills and intuitions about contrastive sound substitutions that come so effortlessly to you and me. For example, illiterate Portuguese fishermen have a great deal of difficulty substituting one sound for another when asked to do so by an experimenter, by swapping a sound, or adding or subtracting a sound. Where you and I can effortlessly chop off the first sound of a word and replace it with another if asked to do so, these illiterate fishermen have difficulty even understanding the task. We might conclude, therefore, that our ability to manipulate speech sounds in this fashion is largely dependent – perhaps *solely* dependent – on our familiarity with an alphabetic writing system.

But, of course, these fishermen were illiterate. Illiteracy may stem from two broad sources: a lack of formal education and/or some sort of learning disability. It certainly might be the case that they were illiterate not because of a lack of formal education, but, instead, because of an inability to learn how to read. Perhaps this inability is also responsible for their failing to learn the sound-substitution task. A number of clever experimentalists have examined this hypothesis, and have devised a rather straightforward method to test it. These researchers have given a similar sound-substitution task to educated adults who are fully literate in a writing system that is not alphabetic in nature. In Chinese, for example, each symbol, or character, represents a whole word, and contains absolutely no information about the component sounds that combine to form the phonetic quality of the word. (There is, typically, some phonetic information that is encoded in a Chinese character, but it is never of the alphabetic sort. Instead, it encodes information about the phonetic quality of the form as a whole. For example, 花, 哗 and 华 all mean different things, but all sound like [xwa] in the Mandarin dialect, as they all have the component '化', a character on its own, which also sounds like [xwa]; [x] is the sound at the end of 'Bach'.) When literate, educated Chinese adults (who have no knowledge of an alphabetic writing system) are asked by an experimenter to perform a sound-substitution task, in fact, just like the illiterate Portuguese fishermen, they can't do it! So, one's ability to manipulate speech sounds is clearly unrelated to general intelligence and instead is rooted in the explicit learning of an alphabetic writing system. Consequently, the ability to manipulate these 'building block'-like sounds in these sorts of language tasks cannot be taken as evidence for their relevance at the linguistic level.

Allow me to make this point in a more concrete way. I lived in China for a few years, teaching conversational English to graduate students at a prestigious university in Shanghai. Sometimes, when meeting with my students, they would need to consult a Chinese–English dictionary to find an English word they didn't know. Since Chinese is not written alphabetically, you might wonder how dictionaries are organized. Most are organized by 'stroke'-order, where a stroke is one of the dots or lines that, combined with others, forms a complete character. For example, 止 has four strokes, 怍 has eight, and 檸 has eighteen. By learning a few simple rules of stroke ordering (which all Chinese do when they learn to read and write), looking up words in the dictionary becomes as simple as it is for you and me. However, some Chinese–English dictionaries are organized by a Roman alphabetic system, called 'hanyu pinyin' ('Chinese spell-sound'). In school, young students learn this alphabet to jump-start their learning of Chinese characters, which take years to master. But the hanyu pinyin system quickly falls into disuse during the course of education. (Importantly, the aforementioned literate adults had no training in hanyu pinyin.) Now, when my students used a dictionary organized by the hanyu pinyin system, they would slowly and laboriously mouth each of the component sounds of the word in their effort to determine its spelling, because they had so precious little familiarity with an alphabetic writing system, and so were never called upon to break words down into smaller, sound-based units. I confess that I used to get impatient with them, because I knew I could find the word much more quickly than they could, even though they were using a Chinese-to-English dictionary. It's not that I was more intelligent than they were – indeed, they were among China's best and brightest – and I certainly didn't have better intuitions about Chinese phonology than they did. Instead, unlike them, I was well-trained in an alphabetic writing system. This made my mastering hanyu pinyin almost trivial. That's the reason I could find words faster than they could in a spelling-based dictionary, and that's why you can so readily understand the concept of contrastive sound substitutions, and consciously manipulate speech sounds accordingly.

Bloch and Trager, once again, express the subtleties of this argument very succinctly. When a researcher is confused about the sound-structural properties of some foreign language, 'This uncertainty cannot be resolved simply by asking the informant. If [the informant] is sophisticated enough to understand such finespun questions, he is probably literate in his native language and hence likely to be misled by the way in which words are written, by the tradition of the schools, and by other equally fallible guides; and if he is unspoiled by education, the chances are that questions about the identity of words will only baffle him'.

2. Neutralizing sound substitution

The two other types of sound substitution – neutralization and allophony – are not nearly as intuitively obvious as contrastive substitution because they do not involve a change in meaning, and so they are not usually reflected in our writing system. In a neutralizing sound substitution, the replacement of one sound with another eliminates the phonetic distinction between words, resulting in homophony. This obviously creates the potential to eliminate *meaning* distinctions: two (or more) words end up being pronounced the same, and so there is no phonetic evidence for their distinction in meaning. But the counter-functional effects of neutralization are never very devastating, since the *real-world context* and/or the *grammatical context* normally makes a speaker's intended meaning clear. As an example of neutralization, consider again the compound word 'phone book', mentioned earlier.

When you say this in a natural way – at a natural speech rate, and in a natural conversational context like 'Where's the phone book!?' – quite possibly your lips will close during the last sound in 'phone', resulting in something that sounds very much like 'foam book'. So, in the context of '-book', 'phone' may end up sounding like 'foam'.

Nonetheless some might feel that the pronunciation [fõʊ̃n] – with an [n] – is somehow a more 'authentic' or a more 'privileged' realization of the word 'phone' than is the alternative pronunciation [fõʊ̃m], with an [m] (for now, you can just concentrate on the [n]–[m] substitution, which is the primary difference in the two forms). In fact, sometimes the word is pronounced [fõʊ̃n], sometimes [fõʊ̃m], and sometimes, as in 'phone call', it may be pronounced [fõʊ̃ŋ] (in which the symbol [ŋ] indicates the 'ng' pronunciation). For [fõʊ̃m] and [fõʊ̃ŋ], the final sound in 'phone' matches the following sound ([b̥] and [k], respectively) in terms of tongue and lip position, but neither of these pronunciations of 'phone' is any less legitimate than [fõʊ̃n] (with [n]). Our intuitions might tell us that [fõʊ̃n] is the *real* pronunciation of 'phone', but I've already emphasized that our feelings about language are of no help in determining its structural properties. In fact, I can just imagine someone protesting, 'I don't say "pho[ŋ]e", I say "pho[n]e", like in "pho[ŋ]e call, or pho[m]e book". I always say it with an "n"!' This person doesn't realize that the same word can have different pronunciations depending on its context, and so mistakenly believes that the word is always pronounced in just one way. The reason our intuitions tell us that [fõʊ̃n] is somehow more real or authentic than [fõʊ̃m] or [fõʊ̃ŋ] is that our notion of the correct pronunciation of an English word is usually based on its pronunciation in isolation; also, it is often influenced by how the word is spelled.

It might help if I use set diagrams to illustrate neutralization. Let's suppose for the moment that the word 'foam' has only one pronunciation, whereas 'phone' has the three that we have just considered, which are dependent on the context in which the word is found. While this is a simplification, for now let's just suppose it's true. If different pronunciations have the same meaning, they are grouped into a set. The ambiguity of [fõʊ̃m] is indicated by the intersection of the two sets in Figure 1.1.

The example of 'phone' and 'foam' shows us that words that are distinct when standing alone may neutralize when other words of certain phonetic shapes are added: the form [fõʊ̃m] corresponds to more than one meaning when [b̥] immediately follows. In other words, the [n]–[m] sound substitution in this phonetic context has the potential to eliminate a distinction in word meaning due to the resultant homophony. This is neutralization.

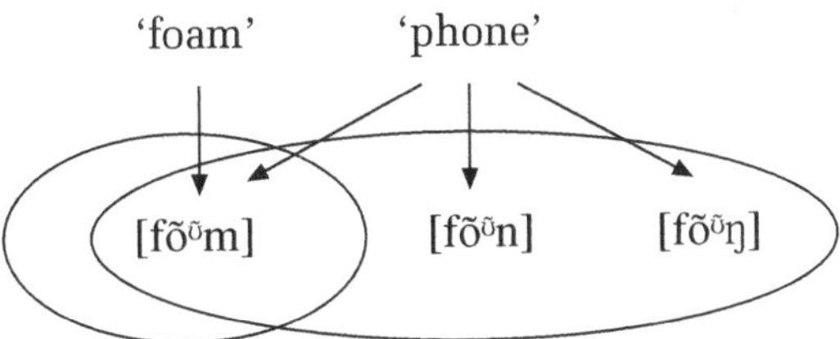

Figure 1.1 Sets for 'foam' and 'phone'

You might now grant that 'phone' has a number of perfectly acceptable pronunciations, and that one of these – [fõ^{ʊ}m] – is ambiguous between 'phone' and 'foam'. But what is a *foam* book? You might imagine that you're about to give the children their bath, and they're crying for their favourite bath-safe book, and you can't find it, and so you mutter under your breath, 'Where's the foam book!?' But I think you'll agree that in most cases the intended meaning of the form [fõ^{ʊ}m] in this phrase will be unambiguously interpreted by listeners as 'phone'. Even when the phonetic distinction between words is neutralized, the real-world or grammatical context of the neutralized form usually serves a disambiguating function. As I said, the functional consequences of neutralization are never very dire.

We've now seen that words that are distinct when standing alone may neutralize when other words of certain phonetic shapes are added. But this doesn't mean that the spelling pronunciation, or the pronunciation that we use in isolation, has any privileged structural status, or is any more real or authentic than other pronunciations. To show this clearly, let's consider another route to neutralization: in some languages, certain words in *isolation* are homophonous, and they only express their full contrastive status when certain sounds are *added*. In a well-known paper written in 1933, the linguist and anthropologist Edward Sapir reported some findings on the Sarcee language of Alberta, Canada. His Sarcee language consultant, John Whitney, provided him with two words that sounded exactly the same to Sapir, and yet Whitney insisted that the words were different. What Sapir heard as [dìníh] corresponded to two meanings for Whitney, 'this one', and 'it makes a sound'. (The grave and acute accents indicate, respectively, lower pitch and higher pitch; Sarcee is a *tone language*, and so the relative pitch – higher or lower – can change the meaning of a word. Changing the pitch in this way is a sound substitution like any other; we'll come back to tone in later chapters.) Although Whitney himself could not actually hear any difference between the two, and could not even sense an articulatory difference in his mouth, he nonetheless *felt* that the words were not identical. After he and Sapir worked at some length to figure out the exact nature of the distinction between the two words, Whitney finally said that he 'felt a "t"' at the end of the form for 'it makes a sound'. Both Sapir and Whitney were rather stumped by this phantom 't' that Whitney could mentally feel, but for which there was no tangible evidence. But as Sapir learned more about the structure of Sarcee, he found that by adding the suffix [í], 'the one who ...', this phantom 't' finally made itself heard: [dìnítʰí]. Suffixing [í] to the *other* [dìníh] ('this one') did not induce the presence of a [t]. Adding other suffixes to the words also resulted in phonetic distinctions between them. So the words phonetically manifested their contrastive status only when suffixed, but were homophonous when the suffixes were subtracted. This source of neutralization is quite different from the English example just discussed, because in English the neutralization occurs upon the *addition* of certain sounds, whereas in Sarcee it occurs upon the *subtraction* of sounds. The Sarcee case, then, clearly shows us that forms in isolation are not linguistically 'privileged' in any sense.

Sapir concluded that Whitney's feelings about the 't' constituted evidence for Whitney's otherwise hidden knowledge of Sarcee's sound system. Despite its physical absence, Whitney could mentally feel its presence, and so the 't' was 'psychologically real' in Sapir's parlance. Sapir proposed that there is an abstract phonological value – a 'phoneme' – that is psychologically somehow more basic, more prominent, than any of the phonetic ways in which this value is phonetically expressed, and that this abstract phonological value may be psychologically present even in the absence of any physical manifestation. (The term 'phoneme', though not necessarily this concept of its meaning, predates Sapir's work by a number of decades. In Chapter Seven we consider the profound influence that Sapir's proposals have had on twentieth-century phonological theory.)

Two years after Sapir's paper appeared, another scholar, William Freeman Twaddell, published a work in which he challenged Sapir's interpretation of the Sarcee phantom 't'. Twaddell wrote, 'In so far as this incident may be interpreted as evidence of any mental reality, it would appear to be rather a morphological class or lexical unit than any phonetic or quasi-phonetic class or unit'. In simpler language, Twaddell didn't deny that there was linguistic significance to Whitney's feelings, but these feelings reflect the distinction in *meaning* between the two words, a distinction for which the phonetic cues are absent when the words are unsuffixed. These feelings, according to Twaddell, don't tell us anything about the psychological organization of the sound structure of Sarcee.

If Twaddell was correct in his interpretation, why did Whitney himself, a native speaker of Sarcee, report his feelings in terms of *sound* and not *meaning*? Let's try to recreate how the difference between the two [dìníh]s might have come to Sapir's attention in the first place. Although Sapir never discussed it, we might imagine that he first encountered the two forms of [dìníh] at different times during his work with Whitney, when the meaning distinction between the two was very clear from the context in which the words were used, and so there would have been no confusion on Whitney's part about their pronunciation. Since he was not specifically comparing and contrasting the two forms, Whitney was probably perfectly happy in pairing one [dìníh] with one meaning and the other [dìníh] with the other, rather like when we say 'pho[m]e book' without giving the ambiguity of [fõʊ̃m] a second thought. Maybe later, Sapir checked his notes and realized that these two different words were pronounced the same way. At that point, he might have asked Whitney to compare the two. If Sapir asked Whitney about the word [dìníh] in complete isolation, without a context that would link the word to one or the other of its meanings, Whitney might have said, 'Hmm, that word can mean two different things!' But when Sapir put the word in two different contexts which induced the two different meanings, only now – when Sapir specifically juxtaposed the two words in a way that brought to the fore their distinction in meaning (though not yet their distinction in sound) – would he engender in Whitney the confusing feelings about the difference between the two words. But, according to Twaddell, these feelings might not tell us anything about the mental organization of the sound system. How can Twaddell be right? Sapir wrote that he and Whitney were searching for a way to phonetically distinguish between the two [dìníh]s. Although they had to give up this endeavour when no phonetic distinction was found, they were still in a sound-based frame of mind; they were still looking for a sound-based explanation for Whitney's feelings. I imagine that Whitney began silently thinking about the two words in different contexts, for example in a suffixing context where a [t] was actually present for the one meaning but absent for the other. Now Whitney could give Sapir an answer that they could be satisfied with. He mentally plugged [dìníh] into different contexts, a [t] popped up for only one of the meanings, and so he could tell Sapir that he 'felt a "t" '. Under this scenario, then, just as Twaddell argued, Whitney was really responding to the difference in *meaning* between the two [dìníh]s, not to a difference in phonological structure.

Whitney was mistaken in a way similar to someone who says, 'I don't say "pho[ŋ]e", I say "pho[n]e", like in "pho[ŋ]e call", or "pho[m]e book" '. Where our English speaker mistakenly thinks that all these 'phone's sound the same because they have the *same* meaning, Whitney was mistakenly setting apart phonetically identical forms that have *different* meanings. In both cases, the confused responses are a consequence of mis-pairing sound and meaning – a consequence of non-bi-uniqueness induced by non-contrastive sound substitution – not a consequence of the supposed 'psychological reality' of elements of the sound system. But Whitney wasn't the one who made the real mistake, however. It was Sapir who was inducing the confusion that Whitney experienced – a confusion that Whitney would never feel in an everyday language context – by asking him to report his feelings about differences in *meaning* in terms of differences in *sound*. But this doesn't make any sense, as Whitney's legitimately confused reaction shows us. Indeed, the task of the phonologist and the task of the language learner/user are very different, and *there's no reason to assume that the methods I employ and the generalizations that I make as a phonologist are the methods employed and generalizations that people make when they are actually learning and using their language*. Sapir, I would claim, was confusing the knowledge that he possessed as a Sarcee *linguist* with the knowledge that Whitney possessed as a Sarcee *speaker*. As a Sarcee linguist, Sapir – a remarkable field linguist by anyone's standards – was busy establishing generalizations about the sounds of Sarcee. As a Sarcee speaker, Whitney was busy extracting meaning from the speech signal.

It was very easy for me to illustrate contrastive sound substitution with words like 'brick' and 'trick' because we have conscious awareness of this phenomenon. This sort of substitution is reflected in the writing system which we are taught, and more importantly, this sort of substitution changes word meaning: it is the change in word meaning that truly resonates with language users, because of its functional importance. But I suspect it took a bit more to convince you that the 'n's of 'phone' and 'phone book' are phonetically distinct from each other, in part because, usually, our writing system only encodes sound changes that produce *changes* in meaning, but mostly because such neutralizing sound substitutions do not play the functionally important role of switching one meaning for another.

3. Allophonic sound substitution

We've now discussed how [fõ$^{\tilde{ʊ}}$m] may be ambiguous between 'phone' and 'foam'. But what about [fõ$^{\tilde{ʊ}}$ŋ]? This form doesn't mean anything on its own, and it can only mean 'phone' in contexts like 'phone call'. In this case, the substitution of [ŋ] for [n] neither changes word meaning nor induces homophony with any other word. Since it is neither contrastive nor neutralizing, this sound substitution must be of a third type. This third and final type of sound substitution is called *allophony*, where 'allo-' means 'same' and '-phon(e)' refers to Sapir's 'phoneme'. These sounds are different phonetic realizations of the same phoneme. But since we are not embracing the theoretical construct 'phoneme' in this book, the term 'allophony' is consequently slightly misleading for us. For our purposes, the term 'allophony' refers to the phenomenon whereby sounds are *phonetically distinct* though *functionally non-distinct*.

Consider again the last sound in the word 'invite' when you say 'invite someone'. There are a few ways in which a speaker of American English might say this word. Each is as good as another to illustrate my point, so let me transcribe this last sound [ˀt̚], which is the way I often produce it. The superscripted question mark-like symbol indicates a glottal stop, in which the vocal folds suddenly and completely shut tight, prohibiting any air from leaving the lungs. You may have trouble recognizing the glottal stop because our orthography does not use a symbol for it, but you make one every time you answer a question negatively with 'uh-uh', as opposed to the positive 'uh-huh'. In the negative form, the silence between the two vowel sounds is the glottal stop ([ʌ̃ʔʌ̃]), whereas the positive form has [h] here ([ʌ̃h̃ʌ̃]). Similarly, when you say 'invite someone' you might feel a slight tightening around your larynx, just before the end of 'invite'. That's the glottal stop. (If you say 'invite' then 'inside', you might feel a difference in your throat at the very end of the words, since 'inside' doesn't have the glottal stop.) The symbol after the 't' indicates that the tongue tip stays up after making contact with the roof of your mouth. We call this an *inaudibly released* 't', or more often an *unreleased* 't', because you don't let the tongue immediately drop from its contact position; you don't immediately release the 't'. Not all English speakers make their word-final 't' in this way, but it's quite common.

Now let's replace 'someone' with 'anyone': 'invite anyone'. In my pronunciation, I no longer make a glottal stop, and since the closure is immediately followed by a vowel, the [t] is immediately released into the first vowel of the next word. In this context, the sound is extremely short in duration, and consists only of a little tap of the tongue tip against the roof of the mouth. We transcribe this tap [ɾ]. Now we have 'invi[ˀt̚]e someone' and 'invi[ɾ]e anyone': two different realizations of 'invite'. The sounds are not the same, but the meaning of the word is. So these two sounds in 'invi[ˀt̚]e someone' versus 'invi[ɾ]e anyone' exemplify a sound substitution in which word meaning is maintained, since both involve the meaning 'invite'. This is an allophonic sound substitution.

It turns out that there are very systematic changes that a sound may undergo, depending on the phonetic character of the sounds that are near to it. As we discuss in great detail in Chapter Six, the [ˀt̚]–[ɾ] substitution is just one example of a fully regular phonological pattern in American English. Basically, words that have [ˀt̚] in final position when a consonant immediately follows (except [ɹ] under certain circumstances), instead have [ɾ] when a vowel immediately follows (again, under certain circumstances). Now, the way I expressed the generalization about glottalization/unrelease versus tapping in English certainly seems like a *rule* that constrains English sound sequences. So haven't I just contradicted my earlier claim that sound substitutions are a consequence of experience with actual words and not a consequence of internalized sound-sequencing constraints? No, I haven't. What I do as a phonologist is quite different from what I do as a learner of a language. As a phonologist, my first task is to document the sorts of sound substitutions I observe. Once I have investigated the phonetic form of many words in many contexts, my next task is to establish the correct generalizations about the patterning of the sounds: what are the systematic properties of the sound substitutions that I have documented? An efficient method of characterizing the observed systematicity is by setting up constraints and general rules on the sorts of sound substitutions and sound sequences that are found in the language. The generalizations that phonologists make about sound patterning are oftentimes breathtaking in their complexity, their scope and their beauty, and if we are eventually going to have a good understanding of the nature of language, establishing the proper generalizations is absolutely essential. But, again – and I'm repeating this for emphasis – there is no reason to assume that the methods I employ and the generalizations I make as a phonologist are the same methods employed and generalizations made when people are actually learning and using their language. As I said earlier, we can *characterize* phonological systems in terms of sound substitutions, but that doesn't mean that this characterization genuinely reflects the cognitive organization of language. In contrast to the views of many linguists, I maintain that when I learned English I wasn't a 'little linguist' formulating and testing hypotheses about the structural properties of my language. Instead, it is the relation between sound and meaning that is most relevant for learners.

Now, it's certainly true that language learners become aware of the sound-sequencing regularities of their language. For example, even infants have different physiological responses when they hear a rare or absent sound sequence of an ambient language in comparison to when they hear a statistically prevalent sound sequence of this language. They can use these rarities and prevalences to help predict the next sound, or, as they get older, even the next word; we touch on this in the next section. But in fact, the sorts of statistical analyses that infants may engage in are not special to language. Instead, they are the automatic response to any patterned perceptual experience. In Chapter Five we'll see that even lower animals have comparable physiological reactions to rare-versus-common patterns of stimuli, indicating that they too engage in complex statistical calculations over their perceptual experience, which is part of an evolution-derived survival-enhancing mechanism. But there is no reason to assume that the statistical analyses that young language learners engage in assist them in determining the *functional* relationships between the sounds of their language, that is, the contrastive, neutralizing or allophonic consequences of specific sound substitutions in specific contexts. Learners must know word *meanings* in order to establish any functional relationships between sounds. After all, sounds only serve a linguistic function if they contribute to the conveyance of meaning. It is these sound–meaning relationships that have functional consequences for young learners, and it is these that surely emerge to them as they master their language.

Subsequent chapters will thoroughly explore allophonic sound substitutions of the English [ˀt̚]–[ɾ] sort. Two sounds that are related in this way are functionally the same, even though they are not physically the same. Although it may seem curious that a sound substitution may take place that seems to have no functional consequences, in Chapter Six I argue that, despite their superficial functional inertness, allophonic substitutions often evolve exactly to stave off the counter-functional consequences of neutralization.

Learning the alternants

When we hear a completely unfamiliar language, we perhaps get some sense of what speech sounds like at the very earliest stages of language learning – an unbroken jumble of sounds that has virtually no discernible structure, neither rhyme nor reason. But because language learners are exposed to a daily barrage of speech, and because speech consists of words that are used over and over again, certain sound patterns are repeated and repeated. These sequences of sounds – exactly because of this repetition – begin to emerge and be recognized amid the chaos.

In any given language, there is actually a hierarchy of frequency among sound sequences. At the bottom of this hierarchy are those sequences that are clustered across word boundaries. Some of these sound combinations might be encountered in relatively low numbers, because there are few limits on what sound may abut another, and so unusual and rare sequences may be found. But within words, there are sequences that are encountered more often, because words are repeated and repeated, and are comprised of the comparatively limited set of word-internal sound combinations that the language has evolved.

Sound combinations found within words but across *morpheme* boundaries are more often encountered than sound combinations across word boundaries, exactly because words are used again and again by speakers. Morphemes are the 'bits of meaning' out of which words are made. So 'six' ([sɪks]) has one morpheme – a *root* – which includes the rare morpheme-internal sequence [ks]; 'sixth' ([sɪks+θ]) has two morphemes, the root 'six' and the ordinal suffix '-th' (word-internal morpheme boundaries are indicated with '+'). The plural form 'sixths' ([sɪks+θ+s]) has the sequence [ksθs], which is never found within the confines of a single English morpheme. Indeed, this sequence is limited to this word and this word only! The almost-too-clever-for-his-own-good indie-rocker Stephin Merritt has exploited this tongue-twisting sound sequence in his intentionally annoying band name 'The 6ths'. The band's two albums to date are called 'Wasps' Nests' and 'Hyacinths and Thistles'!

The sound combinations that are encountered most often are those *within* morphemes. Usually, only sounds at the beginning and the end of morphemes combine in new ways with other sounds, while sound sequences that are internal to the morpheme are usually fairly stable, because these sounds least often recombine such that they end up next to other sounds – they are typically 'trapped' in a morpheme-internal context – and so are the most stable and consistent in terms of their combinatory properties.

Repetition breeds familiarity:

Least often encountered sound combinations:	across word boundaries
More often encountered sound combinations:	across morpheme boundaries
Most often encountered sound combinations:	within morphemes

As mentioned in the previous section, we have experimental evidence showing that children are differentially sensitive to the more common and less common sound sequences they encounter in the speech signal, even at the early pre-linguistic levels of infancy. However, children cannot possibly understand that the speech signal might be structured into words and morphemes until they begin to associate these particular sound sequences with particular meanings. It's exactly because certain chunks of the speech signal are semantically relevant and useful to speakers of the language that they are repeated over and over again in particular real-world situations. Because of this repetition, they are constantly encountered by learners, and eventually emerge to these learners as the functional units that they are for adult speakers. As they learn to associate particular sound chunks with particular meanings, learners are beginning to *parse* – or separate out – the functionally relevant chunks of the speech signal.

Structuring the speech signal into sentences, words, and morphemes emerges as a consequence of patterns of sounds that are heard again and again by language learners, which they come to associate with a particular meaning, due to what we might call the *richness of the stimulus*. At the earliest stages of vocabulary building, the more often a particular sound sequence is encountered, the more readily such a sound–meaning correspondence will be established. And the more often these sound sequences combine and recombine with other sound sequences, indeed, the more likely that learners will take note of these sequences' tendency to combine and recombine in various ways, and so emerge as independent functional units of the language. In this sense, learners' knowledge of the *form* of language is determined to a great extent by the very *function* that language has for speakers.

The only reasonable explanation for our effortless mastery of the inordinate complexities of the linguistic system is the aforementioned 'richness of the stimulus' hypothesis. Learners are bombarded with speech at spectacularly punishing levels. The constant repetition of particular sound sequences in particular real-world contexts will induce their emergence as functional units of the language – words and morphemes. Consequently, languages that have a richer and/or more complex phonological structure should be no more difficult to acquire than languages that have simpler structures, because phonological complexity is necessarily matched by *evidence* for this complexity. Indeed, *no language takes significantly longer to acquire by children – or is significantly more difficult to acquire by children – than any other language*.

We can well imagine the early learner beginning to make sense of the speech stream, encountering patches of increasingly familiar sequences which coalesce into words and morphemes, punctuated by less familiar sequences, which help to cue word and morpheme boundaries. During the learning process, form and function would seem intertwined to an extent that genuinely precludes their unravelling.

As amazing as this accomplishment is, it becomes even more astonishing when recalling that there isn't a one-to-one relationship between sound and meaning. Due to neutralization and allophony, sounds *alternate* with each other: due to the substitution of one sound with another, the same word or morpheme may possess several context-dependent realizations. The variation in sounds that is a consequence of these alternations can provide evidence to learners that words and morphemes have internal structural properties. Learners come to master all the context-dependent realizations of morphemes, such that they establish the one-to-many and many-to-one relationships between sound–meaning relationships that exist in the ambient system. One-to-many relations exist between sound and meaning in the form of neutralization. Many-to-one relations exist between sound and meaning in the form of allophony, although we might just as readily call this allo*morph*y, since we are dealing with different phonetic shapes at the level of the morpheme, not at the level of individual sounds. What I mean is that, for example, at this level of description, the pronunciations [fõ$^{ʊ̃}$n] and [fõ$^{ʊ̃}$ŋ]k (for 'phone') are phonetically distinct though they have the same meaning, and so the forms are allomorphic. As the linguist Jan Baudouin de Courtenay wrote in 1895, 'Strictly speaking ... alternation concerns not isolated phonemes (sounds), but entire morphemes, or even words.'

So let's see how this might work with our 'phone' example. (For the present, let's just ignore the complications introduced by the fact that 'foam' is also a word in English.) Consider a few sentences that a child might hear in the course of a typical day:

> 'Someone answer the pho[n]e!'
> 'Where's the pho[m]e book?'
> 'The pho[ŋ]e cord is twisted again!'
> 'You missed a pho[ŋ]e call from your brother.'
> 'Someone answer the damn pho[n]e!'
> 'Honey, the pho[m]e bill is overdue again.'
> 'Will someone pick up the goddamn pho[n]e already!!'

During this typical day, a child would hear [fõ$^{ʊ̃}$n] at the end of a sentence twice, [fõ$^{ʊ̃}$ŋ] twice, [fõ$^{ʊ̃}$m] twice, and [fõ$^{ʊ̃}$n] with a following vowel once. Due to the real-world contexts in which these sentences are spoken, the child will quite rapidly come to figure out that these three phonetically distinct forms are allomorphs – that is, they are all associated with the same meaning. (They would also, of course, hear many other words which pattern similarly in this regard, thus increasing their exposure to the sound pattern.)

As children begin to make this many-to-one association between sound and meaning, they are learning that several different (albeit similar) sound sequences play a single functional role. That is, [fõʊ̃m], [fõʊ̃n] and [fõʊ̃ŋ] all mean 'phone'. Now the children can use these different sound sequences in their own emerging speech. They'll begin to say [fõʊ̃m], [fõʊ̃n] and [fõʊ̃ŋ] as appropriate, as a consequence of the speech patterns that they have become familiar with. At this point, then, only sounds that actually alternate with each other – the [m], [n] and [ŋ] of the various 'phone's – might emerge from the otherwise stable phonetic background: [fõʊ̃m], [fõʊ̃n], and [fõʊ̃ŋ]. By contrast, the remainder of the form 'phone' – roughly, [fõʊ̃] – does *not* engage in alternation, and so there is no evidence to learners that these phonetic aspects of the various phonetic realizations of 'phone' may be broken down into smaller, reusable bits: if learners encounter no evidence to the contrary, then [fõʊ̃] patterns as a single, unanalysable whole, or *Gestalt*. We might say that sounds in alternation are *foregrounded* for the learner, exactly because they behave somewhat independently from the remainder of the morpheme or word with which they are affiliated: [fõʊ̃m], [fõʊ̃n], [fõʊ̃ŋ]. So alternations set some elements of the word into high relief against the stable phonetic background, and learners quite naturally and expectedly master their patterning.

A moment ago I remarked that alternations add an astonishing element of complexity to the language-learning task. But now, it turns out that it is this very complexity of the pattern that assists learners in the structuring process itself. The richer the set of alternations, the more frequently learners are exposed to these alternations, the more readily they master these alternations. Here again, it is the richness of stimulus that reveals the structural complexities to learners. As I mentioned, languages which have a richer and/or more complex set of alternations are no more difficult to acquire, and take no longer to acquire, than languages with fewer and/or simpler alternations: *complexity in patterns of alternation is necessarily matched by evidence for this complexity*.

It's vitally important to remember that none of this word- and morpheme-internal structuring is possible without learners assigning a *meaning* to the sounds that they hear. So it's only because [fõʊ̃n] and [fõʊ̃ŋ] have the same meaning that [n] and [ŋ] may emerge as alternants of each other in this context. If learners did not assign meaning to these two phonetically distinct forms, then learners would hear [fõʊ̃n] in a variety of contexts and [fõʊ̃ŋ] in others, but they would have no evidence of the allomorphic relationship between [fõʊ̃n] and [fõʊ̃ŋ], and so would have no evidence for the allo*phon*ic relationship between these particular [n]s and [ŋ]s. Indeed, experimental evidence suggests that learners begin to establish the functional relationships between sounds in alternation during about the tenth to twelfth month of life, which is, not coincidentally, just about when they also start to establish systematic associations between sound and meaning: *learning allophonic relations is dependent upon learning allomorphic relations.*

But learners also must contend with one-to-many mappings, whereby one sound shape corresponds to more than one meaning. This, of course, is neutralization, as in 'phone book' and 'foam book'. And the same principles apply as well. Only when learners are able to pair particular sound sequences with particular meanings will it emerge that the [m] in [fõᶷ̃m] may bear a functional relationship to the [n] of [fõᶷ̃n] and the [ŋ] of [fõᶷ̃ŋ]k, or that this [m] may be part of another word entirely, that is, 'foam'.

Of course, children aren't consciously aware of the generalizations that they make. The point is that it's only through vast linguistic experience – exposure to thousands of words on an everyday basis: the richness of the stimulus again – that learners come to extract the relevant patterns from the speech signal. Generalizations about the pairing of sound and meaning can only emerge through experience with an enormous number of examples.

Although primarily concerned with pairing sound and meaning, listeners' experience with repeated patterns may eventually lead to the passive emergence of statistically-derived generalizations, which may account for their ability to reproduce these patterns in novel contexts. This generalizing ability on the part of language learners might also help explain how they can come to use words that they have never encountered before. Indeed, you may have already been wondering: if our knowledge of phonology is based on our experience with the words that we hear, and not based on structural constraints, how is it that we can produce words that we have never heard before? For example, children might never have heard of a 'wicket' before, but they'll know without hesitation that more than one wicket is a set of 'wickets', with the plural marker consisting of [s], as in a fictional company called 'World Wide Wickets'. These children will also know that a fictional company called 'Continental Flange' deals in some way with 'flanges' – in which the plural marker consists of [ɨz̥] – without ever having heard the word 'flanges' before. We clearly have the ability to group morphemes together into novel combinations, and know which allomorph to use, without ever having encountered the word previously. How do we acquire this knowledge, and what does this knowledge consist of?

The issue is far from resolved, but once again, the 'richness of the stimulus' hypothesis might point the way to a satisfying answer. Based on the thousands and thousands of examples that children are exposed to, they build an inventory of forms that take a plural marker. Sometimes the plural marker is [s], sometimes it's [ɨz̥], and sometimes it might be something else. Through constant exposure to the same words in the plural form, and constant exposure to many *other* words taking one or another plural form, the plural marker is eventually set into high relief against the phonetic background of the nouns that it accompanies: bridge[ɨz̥], pocket[s], bush[ɨz̥], potato chip[s]. Once again, through repetition and variation of the plural marker, it is *foregrounded* from the sound-and-meaning background.

In the case of 'wickets' and 'flanges', what specific generalizations might children be making? Linguists have determined that whenever a noun ends in certain stop consonants ([ˀp, ˀt, ˀk]) the [s] form of the plural marker follows in English. (*Stop consonants* are those in which air is completely blocked from exiting the mouth.) The fact is, however, that we really have no way of knowing if children have mastered the plural form by taking note of the consonants which precede the plural marker or by some other means. Indeed, there can be many routes to this generalization. One route might involve automatized routines of movement. For example, after having mastered a manual transmission, my driving a manual car proceeds unencumbered by reflection. I now effortlessly glide from one automatized action to the next as appropriate to the task. It's probably similar with speech. With the constant repetition of sound sequences that is characteristic of all languages, we probably develop automatized actions. So when we pluralize 'wicket', we tap into our inventory of motor routines and employ the one which we have always used before. We move effortlessly from the articulatory posture for [ˀt] to the one for [s] without a moment's reflection. It would never occur to us to move from [ˀt] to [ɨz̥], since we have never engaged in that motor activity when producing a plural noun, because we have never *heard* a plural like that before.

Alternatively, children might exploit the similarity that 'wicket' bears to other nouns, and pluralize 'wicket' accordingly. Children know, for example, that words similar to 'wicket' take [s], never [ɨz̥], in the plural, for example 'ticket[s]', 'planet[s]', 'bucket[s]'. The problem with this hypothesis is that no one has ever come up with a compelling and quantifiable determination of similarity. What are the specific qualities and relations that render some objects similar and others dissimilar? It remains an impressionistic notion for both linguists and psychologists, and so its scientific use remains elusive for the present. This is not to say that children don't exploit some extremely sophisticated diagnostic for similarity, only that similarity has not, to date, been compellingly operationalized by researchers.

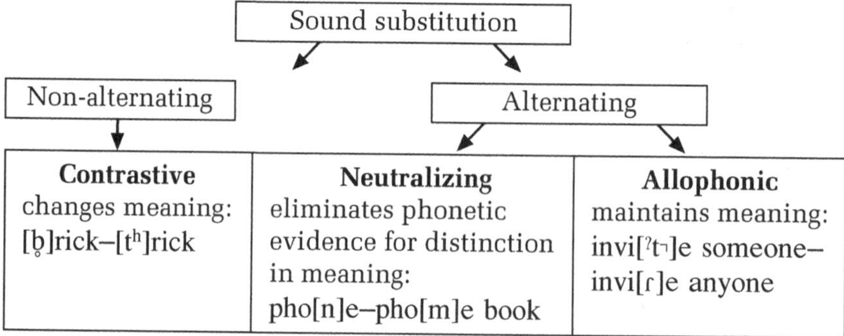

Figure 1.2 Three types of sound substitution

Summary

As speakers of a language, our effortless mastery of sound substitutions derives from our vast experience with the speech that we hear. As shown in Figure 1.2, these sound substitutions can be divided into non-alternating and alternating types. Contrastive substitutions are non-alternating; they change word meaning. Non-contrastive sound substitutions induce alternations. These alternating sound substitutions come in two varieties which result in non-bi-uniqueness between sound and meaning. Neutralizing substitutions create homophones, thus eliminating the phonetic evidence for distinctions in meaning. Allophonic substitutions maintain meaning distinctions.

Neutralizing and allophonic alternations inevitably sabotage bi-uniqueness in phonology, but it is the very property of *non*-bi-uniqueness that may *foreground* the alternating sub-components of words and morphemes from the stable phonetic background, such that learners may effortlessly recycle them in novel forms.

Although one of the main jobs of phonologists is to document the regularities and systematic properties of sound substitutions, there is little evidence that language learners focus their energies similarly. Instead, learners are busy pairing sound and meaning so that they can understand and produce the language around them. It's no wonder that speakers make mistakes about their feelings, or intuitions, about language: sometimes the same sound sequences correspond to different meanings (neutralization), and sometimes different sound sequences correspond to a single meaning (allophony). Furthermore, conscious awareness of speech sounds, and one's ability to consciously manipulate their patterning on demand, reveals nothing about the nature of phonological structure. We do eventually become aware of the regularities of our sound systems, as evidenced by our ability to produce novel forms like 'wickets' and 'flanges', but such knowledge might only emerge after thorough knowledge of words and their meanings is well in place. It seems that learning allophonic relations is dependent upon learning allomorphic relations.

While I certainly don't deny the existence of internal mental states (as a strict Skinnerian behaviourist might), I do believe that we should proceed with extreme caution in our hypotheses about their content. In subsequent chapters I will argue that the nature of linguistic knowledge can only be indirectly ascertained, through direct inspection and documentation of linguistic behaviour across communities of speakers and across generations of speakers, that phonology is best characterized as a self-organized system of substantive social conventions which evolves passively over generations of speakers. The regularities we observe in phonological systems are due to a complex interaction of phonetic and cognitive pressures acting over generations and generations of language use, and can be understood only when considering the communicative function of language itself. Hence, to challenge the inclinations of any would-be solipsists reading this book, *parlo ergo es* 'I speak, therefore you are'.

Further reading

Rule-based and constraint-based approaches to phonology:

Chomsky, Noam and Halle, Morris (1968). *The Sound Pattern of English*. New York: Harper and Row.

Prince, Alan and Smolensky, Paul (2004). *Optimality Theory: Constraint Interaction in Generative Grammar*. Oxford: Blackwell.

The Bloch and Trager quotes (*'The ordinary speaker of English ...'*, *'This uncertainty cannot be resolved ...'*):

Bloch, Bernard and Trager, George L. (1942). *Outline of Linguistic Analysis*. Baltimore: Waverly Press, pp. 40 and 38.

The experiment with illiterate Portuguese fishermen:

Morais, Jose (1985). 'Literacy and awareness of the units of speech: implications for research on the units of perception', *Linguistics* 23: 707–21.

The experiment with educated, literate Chinese adults:

Read, Charles, Zhang Yun-fei, Nie Hong-yin and Ding Bao-qing (1997). 'The ability to manipulate speech sounds depends on knowing alphabetic writing', *Cognition* 24: 31–44.

Sapir's report on his work with John Whitney:

Sapir, Edward (1933 [1949]). 'The psychological reality of phonemes', in David G. Mandelbaum (ed.), *Selected Writings of Edward Sapir in*

Language, Culture, and Personality. Berkeley: University of California Press.

The Twaddell quote ('*In so far as this incident ...*'):
Twaddell, William Freeman (1935 [1957]). 'On defining the phoneme', in Martin Joos (ed.), *Readings in Linguistics I*. Chicago: University of Chicago Press, p. 59.

Evidence for infants' sensitivity to rare versus common sound sequences:
Saffran, Jenny, Aslin, Richard and Newport, Elissa (1996). 'Statistical learning by 8-month-old infants', *Science* 274: 1926–28.

An alternative to 'the richness of the stimulus':
Chomsky, Noam (1980). 'On cognitive structures and their development: a reply to Piaget', in Massimo Piattelli-Palmarini (ed.), *Language and Learning: The Debate Between Jean Piaget and Noam Chomsky*. London: Routledge and Kegan Paul.
Chomsky, Noam (1980). *Rules and Representations*. Oxford: Basil Blackwell.
Chomsky, Noam (1988). *Language and Problems of Knowledge: The Managua Lectures*. Cambridge, MA: MIT Press.

The Baudouin de Courtenay quote ('*Strictly speaking ... alternation concerns not isolated phonemes ...*'):
Baudouin de Courtenay, Jan (1895 [1972]). 'An attempt at a theory of phonetic alternations', in Edward Stankiewicz (ed.), *A Baudouin de Courtenay Reader*. Bloomington: Indiana University Press, p. 175.

On *learning functional relations between speech sounds*:
Werker, Janet F. and Lalonde, Chris E. (1988). 'Cross-language speech perception: initial capabilities and developmental change', *Developmental Psychology* 24.5: 672–83.

2 Contrastive sound substitution

In Chapter One I discussed how sound substitutions are more like Jotto than like Mastermind, because they are constrained by the limits of our linguistic experience. In this chapter I show that the similarities between phonology and Jotto end right there. We know that the English spelling system is far from perfect in visually representing the sounds of spoken language, but more fundamentally, the very nature of a letter-by-letter system actually fails to capture the true nature of linguistic sound systems. In Jotto, the letters are discrete and sequenced. Each individual letter is fully self-contained, having no influence whatsoever on the other letters of the word. So switching B-R-I-C-K to T-R-I-C-K only involves replacing the 'B' with 'T'. The other letters, R-I-C-K, stay exactly the same. But, in contrast to Jotto, sound substitutions bear very little resemblance to our alphabetic writing system. The sounds of language, in fact, mutually interact such that replacing one with another affects the phonetic properties of the word far more than is implied by our letter-by-letter writing system.

There is no question that speech is indeed orchestrated around a gross pattern of alternately *closing down* and *opening up* the vocal tract, resulting in series of *consonant*-like entities followed by *vowel*-like entities. But in this chapter I show how contrastive sound substitution involves numerous phonetic changes that cannot be localized in the speech stream in the way that alphabetic writing suggests.

Three examples of contrastive sound substitution

1. Stops

Consider the three words 'top', 'tot' and 'tock'. Say these words out loud: [tʰɑˀp, tʰɑˀt, tʰɑˀk]. Now try to say *only* the final stop consonants, being careful not to audibly release them: [p˺, t˺, k˺]. If you've said them as I asked – with no preceding vowel, and no audible release – nothing at all will have come out of your mouth, only silence. Yet it can't be the case that replacing one stop with another simply replaces one silence with another, since we hear the words as different from each other, and indeed they each have a different meaning. So this final stop substitution is definitely contrastive in nature. Where does the physical evidence for the contrast actually reside? It's clearly not contained in the oral occlusion of [p], [t] and [k] (where *occlusion* refers to a constriction formed by bringing speech organs completely together, thus forming a seal so that air cannot pass); this would be the case if language were like Jotto, and if our alphabet genuinely reflected the physical properties of speech. Nor does the distinction between these three stops exist only in our minds, like Sapir's specious phantom 't'. Rather, the acoustic distinctions between the three stops reside exclusively on the preceding vowel, and especially in the transition period between the latter portion of the vowel up to the moment of oral occlusion (where *acoustic* refers to the physical properties of the speech signal). This means that we sometimes use different alphabetic symbols to represent identical phonetic values – the 'p', 't' and 'k' all represent silence for the duration of the speech stream that we take each symbol to represent – and we sometimes use a single alphabetic symbol to represent distinct phonetic values. The sound represented by 'o' actually takes on different phonetic characteristics depending on the articulatory nature of the consonant that follows it: the sound represented by the 'o' in 'top' is different from the 'o' in 'tot', which is different again from the 'o' in 'tock'. The same is also true when stop consonants precede vowels. So the acoustic nature of the first sounds in 'pot', 'tot' and 'cot' are, once again, simply silence, and it's the vowel that really does the work. This means, then, that the letters 'p', 't' and 'k' may actually refer to discontinuous acoustic segments of the speech signal: the transition period *before* the stop occlusion is made and/or the transition period *after* the stop occlusion is released: 'a part', 'a tart', 'a cart'.

A key point is that stop occlusions are identical in *acoustic* terms, but not in *articulatory* terms (where *articulatory* refers to the positioning of our speech apparatus); [p], [t] and [k] are made at different *places of articulation*: with the lips for [p], with the tongue tip behind the upper teeth for [t], and with the tongue body touching the soft palate for [k] (if you run your tongue tip back along the roof of your mouth, the front portion is the hard palate, and at a certain point you reach the fleshy section; this is the soft palate). As the shape of the mouth begins to change from a vowel to a stop, or from a stop to a vowel, this has the effect of changing the sound quality. And since each stop is made at a different location in the mouth, the changes in sound quality are unique to each of the different transitions. In fact, the sound quality of a vowel is in a continuous state of flux from right after the mouth opens at the release of the first consonant until the point when the mouth closes again for the second consonant.

What's happening, then, is that the vowel – the mouth's opening gesture – is doing all the work in terms of encoding these phonological contrasts: 'bib' [b̥ɪb̥], 'bid' [b̥ɪd̥], 'big' [b̥ɪg̊], 'dibs' [d̥ɪb̥s], 'did' [d̥ɪd̥], 'dig' [d̥ɪg̊], 'gib' [g̊ɪb̥], 'gid' [g̊ɪd̥] and 'gig' [g̊ɪg̊] all have only a single acoustic value while the mouth is closed for the flanking stop consonants: virtual silence. The opening and closing of the mouth between these two periods of virtual silence is where all the cues to both the vowel *and* the flanking consonants reside. So for the duration of the speech signal that has vowel-like properties, *ten* different distinctions – [ɪ], and each of the nine combinations of flanking consonants [b̥_ b̥], [b̥_d̥], [b̥_g̊], [d̥_b̥], [d̥_d̥], [d̥_g̊], [g̊_b̥], [g̊_d̥], [g̊_g̊] – are represented by the one alphabetic symbol, 'i'. As the great phonetician Peter Ladefoged writes in 2001, 'Many consonants are just ways of beginning or ending vowels. This is particularly true of consonants such as [b̥, d̥, g̊] (he writes 'b, d, g'), each of which has a rapid movement of the lips or tongue before [and/] or after another sound such as a vowel.'

What is the origin of the different sound qualities that result from changing the posture of the lips and tongue during the flow of speech? The answer is actually extremely complicated, and so it's best to start simply. You probably know what a jew's harp is. A jew's harp consists of a stiff metal band which is fixed at one end by being embedded into a metal handle, and which is free at the other end, where it may vibrate between two extensions of the handle (see Figure 2.1).

When the band is flicked, it vibrates back-and-forth. The air molecules in front of the band's movement get pushed closer together, and as the band sweeps back it leaves fewer particles than normal in its trail. These air *compressions* and *rarefactions* propagate outward from the source, and eventually impinge on our ears, which results in an auditory percept, a sound. Because the thickness and stiffness of the band remain stable, the band will always vibrate at the same rate. You can, of course, flick the band with more force or less force, and this

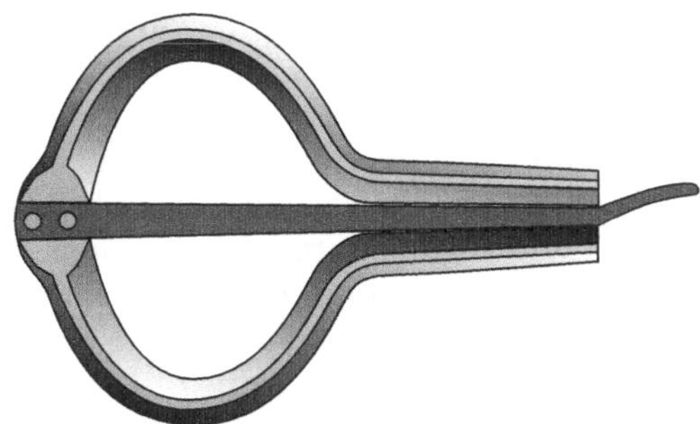

Figure 2.1 A jew's harp

will change the loudness of the resulting sound. But the vibratory rate, hence the pitch, will always remain stable. You can easily confirm this by taking a jew's harp and flicking the band with different strengths while holding it close to your ear. Flick it hard or gently, fast or slowly, and the pitch will always be the same. Jew's harps of different sizes will have different pitches – the larger the harp, the lower the pitch, and the smaller the harp, the higher the pitch – but still, each jew's harp vibrates at one and only one rate.

But if a jew's harp has only one pitch, how do we get that boing-boing/wah-wah effect when we hold it in front of our open mouth? The harp can certainly make sounds which *seem* higher or lower in pitch, depending on the posture of our lips and tongue, and yet the band is still vibrating at its one and constant rate. This riddle is partially solved when we consider that the band's vibratory pattern is actually far more complex than a simple back-and-forth motion. Let's say that the back-and-forth movement of the band is taking place 100 times per second, or at 100 Hertz (Hz). But along with this overall back-and-forth motion, the band is also vibrating at twice this frequency, at three times this frequency, four times, five times, etc., though with decreasing energy (hence decreasing loudness) as the vibratory rate increases. So if the band vibrates 100 times per second, there are also less pronounced vibrations at 200Hz, 300Hz, 400Hz, etc. If a smaller jew's harp vibrates at 200Hz, there will also be lesser vibrations at 400Hz, 600Hz, etc. These multiples of the lowest or *fundamental* frequency are referred to as *overtones* or *harmonics*, and, collectively, as the overtone or harmonic series. These are schematized in Figure 2.2.

We are now part way to understanding the source of a jew's harp's boing-boing effect. There is a whole series of harmonics which accompanies the lowest rate of the band's vibration. Now, setting the band against your mouth amplifies some of these harmonics such that sometimes *higher* harmonics become accentuated and louder, and sometimes *lower* harmonics become accentuated and louder. What happens is, as you reshape your mouth, you are making your oral cavity either longer or shorter. When you pull back your tongue and round your lips, the length of your oral cavity increases. Conversely, when you push your tongue forward and unround your lips, the length of your oral cavity decreases. *Lower harmonics become louder when the cavity is longer, and higher harmonics become louder when the cavity is shorter. The fundamental frequency will always be the same for any given jew's harp, but when you put the harp to your mouth, depending on the shape of your oral cavity, the pitch will seem higher or lower, because higher or lower harmonics will be rendered more prominent.* This is schematized in Figure 2.3.

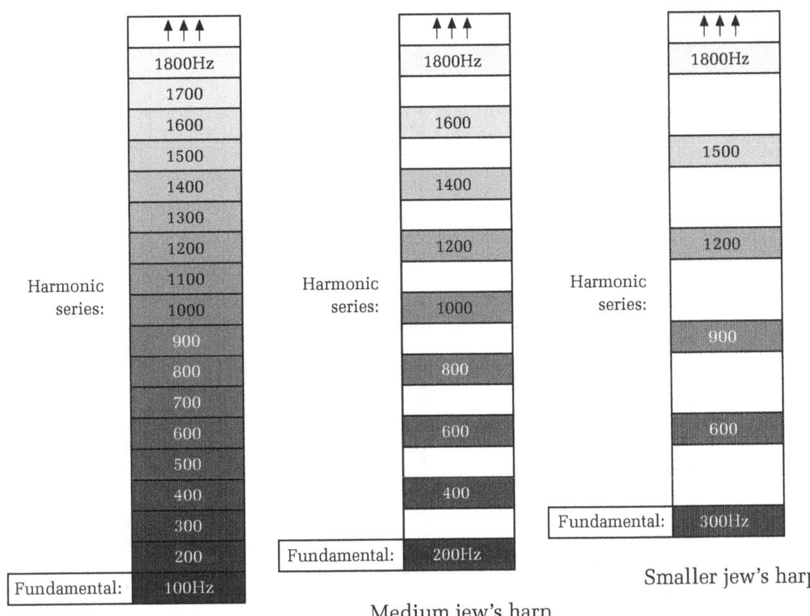

Figure 2.2 Listening to jew's harps held up to the ear: the lowest vibration (the fundamental frequency) is the loudest. This corresponds to the pitch we hear. Quieter vibrations are present at multiples of the fundamental frequency. The lower the fundamental frequency, the more closely spaced the harmonics. Also, the higher the harmonic, the less energy it possesses (suggested by shading).

Forming different vowel sounds is a lot like generating the jew's harp's boing-boing sound. Putting our mouth in an [i]-like posture, as in 'beat', will make a range of *higher* harmonics more prominent, because the tongue is fronted and the lips are unrounded, and so the mouth cavity is *shorter*. Conversely, making an [u]-like gesture, as in 'boot', will make a range of *lower* harmonics more prominent, because the cavity is *longer*. As shown in Figure 2.4, we can plot vowel qualities against the frequency range of louder harmonics to show this pattern. Going from [i] (as in 'beat') to [e] (similar to 'bait') to [a] ('bot') to [o] (similar to 'boat') to [u] ('boot') involves (among other things) incrementally backing our tongue, and, for [o] and [u], incrementally increasing the rounding of our lips. Tongue backing and lip rounding typically go together in vowels, since they both serve to elongate the oral cavity. This increases the acoustic difference between these vowels and those made with a shorter oral cavity.

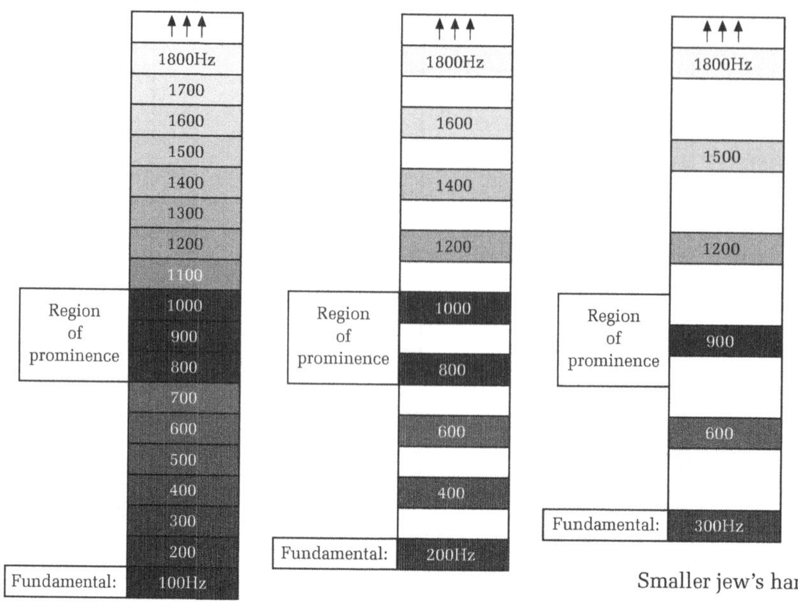

Figure 2.3 Listening to jew's harps held against the mouth: tongue back, lips rounded. A cavity of this length will have a prominence somewhere around 800–1000Hz. The lower the fundamental frequency, the more closely spaced the harmonics, and so the more harmonics that will fall within this region of prominence.

The tongue and lip positioning which accounts for the jew's harp's boing-boing effect may now be seen as also playing a role in distinguishing different vowel qualities. However, there are two major complications to consider. First, for jew's harpists to change the fundamental frequency of the sound source, they must switch to a bigger or smaller harp, because, recall, the band is fixed, and only vibrates at one rate. The situation is obviously different when we speak. Unlike the jew's harp's metal band, the *vocal folds* – which are the source of the vibration when we vocalize – are *not* fixed. The vocal folds can be stretched or squeezed, thickened or thinned, and might achieve many other postures as well. Consequently, when vocalizing, we can quite freely manipulate the fundamental frequency of our voice, and so change the overall pitch of our voice (where *pitch* is the *percept* that is a consequence of the fundamental frequency).

The pitch changes we engage in while speaking are largely independent from those ranges of the harmonic series that are affected

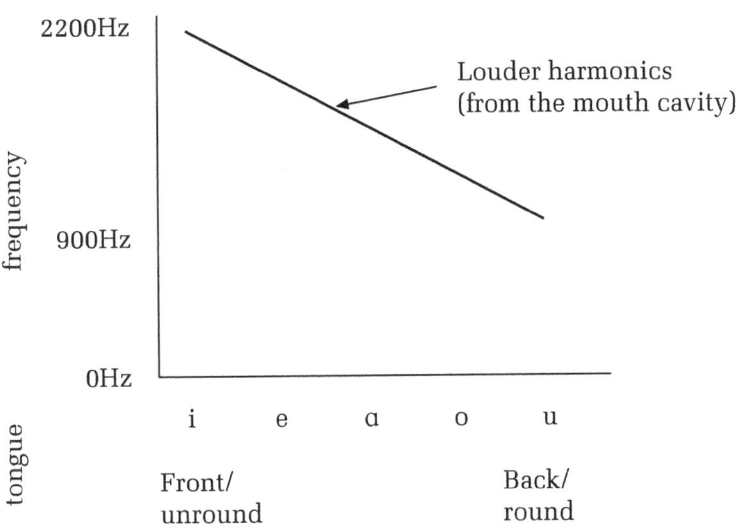

Figure 2.4 As the tongue moves back in the mouth and the lips are rounded, the oral cavity lengthens, and so the region of harmonic prominence becomes lower in frequency.

as we change the position of our lips and tongue. So we can make an [iuiu] wah-wah-like sound while independently changing the pitch of our voice, and the [i] will stay [i]-like and the [u] will stay [u]-like. We can also, of course, maintain a single vowel quality while changing our pitch. So, just like the jew's harp's boing-boing effect, different vowel qualities are a consequence of the shape of the vocal tract and its effect on the harmonic series, and have almost nothing to do with the fundamental frequency itself. That's why a child's high-pitched vowels are understood to be the same as an adult male's lower-pitched vowels. The adult voice might sound richer and fuller, but that's mostly because his vocal folds are bigger and longer, their rate of vibration is slower, so his harmonics are spaced closer together, and so more of his harmonics fall within the region of prominence. Also, since his *mouth cavity* is bigger, this region of louder harmonics might be somewhat lower in frequency than a child's, but not by too much. But for any given vowel quality, whether produced by a child or by an adult, a relatively similar harmonic range will be rendered more prominent, and so the vowels will be perceived as the same.

That's the first complication. Now for the second. Since the vibratory source for vowel sounds is down at the larynx, air molecules all along the vocal tract – and not just those in the mouth cavity – are set into vibratory motion by the repetitive slapping together of the vocal folds. When we make a vowel, we move a section of the tongue towards either the roof of the mouth, or the back of the throat. This means that we are effectively dividing the vocal tract into two separate though connected chambers, one in front of the constriction (in the mouth, as we have just discussed), but also one behind the constriction (in the throat). So, in addition to the harmonics that are accentuated due to the length of the mouth cavity, there are also harmonics that are accentuated due to the length of the throat cavity. In general, the *lower* the tongue position when you make a vowel, the shorter the throat cavity becomes, and so the *higher* in frequency the accentuated harmonics. We can now add this other region of louder harmonics – which derives from the length of the throat cavity – to the first range, deriving from the mouth cavity. As we move from [i] to [e], our tongue continually lowers, eventually bottoming out at [ɑ], only to rise again going to [o] and then [u]. In the throat cavity, the range of harmonic prominence consequently rises as we move the tongue down from [i] to [ɑ], and lowers as we move from [ɑ] to [u]. Look at Figure 2.5.

The distinct sound qualities of vowels derive primarily from particular combinations of these enhanced harmonic ranges, or *resonant frequencies*. These resonant frequencies of the vocal tract are called *formants*. As a good rule of thumb, *the first formant (F1) derives from the throat cavity (always lower in frequency) and the second formant (F2) derives from the mouth cavity (always higher in frequency)*. This is schematized in Figure 2.6. As we make different vowel qualities, we

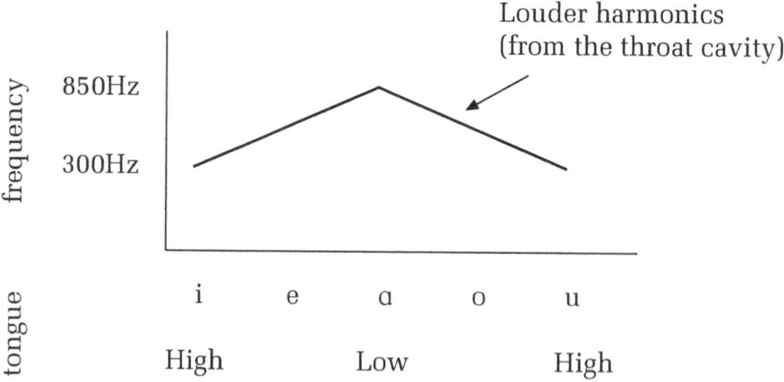

Figure 2.5 As the major front-to-back vowels are made in sequence, the tongue also moves from higher-to-lower-to-higher in the mouth, the throat cavity lengthens then shortens then lengthens, and so the region of harmonic prominence moves from lower-to-higher-to-lower in frequency.

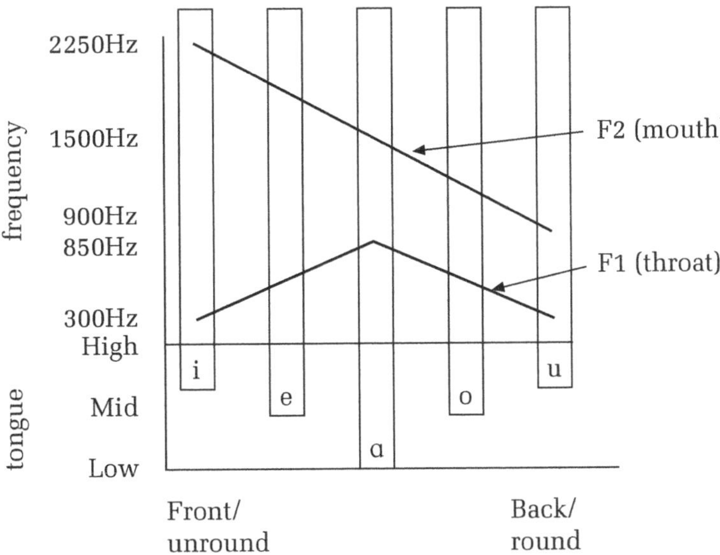

Figure 2.6 Positioning the tongue for vowel sounds divides the vocal tract into two cavities, the mouth and the throat. In the throat cavity, as the tongue is lowered, the cavity gets shorter, and so the first formant (F1) becomes higher in frequency. In the mouth cavity, as the tongue moves back and the lips are rounded, the cavity gets longer, and so the second formant (F2) becomes lower in frequency. The bars are intended solely as a visual aid, calling attention to each vowel quality's approximate formant values.

are changing the size and shape of our throat and mouth. This change in size and shape induces a change in the formant values; as F1 and F2 change in accordance with throat and mouth configuration, different vowel qualities are produced and heard. So, distinct vowel qualities are like chords in music, in which a number of notes combine in an ensemble of sound. Just as an untrained ear hears a musical chord as an ensemble, or a *Gestalt*, so too do we hear the formants of each vowel as a single sound quality, and not as a combination of its distinct elements.

Summarizing now, the rate of vocal fold vibration determines the pitch of the sound, and the particular combination of formant frequencies deriving from the throat cavity and the mouth cavity are independently responsible for the different vowel qualities. The first formant correlates quite well with throat cavity length: *the higher the tongue position, the longer the throat cavity, the lower the F1.* The second formant correlates quite well with mouth cavity length: *the more pulled-back the tongue and rounded the lips, the longer the mouth cavity, the lower the F2.* Each cavity also generates higher formants when the vocal folds are vibrating, but they're less important, and so we're not concerned with them right now.

Now that we have considered the origin of vowel quality distinctions, it becomes quite a bit easier to understand why vowels are able to encode the location of stop occlusions. When moving from a vowel to a [b̥], the mouth cavity may affect the formant structure just up to the point of oral occlusion. As we close the lips, they pass through an [u]-like shape, and so closing the lips lengthens the mouth cavity, and F2 lowers; opening the lips from a [b̥] closure raises F2 at the beginning of a following vowel. So a sudden drop in the second formant at the end of a vowel, followed by silence, can help cue to a listener that a [b̥] occlusion has just been made (as in [d̥ɪb̥s]). After a silence, a rise in F2 at the beginning of the vowel helps to indicate that a [b̥] occlusion has just been released (as in [b̥ɪd̥]). A [d̥] involves raising the tongue tip to make contact behind the upper teeth. This tongue movement has the effect of sending F2 toward about 1800Hz at the end of a vowel. So a move toward 1800Hz, followed by silence, helps cue a [d̥] occlusion (again, as in [b̥ɪd̥]). After a silence, moving away from 1800Hz at the beginning of a vowel helps indicate a [d̥] release (again, as in [d̥ɪb̥s]). Finally, F2 rises as a [g̊] occlusion is being made (as in [d̥ɪg̊]), and it lowers when a [g̊] occlusion is released (as in [g̊ɪd̥]). These *formant transitions* are thus very important cues to the location of stop occlusions, and, clearly, they are not present on the stop occlusions themselves (since there is only silence during the stop occlusion), but rather exist in the *transitions* into and out of these occlusions. Indeed, *the dynamic, transitional portions of the speech signal, as a rule, are far richer in acoustic information, hence far more perceptually prominent, than any sustained, steady-state portions of the speech signal.* Figure 2.7. schematically shows the distinct F2 transitions for every combination of [b̥, d̥, g̊] followed by [i, e, ɑ, o, u].

The situation gets still more complex: in sequences such as [b̥ɹi, b̥ɹe, b̥ɹɑ, b̥ɹo, b̥ɹu, d̥ɹi, d̥ɹe, d̥ɹɑ, d̥ɹo, d̥ɹu, g̊ɹi, g̊ɹe, g̊ɹɑ, g̊ɹo, g̊ɹu], all the [ɹ]s are actually slightly different from each other. As they are, in effect, superimposed on the transition between the stop and the vowel, each [ɹ] bears the distinct mark of the particular stop-vowel formant transition!

Although there are many additional acoustic cues that are present in the formation and release of stop consonants, the important point for now is that the formant structure of vowels, as they are influenced by the location of stop occlusions, provides information concerning where in the mouth the stop occlusion is made.

Now remember why we went into these details regarding the acoustic properties of vowels and stop consonants. Our alphabetic

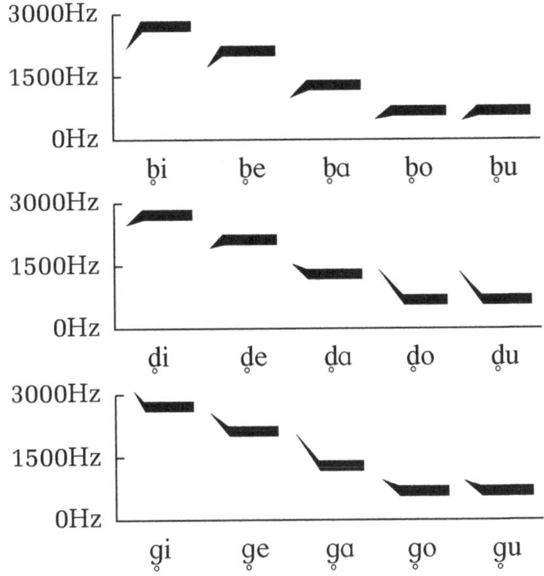

Figure 2.7 Schematic of F2 transitions from consonants [b̥, d̥, g̊] into steady-state vowels [i, e, a, o, u]. Each formant transition has unique characteristics, thus providing information about both the location of the consonant and the location of the vowel.

system is clearly misleading us into believing that phonological structure consists of a linear, element-by-element sequence of sounds. But in fact sometimes distinct alphabetic symbols represent identical phonetic values (as is the case for stops), and sometimes identical alphabetic symbols represent distinct phonetic values (as is the case for vowels). *As we substitute one sound for another, the speech signal undergoes any number of acoustic changes that cannot be localized in the speech stream the way an alphabetic writing system suggests.*

2. Nasals

As described above, stop occlusions consist solely of silence, and so the stops we hear actually reflect the articulatory routes we might take both before and after these silent intervals. By contrast, all other consonants possess acoustic energy during the consonant itself. Let's now consider one of these classes of consonant sounds, the nasals. Figure 2.8 shows how the nasal system connects to the mouth and throat systems.

Like stops, nasal consonants also involve oral occlusions, for example at the lips, behind the upper teeth and along the soft palate:

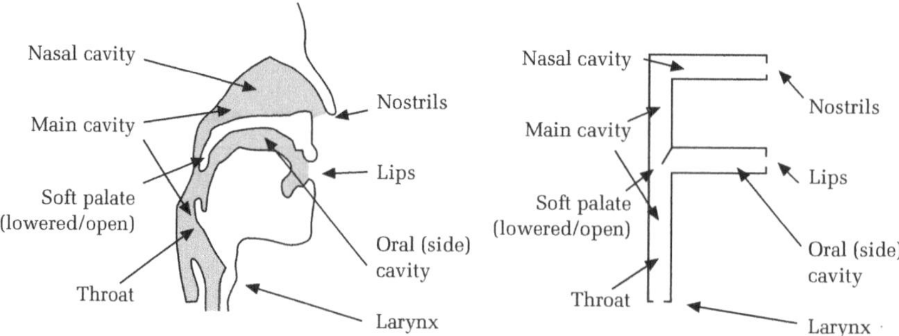

Figure 2.8 The vocal tract cavities, with the soft palate lowered; schematic of same

[m, n, ŋ]. The articulatory difference between stops and nasals is that, for nasals, the soft palate is *lowered*, which opens a passageway into the nasal cavity. When you make a labial stop [b̥], your soft palate is raised, sealing off the nasal cavity, but when you make a labial nasal [m], you lower your soft palate, and the air that would have been otherwise trapped inside your body is instead shunted out the nose. For nasals then, air continually escapes through the nose. Also for nasals, and unlike the stops we've been discussing, the vocal folds continue to vibrate, and so nasals are voiced sounds.

So, despite the fact that they are made with the mouth closed, air can flow quite freely during a nasal consonant (albeit through the nose). This free unobstructed airflow renders nasals more similar to vowels than to stop consonants in acoustic terms. Like vowels, nasals have a fundamental frequency, a harmonic series, and, also, nasals have their own characteristic formant values. But since air passes out the nose, and not out the mouth, the formant characteristics of nasals are quite different from those of vowels.

There are three major differences between the formant properties of nasals and the formant properties of vowels. First, since we can't form constrictions in the nose, and since any occlusion in the throat would prevent the air from getting into the nasal cavity, nasal consonants do not necessarily involve a comparable division of the vocal tract into two separate chambers – the throat and the mouth – as in vowels. Instead, there is, quite roughly, one long tube from the larynx to the nostrils. Consequently, the formant properties that cue nasality are quite stable, regardless of which specific nasal you are making. The first nasal formant is quite low, about 300 Hz. It is low because the larynx-to-nostrils tube is quite long. Second, the nasal cavity's walls are soft with a lot of surface area, and the various sinuses possess many nooks and crannies which may absorb certain components of the complex sound wave. Partly as a consequence of this, the harmonic series of nasals is subject to a greater loss of energy, especially at the higher frequencies. Both of these differences – the low first nasal formant, and the loss of the higher frequencies – help make nasals sound different from vowels, and different from other consonant sounds as well.

Now consider the third difference between nasals and vowels. Vowels may be viewed as possessing a single 'passageway' (albeit consisting of two connected chambers) from the vocal folds to the lips. But nasals are different. Since lowering the soft palate opens the nasal cavity, but doesn't completely seal off the mouth cavity *behind* the oral occlusion, the mouth acts as a *side cavity* which adjoins the main cavity. Depending on the location of the oral occlusion – with the lips [m], with the tongue tip [n], or with the tongue body [ŋ] – this side cavity will be longer or shorter. As you say words like 'Tim', 'tin' and 'ting', reflect on how you make the final sounds, and see if they match up with the following schematics in Figure 2.9.

From our discussion of jew's harps and vowel qualities, we now know about the effect that a longer or shorter mouth cavity has on formant structure: the shorter this side cavity, the higher the formant, and the longer this side cavity, the lower the formant. This means, in addition to the formant structure common to all nasals (which is a consequence of lowering the soft palate), the nasals [m], [n] and [ŋ] will each also have their own unique formant properties. Since [m] has the longest side cavity, its additional formant will be lowest in frequency. Since [n] has a shorter side cavity, its additional formant will be somewhat higher. Finally, [ŋ] has a very short side cavity, and so its additional formant will be highest of all.

Actually, since the formant energy of the side cavity cannot escape through the mouth (since the mouth is sealed shut), it's reflected back into the main larynx-to-nostrils tube. This dumped-in

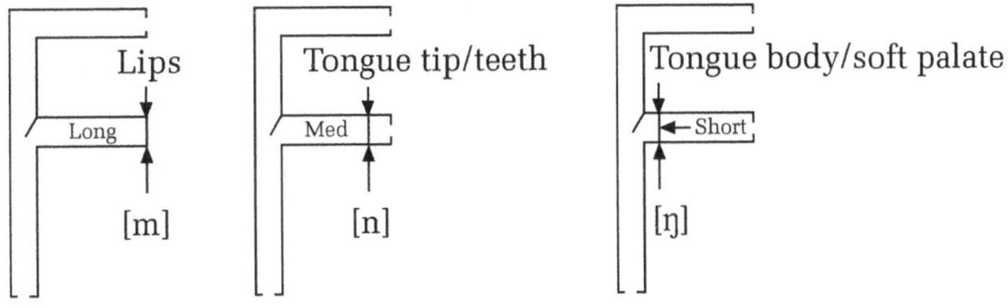

Figure 2.9 Locations of oral occlusion during [m], [n] and [ŋ]. The side cavity (behind the oral seal) affects the acoustic characteristics of the nasal consonant.

energy actually *cancels out* any corresponding energy that is present in the main cavity. The result is that the side cavity formant is not *added* to the main cavity formant structure, but is instead *subtracted* from it, resulting in an 'anti-formant'. This means that there is an energy *valley* for these anti-formants, not an energy peak.

In summary, then, during a nasal consonant the formant structure of the main cavity provides information that we are listening to a nasal sound, and the frequency range of the anti-formants gives each nasal its unique character by providing information on the location in the mouth of the oral occlusion (see Figure 2.10).

What I've provided here, in fact, is quite a simplified discussion. The acoustics of nasal sounds are actually extremely complicated, and can't accurately be characterized as the simple addition and/or subtraction of the oral and nasal cavities' resonant frequencies; the foregoing discussion should be taken as only a very rough first approximation.

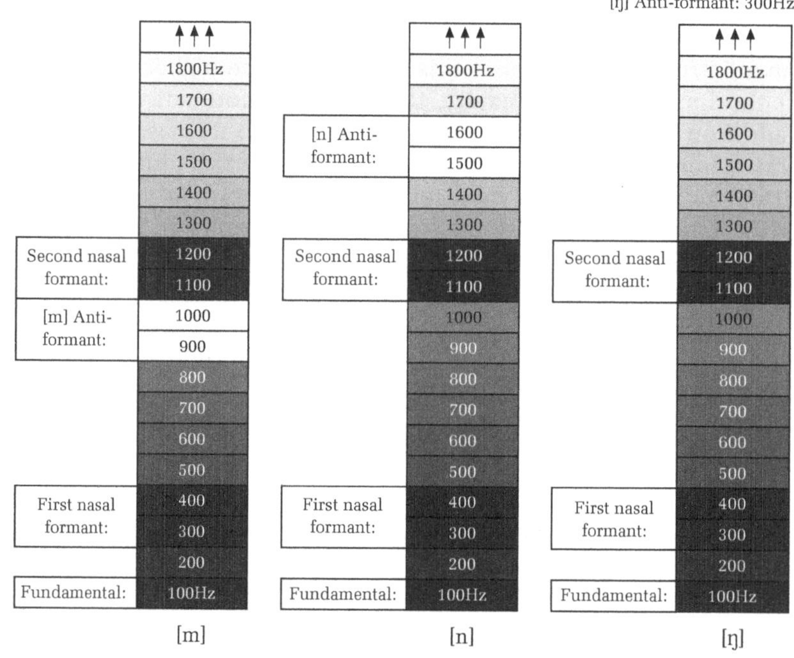

Figure 2.10 Rough schematics of the formant structure of [m, n, ŋ]: the first two nasal formants are found at about 350Hz and 1150Hz (there are higher formants as well). These help cue nasality to listeners. The nasal anti-informants (frequency ranges of reduced energy) increase in frequency as the location of oral occlusion is made farther back in the mouth. These help cue the oral quality of the nasal.

With this caveat in mind, we have, at any rate, now considered three acoustic properties of nasal sounds (their formant properties, their loss of energy in the higher frequencies, and their anti-formant properties), only one of which – their anti-formant properties – helps tell us whether we are dealing with [m], [n] or [ŋ]. But there are very important additional cues to the specific location of the oral occlusion in nasal consonants. Since nasals have oral occlusions, the tongue and lip movements into and out of these occlusions shape the mouth cavity, just as they do for [b̥, d̥, g̊]. Just like stop consonants, this additional set of cues resides on the neighbouring vowels, affecting the formant transitions both into the nasal and out of the nasal, in a way that further informs listeners about the specific location of the oral occlusion.

There is a third cue to the specific location of the oral occlusion during nasals. When moving from a vowel to a nasal, the soft palate does not lower strictly simultaneously with the formation of the oral occlusion. Instead, in virtually every language that has been investigated, the soft palate lowers *before* the oral occlusion is made. So consider the sequence of events for, say, 'on' ([ɑn]): we make a low vowel; we lower the soft palate; and we move the tongue tip towards the upper teeth to form an oral occlusion, giving us a nasal consonant. This means that a good portion of the vowel has air coming out of the nose as well as the mouth. It's hard to notice this, probably because our writing system doesn't indicate it, and so we don't have conscious awareness of it. But try placing your hands tightly over your ears. First say 'bid' or 'bit', then say 'bin'. Probably, you'll feel some vibration in your head – in your nasal passages, specifically – during the vowel for 'bin'. That's the nasalized vowel. Perhaps you recall how I transcribed 'phone' in Chapter One: [fõ$^{\tilde{\text{ʊ}}}$n]. The tilde over the vowel indicates that it is nasalized. So a more accurate transcription of 'on' is [ɑ̃n].

What's especially relevant for our purposes is that, in many languages, the soft palate opens at a different point during the preceding vowel, depending on the location of the nasal's oral occlusion. For example, in Beijing Chinese, the soft palate lowers earlier in the vowel when [ŋ] follows than when [n] follows. These timing differences provide an additional cue to the specific location of the oral occlusion. In Beijing Chinese then, when nasalization on the preceding vowel starts early, the location of the oral occlusion is at the soft palate ([ŋ]); when nasalization on the vowel starts later, the location of the oral occlusion is behind the upper teeth ([n]).

Since our ultimate aim as phonologists is to explain *why* sound systems are the way they are, let me briefly suggest a reason for the greater amount of nasalization on a vowel which precedes [ŋ], as opposed to one preceding [n] or [m]. Recall that [ŋ] has a very short side cavity, and so has a very high frequency anti-formant. In fact, this anti-formant is so high in frequency (above 3000Hz), that it really has very little effect on the overall formant structure of the nasal. When we recall that the harmonics decrease in energy as they get higher in frequency, we realize that this anti-formant – up above 3000Hz – will serve to cancel out only very little energy associated with nasality; it will have very little acoustic effect. By contrast, [m] and [n] have anti-formants of much lower frequencies, due to their longer side cavities. They impose energy valleys in regions that would otherwise have lots of energy (due to the formant properties of the long larynx-to-nostrils tube, nasals have a lot of lower frequency energy). The lower anti-formants for [n], and especially [m], consequently create a rather abrupt loss of energy at the transition from the vowel to the nasal consonant, since vowels also will have a great deal of energy at these lower frequencies due to their own formant properties. The abrupt change in energy distribution – from lots of energy at the lower frequencies, to very little energy here as a consequence of the anti-formant – makes a comparatively sharp *acoustic discontinuity* from the vowel to the [m] or the [n]. But for [ŋ], the *high* frequency orally-induced anti-formant does not affect acoustic quality of the *lower* frequencies, where the vowel formants reside. The result is that the transition from a vowel to [ŋ] is not as clearly encoded in the speech signal. A listener can hear a vowel, and can hear nasality, but, once in a while, will be less able to accurately determine when one ends and the other begins. Consequently, over the generations (which is how all sound patterns evolve and change – over the generations) the nasality might be more likely to become associated with the vowel itself, and so [ŋ] might be implemented with earlier soft-palate lowering.

There is an additional factor at work here. The mammalian auditory system is better at detecting and temporally isolating *increases* in acoustic energy, and is less adept at detecting and temporally isolating *decreases* in acoustic energy, especially *minor* decreases in acoustic energy, as in a vowel followed by [ŋ]. (There is an obvious survival advantage to this property of the auditory system – hearing a twig snap in the wild may make the difference between life and death!) Moving from a vowel into a nasal entails an overall *decrease* in acoustic energy, which, due to the nature of the mammalian auditory system, may result in the auditory impression of a less abrupt acoustic discontinuity between the vowel and the nasal than the acoustic signal actually possesses. Since acoustic energy decreases (as opposed to increases) as a vowel is followed by a nasal, then, once in a while, listeners might not as accurately temporally isolate the various components of the acoustic signal; they may be less able to accurately determine when the vowel ends and when the nasal begins. As speakers do their best to reproduce in their own speech what they hear from others, there may be a consequent tendency to, in turn, *overlap* the relevant articulatory gestures at the level of speech production, in imitation of the auditory signal that they have processed. If nasality from the consonant is overlapped onto a preceding vowel, the result is a nasalized vowel, which mimics the auditory impression of the acoustic signal quite accurately. All this happens very sporadically and very slowly, of course, over generations and generations of speakers; at any given stage of its development, perception and subsequent production is extremely accurate. This, then, is only a suggestion of the *origin* of the pattern.

Nasalization on vowels which *follow* nasals is often not as great as that found on vowels which precede nasals. This asymmetry too may be an indirect result of these physiological aspects of the auditory system. Moving from a nasal into a vowel involves an *increase* in acoustic energy, which the mammalian ear is quite capable of perceiving with temporal accuracy; the acoustic discontinuity at the transition from nasal to vowel will be saliently present in the auditory impression, and, as usual, accurately matched in speech production.

Table 2.1 summarizes our discussion of cues to nasal consonants.

Let's now remember why we got into the phonetic details of nasal consonants in the first place. Contrastive sound substitution does not work the way our writing system implies. It is *not* like Jotto; it is far more complex, affecting stretches of the speech signal that go well beyond the confines of the simple symbol replacement that our letter-by-letter writing system suggests. Look again at Table 2.1, which

Table 2.1 Major cues to nasal consonants

Cues to nasality	*Cues to the location of the oral occlusion*
Nasal formant at about 300 Hz (due to the long larynx-to-nostrils tube)	Location of the anti-formant (due to the length of the side cavity)
Loss of high-frequency energy (due to the soft tissue in the nasal cavities)	Vowel formant transitions into/out of the oral occlusion (due to the articulators moving toward/away from their closed position)
	Duration of nasalization on preceding vowel (due to earlier or later lowering of the soft palate)

outlines the major cues to nasal consonants. Changing the word 'sitter' into 'sinner' entails much more than is implied by a mere switching of 'tt' to 'nn', as nasal sounds actually possess several component parts – preceding the oral occlusion, during the oral occlusion, and following the oral occlusion, all of which possess acoustic information about the sound that is being produced.

Given this subdivision of the totality of acoustic cues to speech sounds, we might further assume that each of them is 'psychologically real' in the sense intended by Sapir. That is, we might suspect that our knowledge of phonology involves a partitioning of nasals into the component parts that our phonetic investigations may reveal. So knowledge of vowel nasalization, the formant transitions, and the nasal anti-formant might each occupy their own individual places in the collection of cognitive entities that eventually combine to produce our phonological system. But I don't think this is the way to go. Despite their separability into component parts, there is no reason to suspect that we treat nasal sounds as anything other than single, integrated wholes, or *Gestalts.* The differences between all the cues to each of the nasals in, say, 'simmer', 'sinner' and 'singer' combine to achieve a single functional result. This becomes especially clear when considering that *the cues to nasal consonants co-vary with each other.* So, a vowel with a lot of nasalization will probably have a lowering of F2 at the end, which will usually be followed by a nasal with a very high anti-formant, which in turn is followed by a raising of F2 if a vowel follows (that's [ŋ]). A vowel with less nasalization will probably have F2 moving towards 1800Hz, followed by a nasal with an anti-formant at around 1550Hz, and then an F2 departure away from 1800Hz if a vowel follows (that's [n]). Since the cues for a given nasal co-vary with each other, and since they don't separate and re-combine with each other in functionally consequential ways, there is little reason for listeners to decompose these cues in the way that a phonetician might: they *collectively* play a *single* functional role in the linguistic system. In this sense, then, finally, our alphabetic writing system seems to fare quite well. Although terribly imperfect, switching one letter with another often yields only a single functional change.

But while these cues strictly co-vary with each other in natural speech, we might set up experimental conditions in which natural speech is *modified*: delete a cue here, switch a few cues around there. By doing so, we might come to understand the importance of one cue over another, and, more basically, we might be able to determine if listeners do indeed decompose the entire ensemble of cues into component parts. For example, we might take the longer vowel nasalization for [ŋ] and switch it with the shorter vowel nasalization for

[n], leaving all other cues the same (this can be done with computers nowadays), and we can see how this affects the perception of the nasal by our experimental subjects. If subjects simply ignore the switch in vowel nasalization, a researcher might conclude that this cue is not terribly significant to the perception of the sound. Some might even argue that the vowel nasalization is a phonetic by-product of the more important, phonologically significant cues to the contrast. But such conclusions are just as wrong-headed as the conclusion that the 'real', 'authentic' pronunciation of 'phone' has an [n], not an [m] or an [ŋ]. We *know* that these cues are noticed and learned by listeners, simply because, for any given language, speakers produce their nasal sounds in the same way that they hear them, with all the phonetic detail intact. Clearly, then, we have full (though unconscious) access to all the phonetic detail we might extract from the speech stream, and there is no reason to assume that language users mentally 'undo' certain cues to arrive at a 'pure' or platonic ideal, such as those that our alphabetic symbols seem to suggest (more on this idea in Chapter Seven). At any rate, we must proceed with extreme caution when performing these sorts of experiments. How people deal with non-natural, doctored speech might not tell us too much about how people deal with normal, everyday speech. In real speech, all these cues co-vary with each other. But in these experiments, listeners are not dealing with the way speech really is, but with a distorted facsimile. Listeners' ability or inability to identify a modified speech signal may not be very telling, since the perceptual strategies that they might bring to bear when cues no longer co-vary with each other may be quite different from those they employ in the context of real spoken language. In general, we should not expect listeners to treat a non-linguistic signal – no matter how similar to language the signal might be – as anything other than non-language. So we should be cautious in assuming that we can learn very much about the structure of language from experiments like these.

You might detect a trend developing here. I see no reason to assume that language users subdivide nasals into their constituent cues the way a phonetician might, because all the cues pattern together in subsuming a single linguistic function. Earlier in this chapter I saw no reason to assume listeners subdivide *vowels* into their constituent formants the way a phonetician might, for this same reason. Nor do I assume that the cues that collectively mark the oral properties of a *stop consonant* – among them, formant transitions *into* the oral occlusion, and formant transitions *out of* the oral occlusion – should be treated as anything but a fully integrated *Gestalt*, despite their being separated by an interval of complete silence. But most fundamentally, as remarked in Chapter One, *I see no reason to assume that language users subdivide the words they learn into distinct sound-components unless there is evidence from alternation to do so. Linguists may subdivide the speech signal into a myriad of constituents, but the only constituents that exist for language users are those which emerge as a consequence of language use, due to the linguistic functions that underlie them.*

3. Vowel harmony

We have now considered two cases of contrastive sound substitution, demonstrating how *phonetically complex changes* may effect a *single functional change*, that is, a *change in meaning*. The various acoustic cues signalling a single functional change may be spread across a sizable temporal domain, or may even reside in discontinuous portions of the speech signal. While alphabetic writing systems do the job of providing a reliable visual code for spoken language, they cannot be taken as a true reflection of either the phonetic or cognitive characteristics of linguistic sound systems.

In our discussions of stops and nasals, we have considered some of the *consonantal* cues which are present in *vowels*. There is also some information about *vowels* that is present in *consonants* (other than stops, which have no energy at all if voiceless), though admittedly not too much.

Consider the word 'fellow'. We can transcribe this word [fɛlow], but here we will just concentrate on [ɛlo]. During the course of saying this portion of the word, I need to get from the position for [ɛ] (tongue mid and front; lips unrounded), to the [l] (tongue tip up behind the teeth, tongue side(s) down, allowing air to pass around the sides and out the mouth), and finally to the position for [o] (tongue mid and back; lips rounded). This sequence of events involves moving my tongue body backwards in the mouth and rounding my lips, while raising and lowering my tongue tip over the course of these other movements. Clearly, since I can't instantaneously jump from one mouth posture to the next, these movements must unfold over time. And since [ɛ], as we know, is so busy accommodating itself to the [l], while also asserting its own '[ɛ]-ness', there is little chance for too much of this tongue-backing and lip-rounding movement to take place before the [l] is implemented (although, in fact, the tongue really *does* start to move toward [o] before the end of the [ɛ] – more on this in a moment). By the same token, the [o] must accommodate to the [l] and assert its '[o]-ness', and so, again, there will be very little opportunity for the movement from [ɛ] to [o] to take place after the [l] is released. This means that the tongue and lip reposturing must take place mostly during the [l] itself. And since the [l] is like nasals and vowels (but not stops), in that it has a harmonic structure and formant properties, this means that there will be acoustic consequences of this reposturing during the [l] itself, in the form of formant transitions: moving the tongue back and rounding the lips when going from [ɛ] to [o] – even through an [l] – will lower F2. So, in addition to the cues that signify the [l], such consonants may also bear the acoustic mark of their surrounding vowel qualities. This means that the [l] of 'fellow' is slightly different from the [l] of 'fallow', which is different again from the [l] of 'follow'. (These same tongue movements take place during stop occlusions too, but since there is no energy in the speech signal during a stop, the only acoustic evidence for them resides just before the stop occlusion, and just after the stop release. At these locations, as I said, there is indeed evidence that the tongue is affected by the vowel on the other side of the consonant.)

Since there are cues to one vowel even through an intervening consonant and on to a neighbouring vowel, then, over the course of generations of speakers, there are opportunities for vowel qualities to get 'unstuck' from their predominantly inter-consonantal position. What I mean is, since vowels are slightly influenced by the articulatory and acoustic properties of their neighbouring vowels – even across intervening consonants – it's possible that vowels might come to have more significant effects on each other. So one vowel might slowly (over the generations, of course) begin to encroach upon another vowel, eventually inducing a significant change to this other vowel's articulatory and acoustic makeup. This sort of vowel-to-vowel interaction is actually quite common in the world's languages, going by the name of 'vowel harmony'. In vowel harmony, one vowel takes on a property or properties of a neighbouring vowel, such that the same or a similar tongue and/or lip position is maintained from one vowel – even through intervening consonants – to a neighbouring vowel.

Let's consider an example, to show what I mean. Consider the Finnish words in Table 2.2.

The [æ] symbol is pronounced just like the 'a' in 'bat'. The tongue is in a low front position. For [ø], the tongue is also in a front position, higher

Table 2.2 Some words of Finnish

Finnish	*transcription*	*translation*	*Finnish*	*transcription*	*translation*
väkära	[vækæɾæ]	pinwheel	makkara	[makkaɾa]	sausage
pöytä	[pøjtæ]	table	pouta	[powta]	fine weather
käyrä	[kæjɾæ]	curve	kaura	[kawɾa]	oats
tyhmä	[tyhmæ]	stupid	tuhma	[tuhma]	naughty

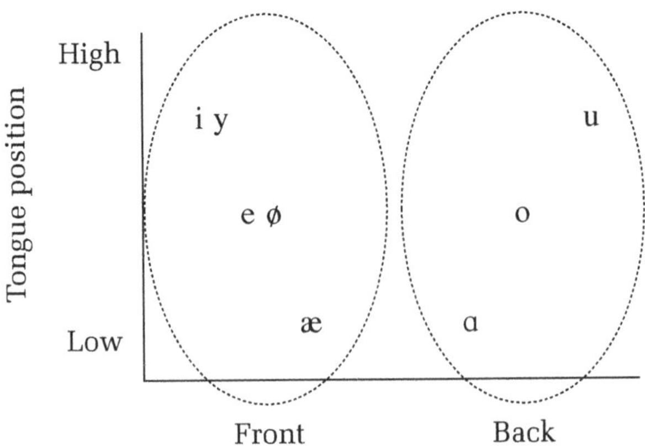

Figure 2.11 A plot of the Finnish vowels

in the mouth than [æ], and the lips are rounded; it's the same as [e], except that the lips are rounded. The [y] is front as well, and is in a higher position still, also with the lips rounded: simply a rounded [i]. Let's now plot these three new vowel qualities along with the five we already know about. Following standard practice, in Figure 2.11 I put the new rounded vowels directly to the right of their unrounded counterparts.

If we now look back at the Finnish words I listed, and compare the vowels in those words to those in the vowel chart, a very interesting pattern emerges. Throughout Finnish, a word has either all front vowels, or a word has all back vowels. That is to say, Finnish vowels are *harmonic* in terms of front/back. (There are certain exceptions to vowel harmony in Finnish, but these exceptions do not bear on the current argument.) I have circled the two sets of vowels – front and back – to illustrate what I mean. For instance, the only difference between [tyhmæ] and [tuhmɑ] is the front or back position of the tongue. Other phonetic aspects of these two words are more or less the same. This means that in Finnish, changing one aspect of tongue posture for the *entirety of the word* (either a front posture or a back posture) while keeping other aspects of tongue posture stable, changes the meaning of the word as well. Changing the tongue position in this way affects the F2 of the first vowel, also the following consonants, and the following vowels as well. (Remember that F2 is affected by tongue backness/frontness.) This means that the contrastive sound substitution is changing *part* of a vowel quality across *more than one* vowel (including the intervening consonants as well)!

Although Finnish uses an alphabet which provides an effective method of visually encoding the spoken language, there is just no way that this alphabetic, symbol-by-symbol system can effectively capture the genuine nature of this sort of sound substitution. Finnish vowel harmony cannot be compellingly represented in an alphabetic system because this single sound substitution affects a shared phonetic sub-component (tongue fronting/backing) of a number of different – independent and unrelated – symbols. Vowel harmony thus requires that more than one alphabetic symbol be changed to reflect only a single phonological substitution. For example, the single sound substitution in 'tyhmä' to 'tuhma' – the replacement of a front tongue position with a back tongue position – requires replacing two symbols: 'u' for 'y' and 'a' for 'ä'. And although the 'h' and 'm' stay the *same*, their phonetic properties actually *change* as a consequence of vowel harmony. So alphabets inevitably *under*-represent the phonetic changes in sound substitution, and, as the case of vowel harmony shows, alphabets sometimes *over*-represent the phonological changes. Of course, once again, Finnish uses an alphabet for writing, and it serves its purpose just fine. But it is a significant mistake to assume that its writing system reflects the genuine phonological properties of the Finnish language.

If you still had faith in the Jotto metaphor, I hope the phenomenon of vowel harmony has shattered it once and for all.

Summary

To sum up, in this chapter I hope to have convinced you that an alphabetic writing system fails to reveal the true nature of linguistic sound systems. This is not a damning criticism of alphabetic writing systems. They were not developed to serve this purpose, and they do quite an adequate job of visually representing spoken language. I am suggesting, however, that it is a serious mistake to employ our alphabetic writing system as a model – even an imperfect model – of phonological structure. A simple, letter-by-letter system does not do justice to the genuine complexities of phonetics and phonology, and, further, tends to confound speakers' (and, alas, many linguists') understanding of the true nature of sound substitution.

In some cases, our writing system employs more than one symbol for an identical phonetic value: 'p', 't' and 'k' are different symbols, yet for the duration of the speech signal that we take each to represent, there is nothing but silence. (Instead, the cues to these consonants reside primarily in formant transitions into and out of the oral occlusion, at the adjacent edges of neighbouring vowels.) In all other cases, a single symbol is employed for a wide array of phonetic distinctions, encoding information about a number of different contrastive sounds simultaneously:

recall that the stretch of the speech stream represented by a single vowel symbol like 'a' contains information about many different phonological contrasts, such as neighbouring stops, the oral quality of a following nasal consonant, and so on. We have also seen that the symbols we use for consonants other than stops present us with same situation, as the sounds that these symbols represent include phonetic details about the flanking vowels as well, as in our discussion of the 'l' in 'fellow' versus 'fallow' versus 'follow', for example. Finally, vowel harmony shows us that a single phonological change may have cues spanning the entirety of a word, and thus requires *multiple* changes to the alphabetic notation to indicate only a *single* phonological change.

It is clear that phonology does not consist of the speech-segment-by-speech-segment chunks implied by an alphabetic writing system. Just consider what's going on as we make a nasal sound between vowels, as in 'loony' [luni]. The various gestures are choreographed in a genuinely balletic fashion, overlapping with each other to produce many and varied acoustic cues for each of the linguistically relevant components of the speech stream (see Figure 2.12). Indeed, it shouldn't be surprising that languages have evolved a property that multiplies the opportunities for listeners to receive the intended message from speakers.

All this being said, there is still no question that speech is indeed orchestrated around a gross pattern of closing down and opening up the vocal tract, resulting in series of consonant-like entities followed

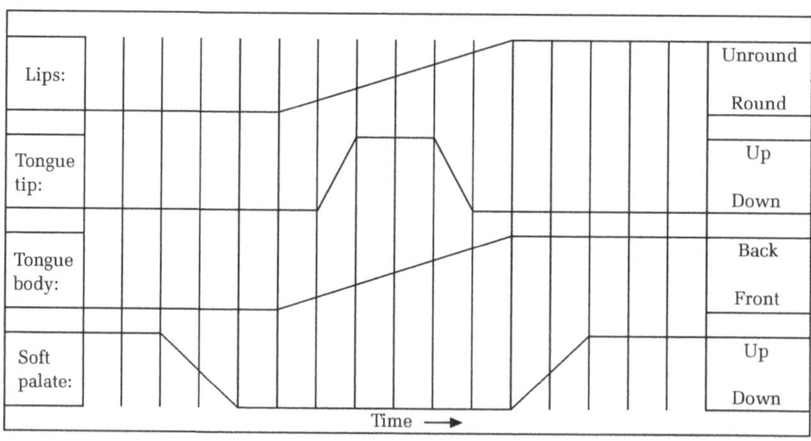

Figure 2.12 The overlapped movements of the articulators for the word 'loony', minus the initial 'l'. Overlapping of the articulatory gestures gives rise to multiple and varied acoustic cues, thus better serving the communicative function of language.

by vowel-like entities. This makes sense, since robust transitions from consonant to vowel give rise to a multitude of overlapping and stretched-out cues that aid listeners in recovering the speech signal, and since, as noted, the sudden increase in acoustic energy as a consonant is released into a vowel is auditorily prominent. Consequently, it is very easy to succumb to the illusion that the components of the speech stream commonly referred to as 'vowels' and 'consonants' are the primary bearers of functionally relevant information. But the results of this chapter instead suggest that *the consonant–vowel sequences that we think we observe are simply artefactual, and it is the transitions between them that are most relevant*, since they are the most informationally rich and often the most auditorily prominent components of the speech signal. Alphabets are hopeless in capturing this fundamental characteristic of phonological systems. Speech is not accurately represented by the writing systems we might employ, even, unfortunately, by the remarkably useful and flexible phonetic transcription system that we will continue to use for the remainder of this book.

This is all old news, actually. In 1880, the linguist Hermann Paul wrote, 'A real analysis of the word into its proper elements is not merely extremely difficult, but is actually impossible. A word is not a united compound of a definite number of independent sounds, of which each can be expressed by an alphabetical sign; but it is essentially a continuous series of infinitely numerous sounds, and alphabetical symbols do no more than bring out certain characteristic points of this series in an imperfect way.' Mikołaj Kruszewski wrote something similar in 1883: 'A sound complex cannot be considered a mechanical juxtaposition of a certain quantity of independent sounds. When combining with one another, sounds – we have in mind here not only their acoustic, but also their physiological aspect – accommodate themselves to one another. This accommodation is the cement which transforms several sounds into one integral complex'. In 1927, Kruszewski's teacher, Jan Baudouin de Courtenay, wrote, 'two types of confusion must … be guarded against: (a) that of letters with sounds …, and (b) that of phonetic-auditory phenomena with their fixed psychological counterparts.'

Our intuitions might tell us that the *real* phonological structure is still accurately represented in a symbol-by-symbol system. So, we might not notice the nasalization on a vowel before a consonant, and we might regard this as evidence that such nasality is simply an *unintended* phonetic reflex, and the real, authentic *intended* value is the nasal consonant itself. But recall that such intuitions are exactly a consequence of our explicit training in alphabetic writing, and do not open any sort of window on to the structural properties of language. We exploit all these cues as listeners, and we reproduce them all as speakers, and so they are all relevant to the linguistic system.

As I discussed in Chapter One, in order to understand the nature and extent of contrastive sound substitutions, linguists have to investigate a huge number of words. Discovering that [tʰ] and [b̥] contrast before [_ɹɪk] is just one single fact; these might be the only two words of the language which substitute [tʰ] and [b̥], just as 'knish' may be the only word in English to have [kn] at the beginning. But although we have only barely scratched the surface of the extensive functional role of contrastive sound substitution, we have gone into considerable detail about the actual complexity of the issue.

Further reading

The Ladefoged quote ('Many consonants are just ways of beginning or ending vowels . . .'):

Ladefoged, Peter (2001). *Vowels and Consonants.* Oxford: Blackwell, p. 47.

On vowel nasalization in Beijing Chinese:

Zhang, Jie (2000). 'Non-contrastive features and categorical patterning in Chinese diminutive suffixation – Max[F] or Ident[F]?', *Phonology* 17: 427–78.

On the phonetics of nasals and their phonological consequences:

Ohala, John J. (1975). 'Phonetic explanations of nasal sound patterns', in Charles A. Ferguson, Larry M. Hyman and John J. Ohala (eds), *Nasálfest: Papers from a Symposium on Nasals and Nasalization.* Language Universals Project, Stanford University, pp. 289–316.

On the importance of acoustic discontinuities in the speech signal:

Mattingly, Ignatius G. (1981). 'Phonetic representations and speech synthesis by rule', in T. Myers, J. Laver and J. Anderson (eds), *The Cognitive Representation of Speech.* Amsterdam: North Holland Publishing Company, pp. 415–19.

On the mammalian auditory system as related to the organization of speech:

Delgutte, Bertrand (1980). 'Representation of speech-like sounds in the discharge patterns of auditory-nerve fibers', *Journal of the Acoustical Society of America* 68: 843–7.

Delgutte, Bertrand (1982). 'Some correlates of phonetic distinctions at the level of the auditory nerve', in R. Carlson and B. Granström, (eds), *The Representation of Speech in the Peripheral Auditory System.* Amsterdam: Elsevier Biomedical, pp. 131–50.

On the auditory prominence of consonant-to-vowel transitions:

Bladon, Anthony (1986). 'Phonetics for hearers', in G. McGregor (ed.), *Language for Hearers.* Oxford: Pergamon Press, pp. 1–24.

Silverman, Daniel (1995 [1997]) *Phasing and Recoverability*. New York: Garland.

Wright, Richard (2004). 'A review of perceptual cues and cue robustness', in Bruce Hayes, Robert Kirchner and Donca Steriade (eds), *Phonetically Based Phonology*. Cambridge: Cambridge University Press, pp. 34–57.

On the perceptual integration of cues to nasal consonants:

Kurowski, Kathleen and Blumstein, Sheila E. (1984). 'Perceptual integration of the murmur and formant transitions for place of articulation in nasal consonants', *Journal of the Acoustical Society of America* 76.2: 383–90.

On vowel-to-vowel influence (through intervening consonants):

Ohman, Sven E. G. (1966). 'Coarticulation in VCV utterances: spectrographic measurements', *Journal of the Acoustical Society of America* 39: 151–68.

On Finnish vowel harmony:

Harms, Robert T. (1997). *Finnish Structural Sketch*. Richmond, Surrey: Routledge Curzon.

The Paul quote ('*A real analysis of the word into its proper elements* ...'):

Paul, Hermann (1880 [1970]). *Principles of the History of Language*. College Park, MD: McGrath, p. 39.

The Kruszewski quote ('*A sound complex cannot be considered* ...'):

Kruszewski, Mikołaj (1883 [1995]). 'An outline of linguistic science', in Konrad Koerner (ed.), *Writings in General Linguistics*, (Amsterdam Classics in Linguistics 11). Amsterdam: John Benjamins, p. 63.

The Baudouin de Courtenay quote ('*two types of confusion must* ... *be guarded against* ...):

Baudouin de Courtenay, Jan (1927 [1972]). 'The difference between phonetics and psychophonetics', in Edward Stankiewicz (ed.), *A Baudouin de Courtenay Reader*. Bloomington: Indiana University Press, p. 281.

Part 2
I speak my mind

3 Neutralizing sound substitution

Recall something I wrote in Chapter One about 'phone books' and 'foam books'. Although one pronunciation of the word 'phone' sounds exactly like 'foam', there is very little chance for miscommunication. And if you think about it, it really couldn't be any other way. Indeed, a language could never evolve towards a state in which its communicative function becomes genuinely eroded. Neutralization may survive, but it will never flourish. By hook or by crook, linguistic communication will proceed unencumbered. Real-world knowledge plays a great role in disambiguating homophonous forms, but in many cases where the phonetic distinctions between words are evolving towards massive neutralization, a language will *co*-evolve means to countervail the threat of ambiguity. As we'll see in this chapter, this response is often phonological in nature, but in some cases it is morphological instead. We'll consider several cases which illustrate this, further finding that *it is impossible to account for the state of a language at a particular point in time without also considering the historical forces that have given rise to this state*: forms that are neutralized in the present may have been phonetically *distinct* in the past. As Baudouin de Courtenay wrote in 1871, 'The mechanism of a language (its structure and composition) at any given time is the result of all its preceding history and development, and each synchronic state determines in turn its further development'.

1. Dutch

Let's begin with a very common phenomenon – so-called *nasal assimilation* – that illustrates how a potentially neutralizing sound pattern evolves.

In Chapter Two I suggested strong caution in putting too much stock in certain experimental methods we might employ to determine the greater importance of one acoustic cue over another. My reasoning, recall, was that many experimental methods rely on a manipulation of the speech signal such that we can't be sure whether listeners are using their usual speech perception strategies while trying to decipher the doctored signal, or whether they are exploiting alternative, atypical strategies; we cannot expect listeners to treat a non-linguistic signal as anything other than non-language. There are, however, alternatives to such experimental procedures that might help us determine the greater importance of certain acoustic cues over others. Some of these alternatives take place in 'nature's laboratory'. In nature's laboratory, the experimental setting may be a speech community that is observed over generations, from which linguistic data is collected and analysed. Specifically, we focus on sound change – what sounds, and under what circumstances, change into what other sounds. It seems like a huge task, and indeed it is; until recent times linguists have assumed that language change can only be *deduced*, but not directly *observed*. But, in the greatest empirical finding of twentieth-century linguistics, the linguist William Labov has spent his career demonstrating that sound change *can* be observed. Labov has painstakingly documented the statistical details of speech patterning within and between speech communities, having conclusively demonstrated that language is in a constant state of flux in both time and space, and that this flux is indeed observable and measurable even over the span of a few years time, and a few city blocks. His work has necessarily covered only several decades so far, but clearly this foundational work can be continued across the generations. Labov's remarkable findings lend credence to the hypothesis that *sounds in alternation in the present often reflect sounds that have gradually changed in the past*. Regarding sound substitutions which are potentially neutralizing, the less perceptually distinct two sounds are in a particular context, then the more likely that they will evolve towards the same phonetic value. At that point, if certain words were previously rendered distinct by these sounds and these sounds only, then homophony is the result. Based on such sound changes, we might formulate hypotheses about *which* particular acoustic cues are more likely to be rendered indistinct from each other in such potentially neutralizing contexts, and which cues are less jeopardized. We can then establish a hierarchy of perceptual prominence among the cues that combine to form a contrast. This is one way in which 'nature's laboratory' can help us determine the greater importance of certain acoustic cues over others.

As an example, let's recall some of the acoustic properties of nasal sounds. There are four major acoustic cues to the location of the oral occlusion among the nasals ([m, n, ŋ]):

(1) the formant transitions out of the nasal consonant;
(2) the formant transitions into the nasal consonant;
(3) the location of the nasal anti-formant during the oral closure, and
(4) the duration of nasalization on the preceding vowel.

Among nasals, certain patterns of potentially neutralizing sound substitution appear in language after language: [n], [ŋ] and (less often) [m] are substituted for the nasal sound which matches the place of oral closure of a following stop consonant. For example, a morpheme that has a final [n] in most contexts may replace that [n] with [m] before morpheme-initial [p], and with [ŋ] before morpheme-initial [k], much like the pattern in English: [n+p] becomes [mp], [n+k] becomes [ŋk] (recall that '+' indicates a morpheme boundary). This sort of sound substitution is called an *assimilation*, since one of the sounds becomes more similar to its neighbour; the nasal *assimilates* to the following stop in terms of its tongue and/or lip configuration. If certain words or morphemes differ only in terms of a final [n] or [m], for example, then this sound substitution will neutralize their distinction, just like 'pho[m]e book', where the labial [m] is found when a labial [b] follows.

Let's consider Dutch, which has a fairly straightforward case of nasal assimilation. Dutch morphemes sometimes have nasal–stop sequences, but these sequences, just like English, always agree in terms of their oral quality, for example *panter* [nt] 'panther', *wimper* [mp] 'eyelash', *anker* [ŋk] 'anchor'. Dutch also has nasal assimilation at morpheme and word boundaries. Here, morpheme- or word-final nasals may assimilate to a following stop, but only if this nasal is realized as [n] in other contexts: [ɪn+trɛk] 'move in', [ɪm+pɑk] 'wrap to', [ɪŋ+kɛik] 'look into'. The underlined sounds in these forms belong to the same morpheme, despite their phonetic differences. Morphemes that have final [n] in some contexts may consequently neutralize with otherwise identical [m]-final and/or [ŋ]-final morphemes. For example, *Han* [hɑn] is a proper name, while *ham* [ham] means 'ham', and *hang* [hɑŋ] means 'bent'. Due to nasal assimilation, *Han bidt* ('Han prays') may be pronounced [hɑm bit], and *Han koopt* ('Han buys') may be pronounced [hɑŋ kopt]. So homophony is induced, but clearly the likelihood for miscommunication – at least in these examples – is virtually nil. Other morpheme-final nasals ([m] and [ŋ]) are stable regardless of the oral features of the following consonant: [ɔm+trɛk] 'circumcise', [ɔm+prɑt] 'talk into', [ɔm+kɛik] 'look back', and also [lɑŋ+ten] 'long toe', [xɑŋ+pɑt] 'corridor', [hɑŋ+kɑst] 'cupboard'.

If we want to understand *why* this sort of sound substitution has evolved, we might begin by comparing the acoustic properties of assimilated nasal sounds with the acoustic properties of *un*assimilated nasal sounds. It is quite possible that the sorts of acoustic cues which are present in the non-assimilated context, but which are missing from the assimilative context, are especially functionally important. My reasoning is rooted in the hypothesis that cues which are robust tend to survive, but in certain contexts certain cues become weakened, perhaps disappearing entirely. Without these cues, the ability of listeners to discern distinctions between sounds which depend on these cues becomes diminished. Consequently, the likelihood that these sounds will be perceived as identical becomes greater.

Let's consider the cues for nasal sounds in certain contexts, to see which cues are absent and which cues are present. First, when a morpheme-initial nasal is immediately preceded by a stop, but is immediately followed by a vowel (for example [ɑp+nɑ]; not a real word, but I'm using it just to clearly illustrate the patterns that we're looking at), then:

(1) formant transitions out of the nasal consonant are present ([...nɑ]);
(2) formant transitions into the nasal consonant are largely absent, since a consonant immediately precedes the nasal ([...p+n...]);
(3) the nasal anti-formant is present ([...n...]), and
(4) there is no nasalization on the preceding vowel, since a non-nasal consonant immediately precedes the nasal ([...ɑp+n...]).

Now consider that we almost never observe an assimilative sound substitution in this context, so [ɑp+nɑ] may very well contrast with [ɑp+mɑ], and perhaps [ɑp+ŋɑ] as well, but in the world's languages we almost never find, for example, [nɑ], but [ɑp+mɑ], [ɑt+nɑ], and [ɑk+ŋɑ]. In these examples, the underlined sounds all belong to the same morpheme, but have assimilated to the preceding stop consonant. This suggests that formant transitions from the vowel into a following nasal are not essential to conveying the location of the nasal's oral closure since, even in their absence, the oral contrasts between nasals are likely to endure over the generations. This also suggests that the amount of nasalization on a preceding vowel is not essential either, because again, even in the absence of this nasalization, the nasal's oral quality survives.

When a nasal sound immediately precedes a stop closure made at a different location in the mouth, for example if we replace the second morpheme of [ɑ̃n+ɑ] with [+pɑ] giving [ɑ̃n+pɑ], this is what we find:

(1) formant transitions out of the nasal consonant are largely absent, since a consonant immediately follows ([...n+p...]);
(2) formant transitions into the nasal consonant are present ([ɑ̃n...]);
(3) the nasal anti-formant is present ([...n...]), and
(4) nasalization on the preceding vowel is present ([ɑ̃n...]).

But recall that this is the context in which we typically observe the assimilative sound substitution, for example [ãn̠+ɑ] and [ãn̠+tɑ], but [ãm̠+pɑ] and [ãŋ̠+kɑ]. Combined with our earlier results, this suggests several things:

(1) The formant transitions from the nasal into a following vowel seem to be very important in the determination of a nasal's place of articulation. Without these formant transitions, the distinctive oral properties of the nasal may eventually be lost.
(2) Formant transitions from the vowel to the nasal, again, are not especially important, since their presence here does not salvage the nasal's oral properties.
(3) The anti-formant is not extremely important for the determination of a nasal's place of articulation, since it is present whether the nasal assimilates or not.
(4) Again, the duration of nasalization on the preceding vowel does not seem crucial to determining the place of oral closure, since its presence here does not salvage the nasal's oral properties.

So, the presence-versus-absence of formant transitions into a following vowel seem to be the best predictor of the survival or loss of a nasal's oral properties, the other cues less so.

Before moving on, it's important to keep certain ideas organized properly. I just said that both vowel nasalization and the nasal anti-formant survive even in contexts where a nasal assimilates to a following stop. This doesn't mean that the *value* of the nasal anti-formant of [n] in [ãn̠+ɑ] is maintained even when it is substituted with the [m] in [ãm̠+pɑ]. Of course, the location of the anti-formant changes upon the sound substitution: it is higher in frequency for [n], and lower in frequency for [m]. So there is *some* anti-formant present, whether we consider the [n] of [ãn̠+ɑ] or the [m] of [ãm̠+pɑ]. The point is that any particular anti-formant doesn't seem to be a sufficiently robust acoustic cue to inhibit the assimilative sound change. Our working hypothesis is that non-contrastive sound substitutions are the product of slow-going sound changes. The presence of formant transitions from a nasal to a vowel seem to be sufficiently robust that the nasal's oral properties have a secure future even in the absence of certain other cues. But in the absence of these nasal-to-vowel formant transitions – as when a stop consonant immediately follows the nasal – other cues seem susceptible to change; they are insufficiently robust to perpetuate themselves in their original form.

To summarize, the cross-linguistic patterning of nasal sounds suggests that (1) the formant transitions from the nasal into a vowel are very important for listeners in their determination of a nasal's oral features, and that (2) the formant transitions into the nasal, (3) the nasal anti-formant and (4) the duration of nasalization on the preceding vowel are somewhat less important for listeners in their determination of a nasal's oral features. (It should be noted that at least one lab experiment has found that the anti-formant is as important as the nasal-to-vowel formant transitions in cueing a nasal's oral features. These results are inconsistent with the suggestive evidence from actual alternations and actual sound changes.)

So far, we have compared the cross-linguistic tendencies in the patterning of nasal sounds to the acoustic cues that are present or absent in a given context, and have tentatively concluded that nasal sounds are more likely to maintain their contrastive oral properties when they are immediately followed by a vowel, and less likely to do so when they are followed by a consonant. But we haven't considered why the loss of these acoustic cues so often leads to a specifically *assimilative* sound substitution ([mp, nt, ŋk]), rather than, say, the uniform presence of a single nasal sound regardless of context (for example [np, nt, nk]). Both of these results are possible outcomes, so why is it only the assimilative pattern that we find?

Although I will argue otherwise, many phonologists believe that the explanation for assimilative nasal substitution lies predominantly – or even exclusively – in the realm of articulation. These phonologists claim that speakers *anticipate* the place of articulation of the stop consonant during the nasal itself, such that the nasal forfeits its own oral properties in favour of the following stop's. However, this articulation-based account of the pattern cannot explain the absence of assimilation in contexts where stops precede nasals: we rarely, if ever, find a pattern like [ɑt̲+ɑ], but [ɑp̲+mɑ], [ɑt̲+nɑ] and [ɑk̲+ŋɑ], even though an articulatory account would predict their occurrence. Indeed, the sound substitutions that we observe can probably *never* be reduced to such one-dimensional, proximate influences on speech, articulatory or otherwise; we observe articulatory anticipation in the present state of the language, but this doesn't mean that the pattern has its origins in present-day articulatory forces. There is a tremendous temptation to explain that which is observable in the present solely in terms of forces that are supposedly active in the present. But in actuality, present-day patterns of alternation result from a dizzyingly complex and long-term interaction of articulatory, acoustic, auditory, aerodynamic, perceptual, functional and social forces. Just as the form that a species takes is not determined anew in each generation, but is the culmination of centuries and centuries of gradual, enormously complex evolutionary pressures, the behaviour of a linguistic sound is the culmination of generations and generations of gradual changes in patterns of usage. In short, it's facile to assume that the explanation for present-day phonetic and phonological patterns reduces to present-day phonetic and phonological pressures.

Instead of focusing exclusively on the current state of the system, the way to understand the origins of nasal assimilation is to work backwards from the present. In many present-day languages, there are no contrastive oral features on nasals which precede stops. However, listeners have always been able to determine that the sound – whatever its oral characteristics – is indeed a nasal. This is because the nasal formant structure is not jeopardized in this context: the vocal folds are vibrating, the soft palate is down, air rushes through the nose, and thus the cues to nasality are robustly present in the speech signal. So listeners clearly hear nasality, and they clearly hear a following stop.

Now, in the case of vowel–nasal–stop sequences, for example [ɑ̃n+p], nasalization is present during the *transition* from the vowel to the oral closure of the nasal, rendering the acoustic signal especially complex during this crucial moment. This may contribute to the tendency for nasals' susceptibility to confusion and, ultimately, their susceptibility to assimilation. By contrast, consider the case of vowel–stop–nasal sequences, for example [ɑt+m]. Nasals before stops tend to assimilate, but stops before nasals almost never do; we don't find languages with [ap̲+mɑ], [at̲+nɑ], and [ak̲+ŋɑ]. This may be due to the absence of a superimposed nasal formant structure during the transition from vowel to stop. This results in a somewhat more transparent acoustic coding of the transition, one which is less susceptible to perceptual confusion, hence more resistant to assimilation.

In general, listeners reproduce in their own speech what they hear in the ambient pattern. So listeners, more or less, produce as many assimilated nasals as are present in the ambient pattern. But as with any reproductive system, exact replication is virtually impossible. Mistakes and elements of randomness are inevitable: some of the nasals which were unidentified by listeners might be implemented correctly as these listeners become speakers, while others may vary among other oral qualities. But in the absence of evidence to the contrary, speakers might be more likely to place their tongue and lips in the position of a sound which they *know* the identity of, that is, the following stop consonant. (They know the value of this following consonant because it is released into a following vowel, and so its cues are salient.) This is not an *anticipation* of the following stop. Rather, it is a guess about the oral properties of the nasal itself. So perhaps a good percentage of these unidentified nasals will be implemented with the same oral properties as the following stop consonant. Consequently, in the next generation of speakers, an increasing number of forms do indeed possess assimilated nasals, which are usually interpreted correctly by listeners. But of course, many forms remain unassimilated, and so are subject to misidentification by listeners. Some of these, again, will be implemented as assimilated. And so the sound change is set in motion. As the generations proceed, more and more forms are spoken with assimilated nasals, such that a pressure to regularize the pattern may eventually be exerted on the remaining unassimilated forms to fall in line with the new norm.

The spread to more forms might initially be constrained to one or other sound, as in the case of Dutch. In Dutch, only the tongue-tip nasal has succumbed to assimilation across morpheme boundaries, whereas the lip and tongue-body nasals have not fallen in line. (Cross-linguistically, tongue-tip and tongue-body nasals are indeed the most susceptible to assimilation; labial consonants are less so, probably due to their robust anti-formant properties.) Eventually, the assimilation may become unconstrained, and *all* nasals might assimilate. And so, what started as a minor phonetic tendency may slowly gain momentum over the generations, first affecting a subset of nasals (as in Dutch at morpheme boundaries), but eventually culminating in the assimilation of *all* nasal consonants which precede stops (as in many other languages, and perhaps someday in Dutch as well). (Within Dutch morphemes, this process has already been completed: recall that all morpheme-internal nasal–stop sequences in Dutch are fully assimilated. It is typical for morpheme-internal sequences to lead the way in such assimilative tendencies, probably because they are the most frequently employed sequences of the speech signal. We delve into the relation between *token frequency* and *the tendency to assimilate or simplify* in Chapter Seven.)

In this scenario, the forces that give rise to speech patterns are *not* created anew by each generation of speakers, nor are they explicable in terms of purely proximate forces. Rather, speech patterns are simply imperfect copies of what is perceived. As a consequence of imperfect replication, certain variant forms may come to hold sway; sound change is the culmination of interacting forces that slowly proceed over generations of speakers. Sometimes, the result is a potentially neutralizing alternation, such as nasal assimilation.

In Chapter Two I discussed how contrastive sounds are actually composed of a number of different acoustic cues that co-vary with each other. Exactly because these cues co-vary, I refrained from suggesting a hierarchy of their importance. Rather, a change in any one cue or combination of cues collectively signals a single functional result – changing word meaning, maintaining word meaning, or potentially eliminating the phonetic evidence for a distinction in word meaning. For this reason, it is unlikely that listeners decompose these cues in the ways that phoneticians and phonologists might. But now, in Chapter Three, I am arguing that certain cues are indeed more important than other cues for a given sound, and that the differences in their importance might influence the way sounds change over time. So which is it? Should the various cues that phoneticians and phonologists might isolate for a given speech sound be regarded as functionally integrated as in Chapter Two, or as independent of each other as in Chapter Three? In fact, it's not contradictory to assert that the cues to contrastive sounds should be treated in both ways. At the *synchronic* ('same-time') cognitive level – the level at which individual language users establish correspondences between sound and meaning – there is no reason to assume that the co-varying cues which collectively possess a single function are decomposed into their constituent parts by the learner/listener. However, at the *diachronic* ('across-time') level – the level of cross-generational sound change – we can readily observe how particular cues might be slowly and passively re-shaped; certain acoustic cues are more susceptible to change over time than other cues. The forces that shape the changes that cues undergo play out over time and over entire speech communities. They do not play out in the 'real time' of individual speaker-hearers, although, to be sure, the individual is the 'conduit' by which patterns travel from one state to another. The same is true in the evolution of species, of course. Generational neighbours are remarkably similar in their genetic makeup, and change is more readily observable over great periods of time, due to the success or failure of traits at the level of the individual organism.

2. Korean, Chinese and Chong

The primary finding for nasals can actually be extended to include other consonants: *any* consonant that is immediately followed by another consonant is less likely to maintain its contrastive qualities than is a consonant that is immediately followed by a vowel. Consonants which precede other consonants are far more likely to lose their release cues and potentially neutralize contrasts.

Consider the case of Korean. Korean has a rather rich inventory of consonants that may be found before a vowel. Look at the list of consonants in Table 3.1, which constitutes the tongue-tip *obstruent* subset of this group. In acoustic terms, obstruents are consonants which lack well-defined harmonic structures; in articulatory terms, they are consonants for which the degree of oral constriction is sufficiently critical that air turbulence is generated (these are *fricatives*),

Table 3.1 The tongue-tip obstruents of Korean that may be found at the beginning of a word

t	tʰ	t'
tʃ	tʃʰ	tʃ'
	sʰ	s'

or that airflow is completely stopped (stops). *Resonants* (also called *sonorants*) are sounds like vowels and nasals which have well-defined harmonic structures and resonant frequencies; they have a more open vocal tract.

All the sounds in the first two rows ([t, tʰ, t', tʃ, tʃʰ, tʃ']) have oral closures made with the tongue tip. Their differences reside primarily in the quality of their release. Releases allow stops to be modified in various ways which may serve a contrastive function: released with a puff of air ([tʰ]), released with closed or nearly-closed vocal folds ([t']; discussed shortly), released with a fricative sound (the [ʃ] component of [tʃ]; [tʃ] is similar to the first sound in 'jeep'), or released with a combination of features ([tʃʰ], as in 'cheap', and [tʃ'], which is not found in English). The superscripted 'h' indicates a puff of air which we call *aspiration*; the vocal folds are spread far apart as the consonant is released, and air rushes out of the mouth. The third column of sounds involves another posture of the vocal folds, one in which they are tensed, and almost completely sealed shut. These are often called *glottalized* consonants, and we indicate them with an apostrophe ([']). Although most glottalized stops are accompanied by a 'pop' at their release (termed 'ejectives'), the Korean version is comparatively quiet. Indeed, although native Korean speakers have no trouble distinguishing their glottalized stops from their plain stops, non-native speakers often find it remarkably difficult to hear the difference. Glottalized stops are not as common as aspirated stops in the world's languages, and glottalized fricatives like Korean [s'] are especially rare. This is because fricative sounds require the vocal folds to be spread far apart, so that a lot of air can rush through the narrow oral constriction and generate noisy, turbulent air, a fricative's defining characteristic. Since the vocal folds must be spread apart for fricative sounds, it is understandable that glottalized fricatives – in which the vocal folds are largely pressed together – should be so rare. This does not preclude the presence of aspirated or glottalized *affricates*, however, which consist of combinations of a stop and a fricative, as in Korean's [tʃ, tʃʰ, tʃ'] series.

As I said, in Korean all these sounds may be found before a vowel, a context where they are necessarily audibly released. But as we have seen in the case of nasal assimilation, when there is no vowel immediately following a stop closure, then it's far less likely that the release characteristics of these sounds will be sustainable. Consequently, there is a definite risk that all the distinctions which rely on the release will be eliminated. So recall that almost all languages have fewer contrasts between their consonants when a vowel does not immediately follow, such as when the consonant is at the end of the word, or when it is immediately followed by another consonant. Korean is no exception to this cross-linguistic tendency. In fact, when a vowel-initial suffix does not follow, all roots ending with [t, tʰ, tʃ, tʃʰ] are indeed made without being released, and so all these sounds are realized [t̚] ([t'] and [tʃ'] are never found in root-final position). For example, [patʰ+e] 'on the field', has aspiration, but [pat̚+k'wa] 'field and' has no audible release of its root-final consonant, and aspiration is not present. The same, by the way, is true for both [sʰ] and [s']; strangely, these also alternate with [t̚] at the end of a word, or when a consonant-initial suffix immediately follows: [osʰ+ɨn] 'as for the clothing', [ot̚+k'wa] 'clothes and'. So any of these sounds may be found when preceding a vowel, including root-finally when a vowel-initial suffix immediately follows. But if any such root finds itself in a position *without* a vowel-initial suffix, [t̚] is substituted. In the same way, [p, pʰ, p'] and [k, kʰ, k'] are substituted with [p̚] and [k̚] respectively in these contexts.

If morphemes differ only in terms of the release characteristics of their final consonant, then, whenever a vowel does *not* immediately follow, they will be phonetically indistinguishable from each other. That is, they will be neutralized. For example, when the words for 'day', 'face' and 'sickle', are in the subject position of a sentence, they are suffixed by the subject marker [i], and are pronounced [nadʒi], [natʃʰi] and [nasʰi] respectively ([t] and [tʃ] alternate with their voiced counterparts when between vowels). However, for 'day and', 'face and' and 'sickle and', the vowel-initial subject marker disappears, and the consonant-initial suffix conjunction [k'wa] takes its place. In this context, all these root morphemes are pronounced identically, with [t̚]: [nat̚k'wa]. The set notation in Figure 3.1 makes this clear.

I should note that some stop-final words may be followed by vowel-initial words. And since speakers do not pause between words in running speech, shouldn't we expect the release cues to survive, at least in this context? Well, probably not. Remember that proximate forces acting on speech production rarely have perfect analogues in the systemic properties of the sound system. At best, such proximate forces might sow the seeds for some future direction the system might take, but many other factors necessarily come into play as time marches on. In the case at hand, it is important to realize that *most*

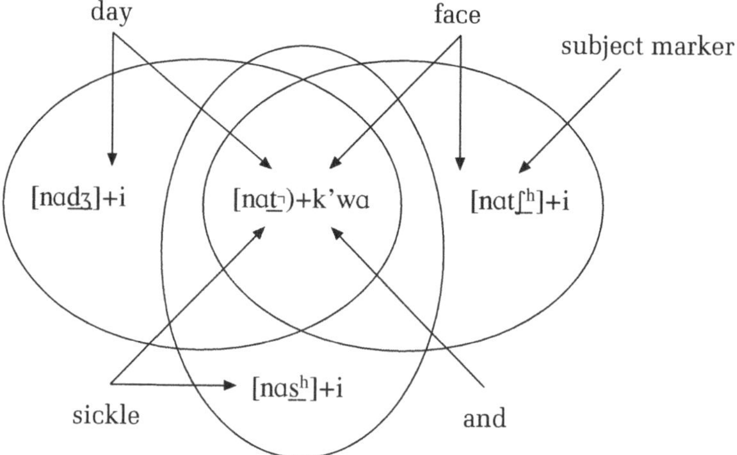

Figure 3.1 The neutralization of Korean 'day', 'face' and 'sickle' when followed by 'and'

words in Korean, and indeed most words in virtually all languages, are consonant-initial, not vowel initial. This being the case, there are not too many actual cases in which these word-final releases might be manifested in a salient manner, because a consonant is likely to follow at the beginning of the next word. With so few opportunities for them to be realized, the likelihood of their being entirely eliminated from this context increases significantly: without the evidence that constant alternation provides, the sound may eventually disappear altogether.

Now an important question: with all these opportunities for morphemes to neutralize in Korean, are its speakers constantly misunderstanding each other? Of course not. This is because the *potential* for homophony is not manifested to any significant degree.

How is the language spared massive homophony? First, *verb* roots in Korean are obligatorily suffixed, and many of these suffixes are vowel-initial. This means that most realizations of verb roots will not substitute an unreleased stop in final position. So verb roots that are *potentially* neutralized are often able to manifest their root-final contrasts.

Second, in much the same way that our English vocabulary is suffused with Latin-based words, Korean has witnessed a massive influx of Chinese words in its distant past which served to partially displace a significant portion of its native vocabulary, particularly its *noun* inventory. Chinese did not have the unusually rich set of root-final consonants found in the native Korean vocabulary: during the era of borrowing, Chinese only had [p̚, t̚, k̚, m, n, ŋ]. So where native Korean has root-final stops whose releases may contrast in the various ways we have seen, the Sino-Korean vocabulary has only unreleased stops (we don't know for sure that stops were unreleased in Chinese, but it seems likely that they were). Since the inventory of root-final consonants was comparatively limited in Chinese, and since roots in Chinese are quite short (almost always consisting of a single syllable), we might suspect that many Sino-Korean nouns are homophonous, being unable to rely on final releases or multiple syllables to increase the number of possible distinctions. But still, there were few instances of homophony in the Sino-Korean noun vocabulary. This is because most Korean nouns of Chinese origin are actually compounds of *two* Chinese roots. For example, the Sino-Korean word [ho], meaning 'good', cannot stand on its own, but it often combines with other morphemes to form nouns: [ho+gi] 'good opportunity', [ho+s^{h}ɑ] 'happy event', etc. So, any limitations on the number of possible contrasts imposed by the smaller inventory of Chinese root-final consonants was offset by these roots' combination and recombination into new and varied compounds. (The nouns discussed above – 'day', 'face' and 'sickle' – come from the comparatively small set of native Korean nouns; they are not Sino-Korean.)

To summarize, Korean verbs have many root-final contrasts that are potentially neutralized when a vowel-initial suffix does not follow, but since verbs are usually suffixed in Korean, there is actually very little neutralization. Korean nouns, though lacking the rich system of root-final contrasts, are usually compounds of Chinese origin. Consequently, there is very little homophony here either. So we have two very different reasons – one for verbs, another for nouns – for the strict limits on neutralization in Korean. The question is, is it just a fortuitous coincidence that both verbs and nouns – for completely different reasons – are so rarely homophonous? Or, perhaps, could this situation have been brought about by design, in the sense that Chinese nouns were *intentionally* turned into compounds of two morphemes in order to increase the number of possible contrasts, and the replacement of native Korean verbs with single Chinese roots was *intentionally* resisted? I hope you agree that neither of these possibilities has any appeal whatsoever. *Intention* has no role to play in the way sounds change over time, any more than it does with the evolution of species.

A more reasonable explanation for Korean's remarkable avoidance of rampant homophony emerges when we consider some of the details of historical Korean phonology. While the ultimate origins of Korean remain murky, the language may bear a distant relationship to the Turkic, Tungusic and Mongolian languages which are spread across the Asian continent, loosely grouped under the name Altaic. The Altaic languages are known for their rich suffixation systems, a characteristic that survives in Korean to the present. Now, Korean and Chinese do not share a common history; they are unrelated to each other. But due to Korea's geographical proximity to such an influential neighbour, Korean vocabulary (especially, as we noted, its noun vocabulary) has been largely supplanted by Chinese compounds, with its much simpler inventory of root-final consonants. Historical records confirm for us that this supplantation was well in place by 1300 years ago. By this period, the Korean vocabulary consisted of two sets – native Korean words, and Sino-Korean words – that had certain differences in their phonological characteristics. For example, historical records tell us that 1000 years ago, native Korean words still retained root-final distinctions between final [t^h], [tʃ] and [$tʃ^h$], and [s^h] even when a vowel did not immediately follow. That is, the sound substitution that we have been discussing had not yet entered the phonology of Korean, and so unsuffixed 'day', 'face' and 'sickle' may have been pronounced something like [nɑtʃ], [$nɑtʃ^h$] and [$nɑs^h$], respectively. By 500 years ago, however, both [t] and [tʃ] alternated with [t̚] as they do today, and 400 years ago [s^h] fell in line with the pattern, and so most of the present-day pattern was finally in place. Probably, due to the absence of following vowels, these consonant releases became weaker and weaker over the generations, until they (and the contrastive sounds which relied on these releases) finally disappeared altogether. Note that all of these changes rendered the native Korean vocabulary *more similar in structure* to the Sino-Korean vocabulary. Specifically, final stops in the Sino-Korean vocabulary were always of the unreleased variety, and so the evolution towards unreleased final stops in the native vocabulary rendered the two systems more similar to each other in this respect. This is a rather common phenomenon: upon the influx of foreign elements, the phonological properties of a language may change; incoming patterns may eventually modify or supplant native ones.

What I'm proposing for Korean is that, as in every language, there always existed a potential for word-final consonants to lose their release features. This does not mean, of course, that they *will* lose their releases, only that the possibility is a very real one. *Sound change is probabilistic, not deterministic.* Even though some sound changes are quite likely to occur, we can never predict when or even *if* they will occur. We can only entertain more-likely and less-likely scenarios. What seems to have happened in Korean is the following: in its pre-history, Korean was probably perfectly happy with its many root-final consonants that always manifested themselves because they were released. However, due to the influx of Sino-Korean morphemes, with its system of unreleased root-final consonants, the *possibility* of the sound change was 'encouraged', and ultimately *actualized.* That is, since the extensive Sino-Korean vocabulary had a fairly simple system of root-final consonants, this eventually had the effect of triggering a change in the native system of word-final consonants (which is a common sort of sound change even without any external 'encouragement'). So when native Korean roots stood alone, and when they were followed by a consonant, they slowly – over the generations – came to conform with the Sino-Korean pattern that was so extensive. However – and this is a key point – it's likely that this change took place *only* because communication was not adversely affected. For *verbs*, obligatory suffixation often induced alternations that guaranteed the survival of root-final contrasts in *most* contexts. So word-final consonants in native Korean verbs could afford to fall in line with the simpler Sino-Korean system exactly because of the alternations that suffixation guaranteed; these alternations resulted in a simplified system of root-final consonants, but, due to the surviving releases in many contexts, significant counter-functional consequences were avoided. For *nouns*, potential homophony due to the loss of root-final contrasts was offset by the compounding process. Indeed, it is almost unimaginable that Korean would have tolerated this simplification if it would have resulted in extensive homophony.

To summarize, look at the timeline in Table 3.2.

So the influx of Chinese nouns into Korean eventually led to a reduced set of root-final consonants. However, this reduction in contrastive sounds was offset by the compounding process, which greatly increased the opportunity for nouns to contrast with each other. The new prevalence of nouns with unreleased root-final consonants may have triggered the loss of releases in the verb system as well. This loss of releases was tolerated because the many vowel-initial suffixes which accompany verbs result in alternations which salvage the contrasts that are dependent on the stop release: cues that unreleased

Table 3.2 A brief history of Korean root-final tongue-top obstruents

1300 years ago	*1000 years ago*	*500 years ago*	*400 years ago*
Sino-Korean vocabulary, with its unreleased final stops, is well-established, supplanting many native nouns with two-root compounds.	Root-final [t], [tʃ], and [s^h] are still found in final position, and before consonants, in native Korean.	Influenced by the Sino-Korean root structure, [t^h], [tʃ] and [$tʃ^h$] become [t˺] in these positions. But verbs alternate, and Sino-Korean nouns are compounds.	[s^h] alternates with [t˺] in these positions as well. Still, there are few adverse functional consequences.

stops obviously lack. There is no *intention* in this proposed scenario. Rather, the Korean phonological system simply evolved passively as a consequence of its communicative function. In Chapters Five and Six we'll explore how this sort of evolution might proceed.

Now let's look at Chinese in a little more detail. As we already know, Chinese root morphemes are almost always single syllables, and have a fairly simple structure in terms of the combinatory possibilities for vowels and consonants (and tones as well). Moreover, there is very little prefixation or suffixation in Chinese, and so alternation is comparatively limited. Indeed, even the sound change we are about to discuss has not resulted in any alternations, neutralizing or otherwise. It has, however, resulted in a reduction in the number of contrasts in root-final position. Sound changes which completely eliminate distinctions are called *sound mergers*. But mergers are different from neutralizations, since the latter necessarily involve sounds in alternation. Upon neutralization, distinctions are eliminated only in certain phonological contexts, and so alternations guarantee that the distinction is expressed in some context or other. So mergers completely eliminate certain contrasts under all phonological circumstances; neutralizing alternations only eliminate contrasts under particular phonological circumstances; under other circumstances, the contrast survives.

In our discussion of Sino-Korean, I wrote that the Chinese spoken during the era of lending had a total of six root-final consonants: [p˺, t˺, k˺, m, n, ŋ]. Some contemporary dialects like Cantonese (spoken in southeast China) retain these six consonants. But others, such as Mandarin (the dominant dialect), have drastically reduced this set to only two members: [n, ŋ]. In Mandarin, all the final stops have been completely lost, and historic [m] has merged with the other two nasal sounds. So, where Cantonese has [sɑm], Mandarin has [sɑn] 'three'; where Cantonese has [nɑm], Mandarin has [nɑn] 'south'. Does this mean that Mandarin has fewer root shapes than does Cantonese? Yes, it does. Cantonese has about 1800 root shapes, but Mandarin, since it has lost all of the possibilities for contrasts that root-final [p˺, t˺, k˺, m] allow in Cantonese, has only about 1300. Of course, Mandarin has not reduced its total number of roots, only its number of root *shapes*. Does this mean that Mandarin has a larger number of homophones than does Cantonese? Yes, it does. Some root shapes in Mandarin have upwards of 20 or more different meanings! So rampant homophony is the inevitable result of the loss of all these root-final contrasts. But does this mean that Mandarin speakers are constantly misunderstanding each other? No, it doesn't. Instead, just as in Sino-Korean, and *un*like related Cantonese or the Chinese spoken long ago,

Mandarin has evolved a huge inventory of two-root compounds, which means that its words are typically twice as long, and so have ample opportunity to maintain phonetic distinctness among themselves. So the rampant homophony that the sound mergers produced has been offset by the *co*-evolution of a compounding process. Of course, as with every language, homophones still exist in Mandarin, but once again, real-world knowledge and grammatical context serve to eschew ambiguity. In Cantonese, probably because it retains its six root-final consonants, the inventory of two-root compounds is not nearly as extensive.

Again, none of this happened by intention or design. There was no external force acting on Mandarin which promoted or dictated the use of compounds. Instead, there are natural, passive pressures on phonology due to language *use* – which, as should be increasingly clear, have a huge influence on language *structure* – that resulted in the evolution of these compounds.

In his book from 2000, San Duanmu, a scholar of Chinese phonology, assumes that the attrition of final stops in Mandarin (as opposed to Cantonese) and the compounding so prevalent in Mandarin (as opposed to Cantonese) are indeed merely a coincidence. For Duanmu, these present-day differences between Mandarin and Cantonese are not rooted in any functional, evolutionary pressures differently affecting the two dialects, but are instead the result of different grammatical constraints acting on the two systems, constraints that are in no way influenced by functional factors: Mandarin speakers have a cognitive, grammatical constraint that imposes two syllables on most words, whereas Cantonese presumably lacks this constraint. *How* and *why* this constraint is present in the minds of Mandarin speakers is not explored by Duanmu.

Actually, Duanmu argues that compounding was far more prevalent in earlier stages of Chinese than many scholars have assumed. For his proposal to go through, Duanmu might further assume that the present-day dialectal difference is due to a Cantonese innovation toward monosyllabicity, rather than a Mandarin innovation toward compounding. Duanmu actually questions the very possibility of large-scale innovative compounding: 'When ambiguities do arise, a speaker can resort to a variety of ways to clarify them. It is unlikely that the entire speech community would come to agree on a single way of disambiguating each of the many homophones.' Now, Duanmu is surely correct when he asserts that the innovations of any individual speaker are extremely limited in their influence on linguistic evolution. However, as Chapters Five and Six explore in great detail, if language is nothing else, it is a system of conventionalized patterns of usage that arise from the minor and limited variations in which speakers naturally engage. The communicative success of certain spontaneous innovations over others – especially in the face of potentially confusing, homophonous forms – may very slowly, almost imperceptibly, drive the linguistic system in new directions. Any individual speaker is not responsible for any individual linguistic change. Rather, there may be a glacially slow accumulation of successful unplanned variants that might take hold in a system, and inch it toward a new state: *linguistic change has its roots in spontaneous linguistic variation*. This variation may be of the *gradual* phonetic sort that culminates in sound changes, or it may be of a more *quantal*, morphological sort, where quantal refers to the addition or change of an entire morpheme or word and not simply a minor change in pronunciation: just as Chinese was undergoing the gradual phonetic loss of its many root-final consonant distinctions, quantal morphological variations may have begun to enter the language. Sporadic compounding innovations that were functionally beneficial may have been propagated and ultimately conventionalized. This, I claim, is the origin of the innovative compounding process in Mandarin: the communicative success of compounds over single-root forms eventually had the effect of turning a spontaneous innovation into a linguistic convention.

In his book from 1933, the linguist Leonard Bloomfield discussed a strikingly similar innovation in a rural southern French dialect, albeit an innovation which only affected a few stray words, and not a broad portion of the vocabulary, as in Chinese. In this French dialect, final [l] has merged with final [t]. For example, where standard southern French has [bɛl] 'pretty', this dialect has [bɛt]. This merger has had further, extra-phonological effects. Because of the sound change, the standard word for 'cock' ('chicken') ([gɑt]) is pronounced [gɑt] here. However, these southern speakers don't use the word [gɑt] anymore. Instead, they use the word for 'chick' ([pul] in Standard French, but [put] here, due to the sound change). The reason 'cock' was changed to 'chick' becomes clear when we realize that [gɑl] is also the word for 'cat', both in the standard dialect and in the rural dialect! Bloomfield writes that 'This homonymy must have caused trouble in practical life; therefore [gɑt] was avoided and replaced by makeshift words.' Although one might believe that the homophone was *intentionally avoided* by speakers, I suspect the new pattern *passively evolved*: these synchronic quantal variations – everyday variations at the level of the morpheme or word – may gradually lead to changes in the conventions of usage. Even when phonology is changing in a potentially homophone-inducing way, by hook or by crook, language inevitably evolves in fulfilment of its communicative function.

Finally, I'd like to briefly consider another language that bears certain similarities to both Chinese and Korean, but differs from both of them in a very crucial way. Chong is spoken by about 8000 people in Thailand and Cambodia. Although Chong is completely unrelated to both Cantonese and Korean, it also has root-final stop consonants that are unreleased (a common property of East Asian languages), for example [kəkɛːp˺] ('to cut with scissors'), [lɛːk˺] ('chicken'). Furthermore, like Korean – but unlike Cantonese – the root-final stop consonants of Chong contrast in terms of glottalization. At this point, a logical guess would be that Chong is like Korean in having a large inventory of vowel-initial suffixes, which provides the opportunity for its glottalized sounds to be realized in a salient way. And while these glottalized stops would alternate with unreleased, non-glottalized stops when unsuffixed, there might still be very few neutralizations, again, just as in Korean. This would indeed be a logical guess about the structural properties of Chong. Unfortunately, it would also be completely wrong. In fact, like all its linguistic relatives in the Mon-Khmer language group – and unlike Korean and its distant relatives in the Altaic group – Chong has no suffixes at all (though it has a rich prefixation system). So Chong has unreleased stops in word-final position, it has root-final glottalized stops, but it has no suffixes. What's going on here? How can all these statements be true?

The best – and consequently most common – way that aspirated (and glottalized) stops are produced is with the aspiration/glottalization *following* the stop closure ([tʰ, t']). Post-aspirates/glottals are better from an auditory perspective: the build-up of air pressure behind the stop closures leads to a salient percept upon their forceful release. However, on rare occasions aspiration/glottalization is timed to *precede* the stop closure. Chong is one of the few languages that has *pre-glottalized* stops, for example [kəsuṵt] 'to come off', [l̤uːṵc] 'soft', [kənoːo̰c] 'nipple', in which the glottalization actually resides on the latter portion of the preceding vowel. (Glottalization on vowels is indicated by the subscripted tilde; the other subscript is not important for now. I have doubled the vowel symbol and placed the tilde under the copy, to indicate that only the final portion of the vowel is creaked, but, still, long vowels contrast with short vowels, as indicated by the colon [ː], which is always used to indicate a long vowel that contrasts with a short one.) This sort of glottalization is usually characterized as a 'creak', because it gives the auditory impression of an old door creaking on its hinges. The vocal folds are tensed and pushed together, and are only intermittently and irregularly blown apart by the critical build-up of air pressure from the lungs.

As I said, pre-glottalized stops are quite rare in the world's languages, probably because they don't provide a very robust auditory contrast to plain stops. If, for whatever reason, pre-glottalized stops should come to evolve in a language, their lack of salience might lead to their eventual demise. Either they would disappear altogether (thus merging with the plain stops), or they would evolve into something else. In Chong, however, pre-glottalized stops survive, and in fact flourish, in that many many words of the language rely on pre-glottalization to remain phonologically distinct from other words. I think, actually, that therein lies the key to their survival. Since Chong is a non-suffixing language (a property that almost surely pre-dates the evolution of the pre-glottalized stops, since it is characteristic of the entire Mon-Khmer group, whereas glottalization is not), and since its final stops are unreleased, pre-glottalization has precious little opportunity to evolve into a more perspicuous form by, perhaps, slowly migrating to the other side of the stop closure. (Such migrations, by the way, are not particularly uncommon. Indeed, some analyses of Korean propose exactly such a migration, in that certain aspirated stops are claimed to derive from [h]-stop sequences where the [h] has migrated to the release position, for example, [h+t] goes to [t^h].) But in Chong, if pre-glottalization were to give up and eventually evolve itself out of existence, the consequences for the language's vocabulary would be rather devastating. My suspicion is, then, that the pre-glottalized stops survive in Chong *exactly because* of their functional importance. Once again, neither intention nor design has played a role in the survival of pre-glottalization in Chong. Rather the communicative function of language is most likely driving pre-glottalization's continued survival, even though the perceptual odds are set against it.

3. Hungarian

As our final example of the limited counter-functional consequences of neutralization, let's consider Hungarian. Like its distant cousin Finnish, Hungarian is a language with vowel harmony. Recall that in vowel harmony languages, the vowels of a word share certain phonetic properties. The Hungarian system is similar to Finnish in that most root forms have either all front vowels or all back vowels. In Table 3.3 I list the Hungarian vowels in terms of their major phonetic properties. The first table lists the vowels in Hungarian orthography, while the second table provides their phonetic transcription. (The significance of the shaded cells is considered below.)

So Hungarian has both round and non-round front vowels, but all its back vowels are round, except for [ɑː]; both back unrounded vowels and low round vowels are extremely rare in the world's languages, and so the Hungarian inventory is quite normal in this regard. The vowels

Table 3.3 The Hungarian vowel inventory

Hungarian vowel inventory (orthographic)

short vowels				
	front		*back*	
	not round	*round*		*round*
high	i	ü		u
high–mid				o
low–mid	e	ö		
low				a

long vowels				
	front		*back*	
	not round	*round*	*not round*	*round*
high	í	ű		ú
high–mid	é	ő		ó
low–mid			á	

Hungarian vowel inventory (phonetic)

short vowels				
	front		*back*	
	not round	*round*		*round*
high	i	y		u
high–mid				o
low–mid	ɛ	œ		
low				ɒ

long vowels				
	front		*back*	
	not round	*round*	*not round*	*round*
high	iː	yː		uː
high–mid	eː	øː		oː
low–mid			aː	

in root morphemes are harmonic (with some exceptions, some of which I'll consider in a moment), and non-alternating. They have either front vowels or back vowels. But Hungarian also has a rich system of suffixation. Unlike roots, most of these suffixes have alternating vowel qualities. Suffixes usually alternate depending on the vowel quality – either front or back – of the root morpheme. If the root is a front root, the suffix takes a front vowel; if the root is a back root, the suffix takes a back vowel. In most cases, the high/mid/low value is set for each suffix individually. So look at the examples in Table 3.4. The first set of roots consists of front words, and so they take the *front* allomorph of the suffixes: [nɛk] 'to' and [tøːl] 'from'. The second set has back roots, and so they take the *back* allomorph of the suffixes: [nɒk] and [toːl], which contain the back counterparts of [ɛ] and [øː], respectively.

However, some *front* unrounded root vowels take *back* vowel suffixes. This is not a deep mystery, however. In the history of Hungarian, these vowels were *back* unrounded vowels, but it seems that they merged with the front unrounded vowels. (This explains the complete absence of back non-round vowels in the present-day system; these are the shaded cells in the previous table.) The fronting of back

Table 3.4 Front words and back words in Hungarian. Compare the vowel qualities in the suffixes.

	front words	
tömeg (crowd) [tœmɛg]	tömegnek (to the crowd) [tœmɛgnɛk]	tömegtől (from the crowd) [tœmɛgtøːl]
öröm (joy) [œrœm]	örömnek [œrœmnɛk]	örömtől [œrœmtøːl]
idő (time) [idøː]	időnek [idøːnɛk]	időtől [idøːtøːl]

	back words	
ház (house) [haːz]	háznak (to the house) [haːznɒk]	háztól (from the house) [haːztoːl]
város (city) [vaːroʃ]	városnak [vaːroʃnɒk]	várostól [vaːroʃtoːl]
mókus (squirrel) [moːkuʃ]	mókusnak [moːkuʃnɒk]	mókustól [moːkuʃtoːl]

unrounded vowels is found in other languages as well, though it's not yet understood why this pattern of sound change should be found. At any rate, these words probably used to be fully harmonic in that they appeared with back vowel suffixes. However, although these root vowels merged with the front vowels, their suffix-taking properties did not change. The result is that they are *disharmonic* in present-day Hungarian: they are now *front* roots which take *back* suffixes. The forms in the first set in Table 3.5 were fully harmonic in the past, and remain harmonic today. The forms in the second set were presumably harmonic in the past, but due to the merger – the fronting of the back unrounded vowels in roots – they are no longer so, as their suffix-taking behaviour shows.

Here's the crucial observation: the suffixes themselves serve to render words distinct even when their root morphemes are themselves homophonous due to the historic fronting of back unrounded vowels. In other words, different suffix allomorphs serve to distinguish roots that have become homophonous. So really there is practically no homophony at all. Indeed, I suspect that *the merger between these root vowels was tolerated exactly because the distinct suffix-taking properties of merged roots maintained the distinction between these otherwise homophonous words.*

Now, it is conceivably the case that many of the alternations that are induced by vowel harmony are neutralizing in nature. For

Table 3.5 Harmonic and disharmonic front vowels in Hungarian. Compare their suffix-taking properties.

Harmonic front unrounded root vowels		
kert (garden) [kɛrt]	kertnek (to the garden) [kɛrtnɛk]	kerttől (from the garden) [kɛrt:øːl]
szín (colour) [siːn]	színnek [siːn:ɛk]	színtől [siːntøːl]
szegény (poor) [sɛgeːɲ]	szegénynek [sɛgeːɲnɛk]	szegénytől [sɛgeːɲtøːl]

Disharmonic front unrounded root vowels (historically back unrounded root vowels)		
híd (bridge) [hiːd]	hídnak (to the bridge) [hiːdnɒk]	hídtól (from the bridge) [hiːdtoːl]
nyíl (arrow) [ɲiːl]	nyílnak [ɲiːlnɒk]	nyíltól [ɲiːltoːl]
cél (aim) [tseːl]	célnak [tseːlnɒk]	céltól [tseːltoːl]

example, one could imagine two Hungarian suffixes [it] and [yt] that *both* alternate with [ut] when affixed to a back-vowel root. This would render the two suffixes homophonous. But, in fact, this never happens. Despite all of its suffixes and all of its alternations, suffix neutralization doesn't present any problems whatsoever for Hungarian.

So how did this avoidance of massive neutralization come about? The answer stems from an important distinction between roots and suffixes (or more broadly, between roots and *affixes*, which includes prefixes as well). Roots – nouns, verbs, adjectives – come from the 'open class' vocabulary. Every language has hundreds and hundreds of open class items, and moreover, every language allows for the possibility of new nouns and verbs to enter usage. This is what makes this class 'open'. By contrast, the 'closed class' – grammatical markers, agreement markers, affixes in general – has many fewer members. It is a 'closed' set because the inventory of items here rarely undergoes augmentation by new members. Now, in language after language, closed class items are *shorter* than open class items; they almost always exploit only a subset of the contrastive sounds found in the open class vocabulary, and they are much more likely to engage in potentially neutralizing alternations. This makes perfect sense, of course. In every language there are many more nouns and verbs to keep distinct than there are grammatical markers.

Hungarian is quite typical in this regard. Its affixes are usually shorter than its roots, and, due in part to vowel harmony, its affixes do

Table 3.6 Suggested history of Hungarian vowel harmony vis à vis vowel fronting

Vowel harmony into suffixes	*Vowel fronting in back unrounded roots*
Tolerated, since there are fewer suffixes, and so they rarely neutralize	Tolerated, since disharmonic back suffixes cue root distinctions
Time→	

not exploit all the contrastive sounds that are found in the language at large. Indeed, I suggest that it's *exactly because* the inventory of suffixes is from the closed class that these morphemes were susceptible to vowel harmony in the first place. Because there are fewer contrasts required of the closed class, there were few functional pressures exerting resistance against the alternations that vowel harmony induced. So vowel harmony is potentially neutralizing, but since there are far fewer suffixes than roots, this potential is never manifested to any significant degree.

Vowel harmony into suffixes was tolerated because it was very unlikely to induce neutralization, and the fronting of back unrounded vowels in roots was tolerated because the presence of *back* suffixes with these particular roots eliminated the possibility that they would neutralize with those front roots which took *front* suffixes. This suggests the historical sequence of changes in Hungarian shown in Table 3.6.

To make my point more clear, just imagine if Hungarian vowel harmony were to go the other way – from suffixes to roots. What good would it do to exploit many contrasts in affixes, and fewer in roots? No good at all. In fact, it would do great harm in that the open class vocabulary would undoubtedly suffer from massive neutralization. Many of the vowel contrasts required of the open class vocabulary would be undone by the affix-to-root vowel harmony. Indeed, it is no coincidence that vowel harmony does not go from suffix to root in Hungarian. In fact, among the world's languages, almost all cases of vowel harmony go from root to affix, not affix to root. The functional advantages of this directional asymmetry should now be perfectly clear.

Summary

In this chapter we've begun to explore in greater detail the idea that sound alternations are the synchronic manifestation of slow, diachronic pressures on phonological systems. In particular, we considered reasons why certain sound substitutions might reduce the number of contrasts in certain contexts. Such sound substitutions clearly have the potential to neutralize distinctions, but this potential is rarely if ever manifested to any significant degree. If root morphemes alternate in this fashion (as in Korean) the system may co-evolve morphological strategies to minimize the functional damage. But typically, the affix inventory has fewer contrastive sounds (as in Hungarian). It's exactly because fewer contrasts are required of this class that it might be susceptible to such assimilations in the first place. So again, the functional damage is minimal.

Further reading

The Baudouin de Courtenay quote (*'The mechanism of a language ...'*):

Baudouin de Courtenay, Jan (1871 [1972]). 'Some general remarks on linguistics and language', in Edward Stankiewicz (ed.), *A Baudouin de Courtenay Reader*. Bloomington: Indiana University Press, p. 63.

On Dutch:

Booij, Geert E. (1995). *The Phonology of Dutch*. Oxford: Oxford University Press.

A few of William Labov's major works:

Labov, William (1966). *The Social Stratification of English in New York City*. Washington, DC: Center for Applied Linguistics.

Labov, William (1972). *Language in the Inner City: Studies in the Black English Vernacular*. Philadelphia: University of Pennsylvania Press.

Labov, William (1994). *Principles of Linguistic Change. Volume 1: Internal Factors*. Oxford: Blackwell.

Labov, William (2001). *Principles of Linguistic Change. Volume 2: Social Factors*. Oxford: Blackwell.

On the perceptual role of the nasal anti-formant:

Kurowski, Kathleen and Blumstein, Sheila E. (1987). 'Acoustic properties for place of articulation in nasal consonants', *Journal of the Acoustical Society of America* 81.6: 1917–27.

On Korean:

Lee, Iksop and Ramsey, S. Robert (2000). *The Korean Language*. Albany: State University of New York Press.

Martin, Samuel E. (1992). *A Reference Grammar of Korean: A Complete Guide to the Grammar and History of the Korean Language*. Rutland, Vermont: C. E. Tuttle.

Sohn, Ho-min (1999). *The Korean Language*. Cambridge: Cambridge University Press.

On Chinese:

Duanmu, San (2000). *The Phonology of Standard Chinese*. Oxford: Oxford University Press.

Bloomfield's French anecdote:
Bloomfield, Leonard (1933). *Language*. London: George Allen and Unwin, pp. 397–8.

On Chong:
Silverman, Daniel (1996). 'Phonology at the interface of phonetics and morphology: root-final laryngeals in Chong, Korean, and Sanskrit', *Journal of East Asian Linguistics* 5: 301–22.
Thongkum, Theraphan L. (1991). 'An instrumental study of Chong registers', in J. Davidson (ed.), *Essays on Mon-Khmer Linguistics in Honour of H. L. Shorto*. London: School of Oriental and African Studies, University of London, pp. 141–60.

On Hungarian:
Kálmán, Bela (1972). 'Hungarian historical phonology', in Lorand Benkö and Samu Imre (eds), *The Hungarian Language*. The Hague: Mouton, pp. 49–83.
Linebaugh, Gary (2004). 'Hungarian vowel harmony and neutral vowels', unpublished manuscript.
Siptár, Peter and Törkenczy, Miklos (2000). *The Phonology of Hungarian*. Oxford: Oxford University Press.

4 Allophonic sound substitution

Consider the nasal sounds in the two words 'runs' and 'runner'. Whether written in English or transcribed phonetically, the same nasal symbol is used for both words, that is, 'n'. These two sounds are indeed quite similar, as both are made with the tongue tip up, the soft palate down, and the vocal folds vibrating. The major differences between them are that (1) the [n] of 'runs' is longer than the [n] of 'runner', and (2) the [n] in 'runs' is followed by another consonant, whereas the [n] in 'runner' is released into the following vowel. These articulatory differences, as we now know, have acoustic consequences. Specifically, the 'n' of 'runner' has formant transitions as the following vowel begins, whereas the 'n' of 'runs' lacks such transitions, since another consonant immediately follows. But although these two 'n's have systematic phonetic differences, most phonologists do not characterize them as alternants of each other. Instead, they regard them as one and the same sound, and would object to a characterization of this pattern as a genuine sound *substitution*. Nonetheless, I maintain that *any* systematic phonetic distinction that results from combining morphemes qualifies as a sound substitution, since there is inevitably *some* sort of phonetic change that sounds undergo as they combine with morphemes of distinct shapes. Moreover, the 'runs'–'runner' nasal alternation should be regarded as a specifically allophonic substitution, not a neutralizing substitution, since there are no words with which either form of 'run' might be confused. That is, this sound substitution maintains meaning.

From such minor, seemingly negligible phonetic differences, greater differences may ultimately emerge somewhere down the generations of language use. Indeed, although these two nasal sounds are indeed quite similar, I argue in this chapter that *articulatory or acoustic similarity between sounds is neither a prerequisite, nor a diagnostic, for allophonic relatedness*. Due to the gradual way sounds change over the generations, most sounds that alternate with each other are indeed quite similar in their phonetic characteristics. But whether these sounds are phonetically similar or not, all that matters to learners is the consequences their substitution have for word meaning: whether it changes word meaning, eliminates word meaning distinctions, or maintains word meaning. In fact, allophonic alternation reveals a remarkable cognitive characteristic on the part of language learners: *functional identity overrides physical similarity in the determination of category membership or non-membership*. To show this clearly, I consider three further cases of allophonic alternation: another case from English, one from Corsican, and one from Taiwanese Chinese. These will be followed by two examples – from Akan and New York English – which show that the *only* way sounds can be allophonically related is if they *alternate* with each other, that is, if they partake in a sound substitution which maintains meaning.

Three cases of allophonic alternation

1. English

We first consider another example of allophony from American English, one in which the phonetic distinction between the allophonic alternants is greater than that in our 'runs'–'runner' example. In a natural, everyday way, say the words 'fill' and 'filling', and think about the way you make the two sounds represented by 'l'. For most speakers of American English, these two sounds are made quite differently from each other. For 'filling', your tongue tip makes contact just behind the upper teeth (the same location as [t] and [n]), but also one side of your tongue is lowered (or both sides), allowing air to continually escape from your mouth. Consequently, 'l' sounds are called *lateral* sounds, since air flows around the side(s) of the tongue. Begin to say the word 'filling', but just before you release the l-sound into the following vowel, instead, sustain the 'l'. If you make the sound in a natural way, this should confirm its articulatory configuration for you. Since the tongue is pushed forward in your mouth, the length of the oral cavity is rather short. This raises the relevant formant frequency of the sound, making it sound bright and clear. We often call this a 'clear l', and transcribe it, simply, [l].

Now reflect for a moment on the 'l' sound in 'fill'. Again, if you say it in a natural way, your tongue is probably *not* pushed forward to the extent found in 'filling'. Your tongue tip might not even make contact behind the teeth. If you say 'fill' and sustain the last sound, you can know for sure. With the tongue pulled back, the oral cavity lengthens, and so the relevant formant is lowered in frequency. This sound is often referred to as a 'dark l', and is transcribed with a tilde through the middle of the symbol: [ɫ]. These two sorts of 'l's were referred to by Bloch and Trager when discussing the word 'little', remarked upon in Chapter One: the first 'l' is clear, the second one dark, even though speakers might feel they are the same.

In American English, as in a number of other languages, these two 'l' sounds systematically alternate with each other. When an 'l' sound finds itself in front of a vowel, the clear version, [l], is produced. Elsewhere, the dark version, [ɫ], is found. So we have 'fill' [fɪɫ] (dark l), but 'filling' [fɪlɪŋ] (clear l), 'fool' [fuɫ], but 'foolish' [fulɪʃ]. Neither [ɫ] nor [l] alternates with any other sound in the language: no other sound alternates with [l] when a vowel follows, and no other sound alternates with [ɫ] when a vowel does *not* follow, and so this alternation never induces homophony. Consequently this is an allophonic sound substitution. You might feel that I'm just splitting hairs by regarding these sounds as genuine allophonic alternants of each other, and that they are really just tiny variants of the same sound, in just the same way that most phonologists regard the [n]s in 'run' versus 'runner' as one and the same. But in the same way that I disagree with these phonologists about 'run' and 'runner', I also disagree if you claim that the phonetic difference between these 'l's is negligible. I'll repeat my assertion that *any* systematic distinction which results from adding or subtracting morphemes qualifies as a sound alternation. At any rate, by this point, you should always be suspicious of your intuitions about sound structure. You *feel* these sounds are so similar mostly because they serve the same linguistic function: whether [ɫ] or [l] is used, the meaning of the morpheme stays the same.

The American English [ɫ]–[l] alternation indicates – perhaps more clearly than our 'run'–'runner' example – that phonetically distinct sounds may yet be equivalent in terms of their linguistic function. But there are further implications of this pattern. Recall the claim I made in Chapter Two that knowledge of allophony need not consist of learners deconstructing the multiple phonetic cues into their component constituents. Instead, what matters is that the ensemble of cues serves a single linguistic function. In the case of 'runs'–'runner', we might incorrectly suspect that learners are taking note of the presence versus absence of following formant transitions in their determination of allophonic relatedness. This is due to the isolability of this particular cue from the entirety of the cue complex: sometimes it's present, sometimes it's absent. But the physical nature of the difference between [ɫ] and [l] is not parallel to the difference between released and unreleased nasals, as one would be hard-pressed to characterize the distinction between the dark l and clear l in terms of adding or subtracting acoustic cues from otherwise identical sounds. Instead, there is a qualitative distinction between the two that is not phonetically isolable from the speech signal; the phonetic difference typically involves the genuine substitution of one tongue gesture for another. Yet these sounds are indeed allophonically related, just as released and unreleased nasals are allophonically related. Is there any reason to insist that English learners might treat the distinction between released and unreleased nasals differently from how they treat the difference between clear l and dark l? I really don't think so. The *qualitative, functional* consequences are the same in either case – the maintenance of meaning – and therefore there is no reason for learners to respond differently to the *quantitative, phonetic* differences between the two pairs. The two sound substitutions are different in terms of the nature and degree of difference between the respective alternating sounds, but the functional consequences are the same in both cases – meaning is maintained.

2. Corsican

The [l]–[ɫ] allophonic sound substitution in English involves sounds that are indeed similar to each other but quite different from all other sounds of the language. So there's little chance of confusing either of these sounds with any other. But now we'll consider a more complicated case, one in which allophonic alternants are far more similar to *other* contrastive sounds of the language than they are to each other.

Consider the following words from Corsican, concentrating on the underlined consonants: [p̲eðe] 'foot' versus [u b̲eðe] 'the foot'; [t̲eŋgu] 'I have', versus [u d̲eŋgu] 'I have it'; [k̲aza] 'house' versus [a g̲aza] 'the house'. You'll notice that [p] and [b] alternate with each other, as do [t] and [d], and [k] and [g]. The [b, d, g] alternants are present when a vowel precedes them, and the [p, t, k] alternants are found when there is no preceding vowel. The difference between [p, t, k] and [b, d, g] is that the vocal folds are set apart from each other for the former set, while the vocal folds are close together and set into vibratory motion for the latter set. So the major difference between [p, t, k] and [b, d, g] is that the former set is *voiceless*, and the latter set is *voiced*. Most other aspects of these pairs of sounds – that they are stops, and the locations of their respective oral closures – are the same. Now, although we've only considered a mere three examples, further investigation of Corsican would show that voiceless stops ([p, t, k]) regularly alternate with their voiced stop counterparts ([b, d, g]) such that the voiceless variants are found when *not* between two vowels, and the voiced variants are found *only* between two vowels (that is, *intervocalically*), just as our examples show. This is actually a very common pattern in the languages of the world. In Chapter Six we consider the phonetic reasons for its prevalence.

Since we don't yet know enough about the other sounds of the language, we can't conclude whether this alternation is allophonic or neutralizing. So let's consider another alternation in Corsican, one on which our answer will hinge. I'll have to introduce several new symbols, two of which represent sounds that are not usually found in English: [b̲okːɑ] 'mouth' versus [ɑ β̲okːɑ] 'the mouth'; [d̲ente] 'tooth' versus [u ð̲ente] 'the tooth'; [g̲olɑ] 'throat' versus [diɣ̲olɑ] 'of throat'. (I should point out that Corsican has long voiceless stops as well. For these so-called 'geminate' stops, the oral closure is held longer than the so-called 'singleton' stops. As with long vowels, we indicate these with a colon following the consonant symbol, as in [bok̲ːɑ]. These geminate stops are never voiced in Corsican. English has geminates only in compounds, like 'rat-tail'. We are already familiar with the voiced stops (underlined) in the first members of these three word pairs. But these stops are slightly different from the word-initial 'b, d, g' of English, because the English sounds very often lack vocal fold vibration until the stops are released. We have been transcribing these [b̥, d̥, g̊], the hollowed circles indicating their overall voicelessness. But the genuinely voiced stops of Corsican contain vocal fold vibration for most of the stop closure itself, and so our transcription lacks the hollowed circles: [b, d, g]. These voiced stops may be found at the beginning of a word in Corsican. Consequently, they are contrastive with [p, t, k], which, as we've just seen, may also be found in this position. But when these [b, d, g]-initial words are preceded by a vowel, the fricatives [β, ð, ɣ] substitute for [b, d, g] respectively. Of these three sounds, only [ð] is found in English, exemplified by the first sound in the word 'this': the vocal folds are vibrating, the tongue touches the upper teeth, and air continually flows out of the mouth in a turbulent fashion. For [β], the lips are close enough together so that a slight turbulence is created as air rushes through the narrow opening. The [v] sound is the closest we have in English to the Corsican [β], although [v] is made with the lower lip against upper teeth, not with both lips. Finally, for [ɣ], we make a [k]/[g]-like tongue gesture, but again, the tongue and soft palate do not come into full contact, and instead are sufficiently close so that the air rushing through the narrow passage becomes turbulent. As [β], [ð] and [ɣ] are all voiced, the Corsican sounds under discussion constitute a series of *voiced fricatives*.

What's especially interesting is that the voiced stops alternate with the voiced fricatives, but they may also *contrast* with those voiced stops that alternate with the voiceless stops! This is a bit confusing, so once again, it may be helpful to envision this situation with set-theoretic notation.

Figure 4.1 characterizes the fact that voiced stops alternate with two different sounds of the language (indicated by the two circles).

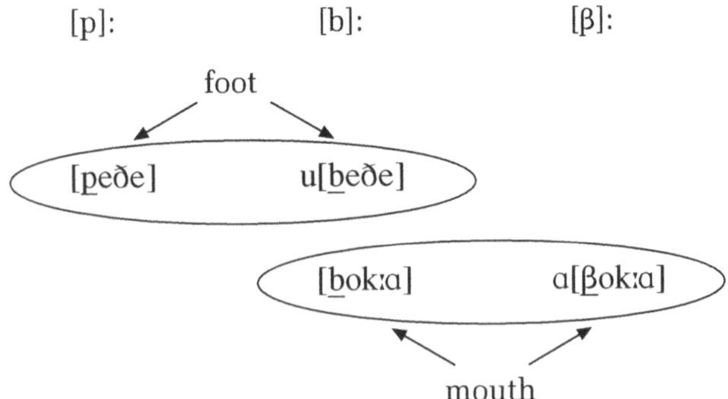

Figure 4.1 Multiple alternation in Corsican

Now the important question arises: are these alternations allophonic, or might they potentially induce neutralization? The set notation provides us with a clear answer: the sets will never intersect. The voiced stops that alternate with the voiceless stops are *only* found between vowels, whereas the voiced stops that alternate with the voiced fricatives are *never* found between vowels. Consequently, there is never an opportunity for the presence of a voiced stop to induce neutralization. So if the words in this set-theoretic example were otherwise identical, the alternations would never induce neutralization. For example, [pa] would alternate with [a+ba], but [ba] would alternate with [a+βa], and so each contrast is inevitably preserved.

We know that there are phonetic differences between stops that follow a vowel, and stops that do not follow a vowel. The former have formant transitions preceding the stop closure, while the latter may lack these transitions. So the two different [b]s in our set notation are similar, but not identical. The important point is that these [b]s are quite similar to each other while being rather *less* similar to the sounds with which they respectively alternate: the underlined consonants in [u beðe] and [bokːa], although not allophonically related, are very similar to each other, while the underlined consonants in the pairs [peðe]–[u beðe] and [bokːa]–[a βokːa] respectively are less similar to each other, but *do* allophonically alternate. Now, I have already suggested strong caution in employing similarity as a diagnostic for linguistic relatedness, because we still lack a reliable determinant of what similarity actually consists of. So for now I'm simply appealing to an unscientific, impressionistic notion of similarity. But the point is that similarity – however it may eventually be quantified – is clearly not playing a role in Corsican allophony, as learners do not mistakenly group the two voiced stops into the same category. We know this simply because children master all the complexities of the language without making mistakes: they come to speak the same language that their parents speak. So phonetic similarity is neither a prerequisite, nor a diagnostic, for allophonic relatedness.

In short, Corsican (and the many other languages which have comparable patterns) shows us quite clearly that phonetic similarity is not isomorphic with functional identity. Rather, the maintenance of meaning upon alternation is both necessary and sufficient for learners to determine allophonic relatedness.

3. Taiwanese

Implicit in our discussion of Corsican is a further proposal about the nature of allophony: very dissimilar sounds may be functionally identical, provided, merely, that they alternate with each other. Let's consider the case of Taiwanese tone alternation in this light. Taiwanese, like all Chinese languages (as well as many North American, Mexican, African and other Asian languages – indeed, like the majority of the world's languages) is tonal. Recall that in tonal languages, pitch may behave just as consonants and vowels do, in that they may be substituted for one another in a contrastive, neutralizing or allophonic way. In Taiwanese, tones at the end of a phrase alternate with tones *not* at the end of a phrase. In Table 4.1, tones are indicated with superscripted diacritics. A high (H) tone is indicated [´], a mid tone (M) is

Table 4.1 Tone alternations in Taiwanese

At the end of a phrase	*Alternates with*	*Not at the end of a phrase*
H# [tsīn p^há̲ŋ] very fragrant	⇔	M [p^hā̲ŋ tsûi] fragrant water
LH# [p^hē wě̲] leather shoes	⇔	M [wē̲ tuà] shoe laces
M# [wì pī̄] stomach ailment	⇔	L [pì̲ lǎŋ] sick person
L [k^hí ts^hù̲] build a house	⇔	HL [ts^hû̲ tîŋ] roof top
HL# [tuà hâ̲i] big ocean	⇔	H [há̲i kǐ̲:] ocean front

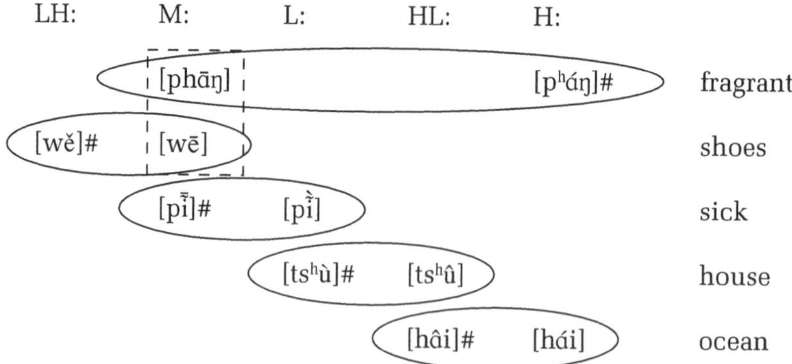

Figure 4.2 The mostly allophonic nature of Taiwanese tone alternation

indicated [¯], and a low tone (L) is indicated [`]. These marks may be combined to indicate a gliding, or *contour* tone, during which the tone rises or falls in pitch. So [^] indicates a HL falling tone, and [ˇ] indicates a LH rising tone. Even if you can't envision the actual pronunciation of these words, just keep your eye on the changing tone symbols; the alternating tones are underlined. (Don't worry, I'll try again to acquaint you with tone production in Chapter Five.) Although the tone symbols appear over the vowel, they are actually pronounced during both the vowel(s) and the final nasal. Cross-hatching here (#) indicates phrase-final position.

If you carefully check the tonal alternations on display here (underlined) you'll notice that they are usually allophonic, and not neutralizing. Our now-familiar set notation makes this more clear (Figure 4.2).

The tones found in phrase-final position are all distinct from each other, and except for the case of [pʰāŋ] and [wē], the non-final tones are distinct from each other as well (recall, [pì] is a phrase-final form). Since both LH# ([ˇ]#) and H# ([´]#) alternate with M ([¯]) when in non-final position, tone substitutions are potentially neutralizing here. I have placed a dashed rectangle around these two forms to draw attention to them. Now, [pʰāŋ] and [wē] are not neutralized because the consonants and vowels are different. However, consider words like [tě]# 'tea' and [té]# 'earth'. When in non-final position, these neutralize, becoming [tē], as shown in Figure 4.3.

At any rate, the potentially neutralizing pattern is not the main topic of our investigation. Instead, let's stay focused on allophony. When discussing Corsican consonants, I suggested that language learners come to ignore phonetic similarity or dissimilarity as they

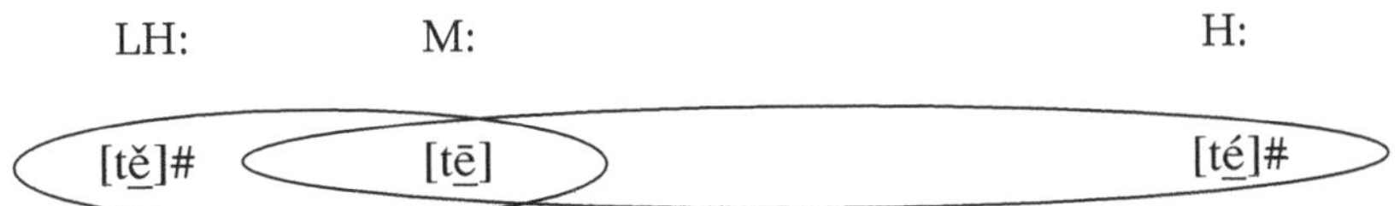

Figure 4.3 Neutralization in Taiwanese

determine the allophonic nature of the sound substitution, even when contrastive sounds bear more resemblance to each other than they bear to their respective alternants. Instead, learners focus their attention on the functional consequences of the sound substitution. The same thing is happening in Taiwanese. Tones in alternation may be less similar to each other than they are to tones with which they don't alternate. This is made perfectly clear in the set diagram in Figure 4.2, as the final alternant of one tone is the same as the non-final alternant of some other tone. But Taiwanese tone allophony reveals something even more remarkable, casting even graver doubt on the hypothesis that phonetic similarity plays a role in the determination of allophonic relations. In Taiwanese there is really no simple generalization we can make about the relationships between final versus non-final tones. The two sets have little in common in terms of their phonetic properties, and moreover, the phonetic nature of the alternation itself is strikingly different from one pair to the next. That is, the phonetic difference within one set of alternants is completely dissimilar to the phonetic difference within the other sets of alternants; they are all changing in their own independent ways. In short, Taiwanese tone allophony is something of a phonetic mess. This is quite different from the situation in Corsican, where the sets of alternants differed in very regular ways – in terms of voice-or-voiceless, and in terms of stop-or-fricative. But since Taiwanese children master their tonal alternations just as readily as Corsican children master their consonant alternations, there would seem little reason to maintain the hypothesis that phonetic similarity plays a role in the determination of allophonic relations. Again, all that matters is that meaning is maintained upon alternation.

Physical similarity versus functional identity

Allophones may be viewed as belonging to one single functional category among many. Therefore, as learners determine the allophonic relatedness between sounds, they are engaging in a form of category formation. Given the conclusions we have drawn from the allophonic patterns of Corsican and Taiwanese, it's clear that any theory of category formation (be it linguistic sound categories or otherwise)

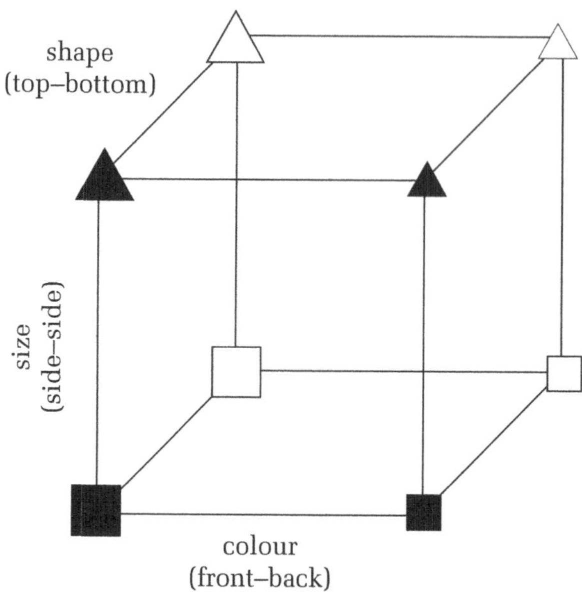

Figure 4.4 Similarity and difference across three dimensions: colour, size, shape

which relies too heavily on physical similarity is unable to account for these and other such patterns. Instead, the functional identity of these linguistic objects clearly overrides their physical dissimilarity.

The relevance of functional identity in category formation is experimentally investigated in a landmark paper from 1961 by the psychologists Roger Shepard, Carl Hovland and Herbert Jenkins. These researchers tested subjects' ability to group visual stimuli into sets that possess either similar or dissimilar members. For example, the schematic in Figure 4.4 portrays an evaluation of similarity between eight members along three dimensions: colour, size and shape.

Here, colour, size and shape fully cross-classify. From these cross-classifications, many groups can be formed which consist of more-similar or less-similar members. Figure 4.5 shows the six logical breakdowns of the eight forms, each consisting of two groups with four members each. Group Type I contains groups with members that are maximally similar, here, on the colour dimension – black shapes group together, white shapes group together. Group Type II consists of groups with qualitatively less similar members, requiring two dimensions to be considered for classificatory purposes – black triangles and white squares group together, white triangles and black squares group together. Group Types III, IV and V consist of groups requiring

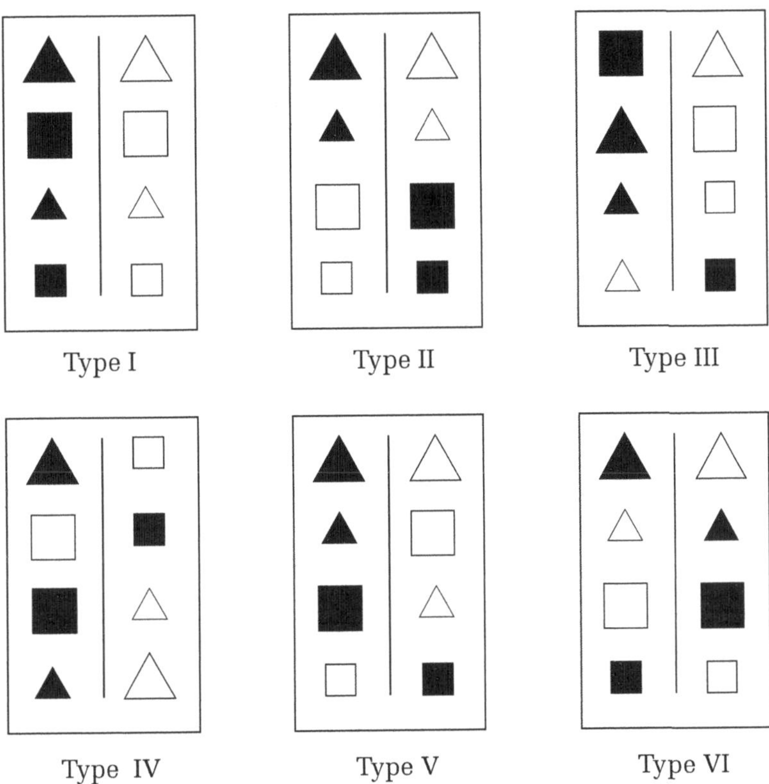

Figure 4.5 The six logical breakdowns of the eight forms, each consisting of two groups with four members each

mention of all three dimensions. For example, in Group Type III, large black shapes and the small triangles group together, large white shapes and the small squares group together. Finally, Group Type VI requires learning the qualities on all three dimensions for each individual member – the large black triangle, small black square, large white square, and small white triangle group together; the large white triangle, small black triangle, large black square, and small white square group together.

In these six group types, physical similarity plays an increasingly insignificant role as we go down the list. In the limiting case (Group Type VI), physical similarity cannot be harnessed at all as an aid in classification. Indeed, attempting to do so actually confounds the process of categorization.

In the actual experiment, these colour–size–shape figures were not employed. Instead, pictures of actual objects were used which differed along similar dimensions. Experimental subjects went through a number of sets of stimuli, with each set conforming to one of the six group types. Subjects were trained to associate a prescribed verbal response to each of eight stimuli within the given set. Four of the stimuli were associated with one verbal response, the other four with another. The pictures of objects used in the experiment did not bear *intrinsic* functional relationships to each other. Rather, their relationships were to be learned by subjects as the experiment progressed. After each response, subjects were provided with immediate feedback as to the correct response to the stimulus flashed, and were then presented with the next stimulus, and so on. After exposure to one set, stimulus presentation moved on to the next set, until 32 consecutive correct responses were produced.

Subjects were successful at learning all six sorts of groupings, but showed a clear facility with learning groups consisting of more similar members (I, II). Learning groups with the least similar members (VI), while slowest, nonetheless improved the most over time, and ultimately patterned similarly to all other groups in terms of their learnability.

How are these findings on category learning relevant to our investigation of learning allophonic relations? First, these findings suggest that learners may experience an initial difficulty, but an ultimate success, in discovering that phonetically disparate allophones should be grouped together. That is, in such cases as the Corsican [t–d]/[d–ð] type alternation, and in those unusual circumstances when allophones have strayed quite far from each other in terms of their phonetic quality, as in Taiwanese, the functional identity of phonetically distinct allophones is indeed learnable, although the category may take marginally more time to master. Thus, despite the initial boost that similar stimuli may receive in terms of category grouping, this boost is quickly overridden by functional cues to category membership.

With respect to learning allophonic relations, initial semantic feedback regarding category membership may fall on deaf ears, for just as experimental subjects do not immediately learn the intricacies and subtleties of category membership, so too early language learners are unaware of the sameness or distinctness in meaning that accompanies sound substitution. As discussed in Chapter One, functional relations between sounds cannot be learned until meaning is: learning allophonic relations is dependent upon learning allomorphic relations. But just as experimental subjects who, when provided with feedback, are ultimately able to group unlike elements together, so too may language learners, over time, exploit the lexical semantic feedback provided them regarding meaning changes or non-changes in order to replicate the functional categories of the adult system, regardless of the phonetic values of these elements. In essence, *the determination of identity or non-identity between stimuli is significantly affected by function – of categorization demands – rather than being an inherent component of the stimuli themselves.* This approach to categorization therefore implicates the relevance of *function* over *form* in order to arrive at – or derive – the proper features necessary for effective category delineation.

But there is additional significance to Shepard, Hovland and Jenkins' findings. Until this point I have merely noted that phonetically unusual phonological processes, such as those found in Taiwanese, are rare consequences of historical change. But why are certain patterns so rare, and others so common? That is, given the possibility that the long march of history will take its toll on the phonetic order of a phonological system, why are not all phonological systems in a state of phonetically transmogrified disarray? A conceivable answer emerges when considering the learning curve involved in forming categories out of dissimilar elements. Recall that in Shepard, Hovland and Jenkins' experiment, subjects initially performed better on lower-numbered group types (forming categories out of elements with physically similar members), and initially performed rather poorly on higher-numbered group types (where physical similarity played an increasingly insignificant role), but that performance here improved dramatically over time as feedback was provided. It is reasonable to assume that linguistic category formation proceeds along similar lines. That is, categories with dissimilar members might indeed take a bit more time to master. Such categories may initially be mistakenly filled with similar members, which would be in keeping with the majority of the more readily learnable categories. Now, over time, such 'incorrectly' formed categories may be 'corrected' with sufficient feedback (sufficient exposure to allophonic alternations – which do not change meaning), but some incorrectly regularized forms may take hold, and consequently change the system towards a more regular state. The question is, which categories with dissimilar members should be most susceptible to a change toward regularity, and which categories should most likely maintain their dissimilar members? This may depend on the amount of feedback available to the learner. If there is a great deal of feedback in the form of exposure to frequently employed words in alternation, categories with dissimilar members should ultimately be successfully learned. Moreover, if there is little-to-no exposure to a given irregular pattern at *early* stages in the learning procedure, these irregularities too will probably be learned correctly later on, as feedback begins after the mature system is well in place – certain archaisms may survive exactly due to their rarity of usage among children. However, those irregular categories with existing though minimal feedback at the early stages of language learning – again, in the form of minimal exposure to less frequently employed items – will likely be the most susceptible to regularization, as minimal amounts of feedback may be insufficient for the proper generalizations to emerge for the learner. The result is that the learner might fill the category with likely candidates – those that conform to the regularities of most other categories in that they possess phonetically similar members.

Now, we can't import wholesale the results of lab-based experimental work to the issue of language acquisition, nor can we necessarily take results ascertained through one modality – vision – and apply them to another modality – the hearing of linguistically relevant sounds. Nonetheless, there is a striking parallel between Shepard, Hovland and Jenkins' findings and what we observe in linguistic patterning. In language after language, irregular patterns are typically found both among the *most* frequently used items, and the *least* frequently used items. Words of moderate frequency are typically the most regular in terms of their linguistic patterning. The linguist Charles Hockett expressed these ideas in his book of 1958:

> Other things being equal, irregular forms of high frequency are less apt to be replaced than are rarer ones ... [If] an irregular form is frequently used, a child learning his native language will hear it many times, and may never come out with any analogically produced regular alternant. Even if he does, he probably already knows the inherited irregular form and may reject his own innovation.

However,

> For a rarer irregular form this argument applies in reverse ... Under some circumstances, extreme rarity may preserve an irregular instead of helping to lose it. The process, however, is quite different. The word *spake* (past tense of *speak*) and *beholden* still occur from time to time; it would seem that the rarity and irregularity of the forms constitute an integral factor in their peculiar archaic flavor, and it is because of the latter that the forms are used.

The initial tendency to group similar things together, and, in the face of a paucity of feedback, the likely assumption that other forms pattern similarly to the norm, may account for such patterns both morphological and phonological in nature. In Taiwanese, then, although we don't have an understanding of the *origin* of the marked irregularity of the tonal system, it may nonetheless be due to the punishing frequency with which learners are exposed to allophonic alternations that this highly irregular pattern has survived.

Two cases of mistaken identity

1. Akan

Sounds that alternate in an allophonic fashion are traditionally said to be in *complementary distribution*, where 'complementary' is used in its geometric sense. That is, subtracting one angle from 90° yields its complementary angle. For example, 60° is the complement of 30°; 60° plus 30° gives us a perfect right angle. In phonology, then, the group of sounds that engages in allophonic alternation gives us the total set of allophonic alternants. The set consists of non-intersecting subsets such that each subset is the complement of the other(s). So American English [ɫ] and [l], due to their allophonic alternation, are in complementary distribution because we may find one exactly where we may not find the other, and vice versa.

However, there is another source of complementary distribution, one that does not involve alternation at all. Look at the words from Akan in Table 4.2, a language of Ghana. I've arranged the words according to the quality of the underlined consonant–vowel sequences.

There is an interesting generalization to be made here. Before front vowels ([i, ɪ, e, ɛ]), we can find [tç] (this is somewhat similar to English 'j' in 'jeep'), and preceding the other vowels ([u, ʊ, o, ɔ, ɑ]), we can find [k] ([ɪ] as in 'bit'; [ɛ] as in 'bet'; [ʊ] as in 'book'; [ɔ] as a New Yorker pronounces 'bought'). Since these two sounds are not found in other contexts in Akan (although an important exception will be discussed in a moment), we may say that [k] and [tç] are in complementary distribution, since [k] may be found exactly where [tç] may *not* be found, and vice versa.

Despite their apparent complementary distribution, [k] and [tç] *never* alternate with each other in Akan. The only circumstances in which we encounter [k] or [tç] in Akan is when a vowel immediately follows *within the same morpheme*. If we were to investigate the way in which morphemes combine into words in Akan, we would find that there are no cases of one morpheme ending with a consonant, followed immediately by another morpheme beginning with a vowel. So we can't find even a single morpheme that has an allomorph that ends in

Table 4.2 Front and back words in Akan

Front words		*Back words*	
[tçim]	umbrella	[kun]	kill
[tçɪtçɛ]	divide	[akomɑ]	the heart
[ɔtçe]	river	[kɔʔ]	go
[tçɛ]	divide	[kɑ]	to bite

[k] when an [u] immediately follows in the next morpheme, but has another allomorph that ends in [tç] when an [i] immediately follows in the next morpheme. This means that there is simply no opportunity for [k] and [tç] to alternate with each other. But still, the sounds are in complementary distribution.

What is the origin of these sounds' complementary distribution? Although we don't know for sure, it is quite possible that [k] and [tç] used to be quite similar in their phonetic attributes – probably, quite like [k] – but over the generations, the sound moved towards [tç] (or *palatalized*) when it preceded front vowels. There are well-understood reasons for this sort of sound change. The first point to consider is that both the tongue body and the roof of the mouth have a fairly large surface area, and so there is a fair degree of 'wiggle room' here. What I mean is that we can form a constriction at different places in this region without significantly changing the acoustic character of the consonant, and so it won't be rendered confusable with another contrastive consonant. In English, for example, the [k] in 'coo' [k^{h}u]) (with a back vowel) is made quite a bit farther back along the palate than is the [k̟] in 'key' [k̟^{h}i] (with a front vowel); the diacritic indicates that the tongue is more forward along the palate. So, it is quite possible that in the history of Akan, the tongue-body consonants that preceded front vowels were more forward than those that preceded back vowels. But this is only the beginning of the story. For these more-forward tongue-body consonants, the tongue actually makes more surface contact with the roof of the mouth than it does for more backward sounds. Because of this increased contact area, the release of a (front) [k̟] may be less sharp, less 'clean' than the release of a (back) [k], such that the air rushing through at the release is more likely to become turbulent. This will be especially true when vowels like [i, ɪ, e, ɛ] follow, since the tongue body remains fairly close to the roof of the mouth. Turbulent air, as we now know, is a characteristic of fricative sounds, which is exactly what we find in the latter portion of Akan's [tç]: [ç] is a palatal fricative. So the sound may have gone through an intermediate stage of [k̟ç]. The last piece of the puzzle is the change from [k̟ç] to [tç]. It is quite likely that the place of oral closure of [k̟ç] might now be susceptible to change, because the formant transitions from the palatal fricative into the following vowel are not dissimilar to those of tongue-tip consonants. These fricative-to-vowel formant transitions are far more robust that those of the [k̟] itself, since the [k̟] is not immediately released into a vowel. In time, the [k̟] may indeed become a [t], giving us the [tç] that we see in Akan today.

In short, in the context of front vowels, there may have been a very gradual shift from [k] to [k̟] to [k̟ç] to [tç]. Furthermore, *none* of these changes would have affected [k]s which preceded back vowels, because the articulatory, aerodynamic, and acoustic conditions were not comparable.

So now I've now offered a hypothesis – rooted in historical phonetics, or *palaeophonetics* – for the present-day complementary distribution of [k] and [tç] in Akan. But now let's return to the main issue. What is the present-day linguistic significance of this complementary distribution? Are [k] and [tç] related in the same way that allophonic alternants are related, which, recall, are in complementary distribution by definition? In many languages, this is an impossible question to answer, due to a lack of linguistic evidence. Despite this lack of evidence, many phonologists (though not I) are satisfied with the guess that sounds in complementary distribution that do not alternate *are* functionally related in the same way that sounds in allophonic alternation are, provided that the sounds are phonetically similar to each other. In Akan, however, there is actually compelling linguistic evidence showing that [k] and [tç] are *not* treated as functionally equivalent. Getting at this evidence will require us to delve further into the phonology and morphology of the language.

Reduplication is a process whereby all or part of a word is copied, and a predictable change in meaning results. In Akan, one way to form a verb is to prefix a copy of a word's first consonant and vowel to the base word itself. The consonant copies exactly, but the vowel is always a high vowel, although its front/back/round quality is usually copied from the original word. Take a look at a few examples: [si+siʔ] 'stand'; [bu+buʔ] 'bend'; [si+seʔ] 'say'; [su+soʔ] 'seize'. When the original vowel is high, the prefixed vowel is a perfect copy. But when the original vowel is not high, it is raised in the copy, with its other features remaining as they were. So [e, o] raise to [i, u], respectively. These copied consonant–vowel complexes are fully-fledged morphemes, by the way, since they change the meaning of the word in a predictable way: in the Akan process we are looking at, the reduplication creates verbs. What makes reduplication unique is that the shape of the morpheme is largely or wholly dependent on the shape of the base word.

Now, remember that [k] and [tç] in Akan seem to be in complementary distribution but not in alternation with each other: [k] isn't found before front vowels, and [tç] isn't found before other vowels. The big question is, what happens when a [kɑ-]-word is reduplicated, which involves the replacement of [ɑ] with [i]? If [k] is replaced with [tç], then we have linguistic evidence that [k] and [tç] are functionally related in Akan. But if [k] is *not* replaced with [tç], and remains [k], we have evidence that [k] and [tç] are *not* functionally related in Akan.

This would, moreover, falsify the claim that the two sounds are in perfect complementary distribution.

So what happens? Look at the following words for the answer: [tçɪ–tçɛ] 'divide', [ki–kɑʔ] 'bite'. The first word is just as we expect it to be, with [tç] preceding the front vowel in both morphemes. But look at the second example. When [kɑ-] reduplicates, the [k] remains [k] even though it comes to precede [i]. So, in the one circumstance when [k] and [tç] finally have the opportunity to alternate with each other, still they remain oblivious to each other's existence, and retain their functional non-identity. This creates an exception to the generalization that [tç] is always found in the context of a front vowel. But as I've demonstrated several times, the generalizations that language researchers make are not necessarily the same generalizations that language users make. Phonologists might observe the almost-perfect complementary distribution of [k] and [tç] and conclude that the two sounds are allophonically related. But Akan speakers are making no such generalization, as the lack of alternation upon reduplication shows so clearly.

So what is the *origin* of this pattern? Akan reduplication suggests that the [k]-to-[tç] sound change occurred prior in history to the introduction of the reduplication process itself, as displayed in the proposed timeline in Figure 4.6.

This historical reconstruction of the Akan pattern offers a straightforward account of the present-day facts. At some point in the history of the language, [k]s which preceded front vowels palatalized to [tç]. This only occurred within morphemes, because [k] never came to precede a front vowel across a morpheme boundary. At a later point in time, the reduplication pattern was introduced into the language, perhaps through a process of language contact (just as English now has reduplications like 'fancy-schmancy', due to contact with Yiddish). This process introduced a new sound pattern into the language (or, rather, reintroduced an old sound pattern), for example [ki], as in [ki–kɑʔ]. The [k] component of *these* [ki]s did *not* palatalize, however, because there were no alternations that established a functional relationship between pre-existing [tç] and new [ki]. Consequently,

early form	*palatalization*	*reduplication*	*present-day form*
kɑʔ (bite)	–	ki–kɑʔ	ki–kɑʔ
kɛr (bind)	tçɛr	tçi–tçɛr	tçi–tçɛr
time ⟶			

Figure 4.6 A suggested diachrony for Akan

these new [ki] morphemes were simply added to the inventory of morphemes of Akan without inducing a [k]–[tç] alternation. So in the new reduplication context – and in this context only – [k] comes to precede [i] within a morpheme, and the present-day pattern is accounted for.

Let me emphasize that this scenario is merely a proposed reconstruction, and that we don't really know the detailed history of Akan. Linguists have developed several methods to investigate how present-day phonological patterns have come into being. The surest method is to study old linguistic descriptions or historical texts, which may provide quite reliable evidence about a language's past. Our discussions of historical Korean and Chinese in Chapter Three were based in part on such texts. Unfortunately, very few languages have been carefully documented over a period of centuries, and so this method is not usually available. Alternatively, we can compare the sound pattern in one language to several of its closest and most obvious relatives. We look at words in each of the languages that clearly have a common historical origin (based upon their comparable meaning and their similar phonetic properties), and compare their phonological properties. The sorts and prevalences of differences and similarities between the sounds of these related languages can sometimes make it obvious which sounds have evolved into which other sounds, which sounds are older (often, the sounds shared by more of the relatives) and which sounds are more recent innovations (often, the rarer sounds). This is known as the *comparative method*. The method we have just employed in our discussion of Akan is known as *internal reconstruction*. In this method, as I just demonstrated, we consider the sounds in a single language at a single point in time. Based on how the sounds phonologically interact with each other, we might reconstruct their historical origins.

Back to Akan now: despite the ease with which we can express this sound change in terms of the individual sounds, the very fact that only a subset of morphemes starting with [k] underwent the change to [tç] strongly suggests that there was *never* a notion of 'k-ness' in the minds of Akan speakers, such that all instances of [k] were organized into a single phonological category. Rather, the sound change seems to be the result of a generalization that learners made over *words*, not a generalization made over component sounds themselves. There were phonetic reasons for words of certain phonetic shapes to undergo a sound change. However, since there were no alternations, there was no functional reason for learners to analyse these words' internal structure; there was no linguistic motivation prompting learners to break down these *Gestalts* into smaller, isolable components, like [k]-[i] and [k]-[ɑ], and so the [k]s from

[ki] and the [k]s from [ka] do not emerge as functionally related to each other: *structuration is dependent upon alternation.* As I've already noted, expressing phonological patterns and changes in terms of the isolable sounds themselves may be the best way we can talk about linguistic generalizations. But of course, the generalizations we make as linguists are not necessarily the same as the generalizations we make as learners, as Akan has just shown once again.

So what about the future of Akan? We might speculate that those rare words like [ki–kɑʔ] will eventually become [tçi–kɑʔ], with the stop again undergoing palatalization. It would be tempting to view such a change as a 'regularization' of a stray pattern, due to a pressure that is pulling these [k]s back in line with the [tçi] pattern that is found elsewhere in the language. But I think this would be a mistaken analysis. We have reliable linguistic evidence that learners do not establish any relationship between [tçi] and [kɑ] in the first place, and so there is no reason for them to treat these rare [ki] morphemes as having strayed from any other pattern in the language, including [tçi]; even though this may be what happened in the history of Akan, history cannot possibly be recapitulated inside the heads of modern speakers. Instead, the same phonetic pressures that gave rise to the [ki]-to-[tçi] change in the past may once again act on [ki]. This has happened in the past of Akan, and it could happen again in Akan, since reduplication has re-introduced [k]-front vowel sequences into the language. But we just don't know, of course. Sound change is not deterministic, but probabilistic. We can no better predict the evolution of a sound than we can the evolution of a species. So even though some sound changes are quite likely to occur, we can never predict when or even *if* they will occur. We can only entertain more-likely and less-likely scenarios.

2. New York English

In Akan, the [k]-to-[tç] change only showed its effects within morphemes, never having the opportunity to affect sounds across morpheme boundaries. Sound changes of this exclusively morpheme-internal sort may produce complementary distributions in which sounds don't alternate with each other, even when given a unique opportunity to do so, as when a process of reduplication creates the very pattern that the sound change has elsewhere eliminated. A language spoken much closer to home – closer to *my* home, anyway – provides us with further evidence for this. New York English has an unusual vowel quality that is sometimes referred to as a *tense 'a'*, as in the word 'ban'. For this vowel, the tongue is in a somewhat higher position than it is for, say, 'bat' [b̥æˀt̚], and there is a little schwa-like vowel that follows, creating a *diphthong* (two sequenced vowel qualities). We'll transcribe this sound [æ̝ə̆], in which the first diacritic indicates the slight tongue-raising that accompanies this sound, the [ə] represents the little schwa, and the second diacritic indicates that this schwa is particularly short in duration: [b̥æ̝̃ə̆̃n]. I realize that [æ]–[æ̝ə̆] is a very subtle distinction, and non-New Yorkers are often either perplexed or amazed when I demonstrate it for them. If you have trouble conceptualizing it, at least you can observe the transcriptional distinction between the two. In New York, [æ] and [æ̝ə̆] are in complementary distribution, but never alternate with each other, just like [k] and [tç] in Akan. Specifically, the [æ̝ə̆] may be found before voiced stops, most of the fricatives, and [m] and [n], but only when these sounds are not immediately followed by another vowel within the same morpheme. There are additional distributional restrictions, but we can ignore them for the present. The [æ] may be found in complementary contexts.

This description is consistent with the pronunciations of 'ban' [b̥æ̝̃ə̆̃n] and 'bat' [b̥æʔt̚]. For 'ban' the vowel precedes [n], which is not followed by another vowel within the same morpheme, and so we find [æ̝ə̆]. For 'bat' the vowel is followed by [t], and so we don't find [æ̝ə̆]. Now, if a following vowel is in the same morpheme, again the lax vowel is used. So for example, the pronunciation of 'banner' – meaning 'pennant' – is [b̥æ̃nəɹ], because a vowel ([ə]) follows the [n] within the same morpheme. Especially interesting is that a person who *bans* something is a 'banner', pronounced [b̥æ̝̃ə̆̃nəɹ]. Here, the tense 'a' of the verb 'ban' remains tensed even though a vowel now follows the [n]. This is because this second vowel is *not* in the same morpheme as the preceding [n]. In phonological terms, 'ban+er' and 'banner' differ only in terms of tensing, but in morphological terms, 'ban+er' has two morphemes, and 'banner' has one. The upshot is that [æ] and [æ̝ə̆] are in complementary distribution within morphemes, and so they are never responsible for a contrast between individual morphemes (there will at least be a following consonant that is different as well). But they can come to constitute a minimal phonological contrast when two words have different morphological structures: words with more than one morpheme can differ from words with only one morpheme solely in terms of the [æ]–[æ̝ə̆] distinction. Some additional examples include 'adder' [æ]dder (a species of snake) versus 'adder' (add+er) [æ̝ə̆]dder (one who adds); 'cannibal' c[æ̃]nnibal versus 'cannable' (can+able) c[æ̝̃ə̆̃]nnable (able to be canned).

The unusual mixed status of the [æ]–[æ̝ə̆] relationship – that these vowels are in complementary distribution within morphemes, but may contrast when morphemes attach – can be traced directly to the historical origins of their phonetic distinction. Since the Middle

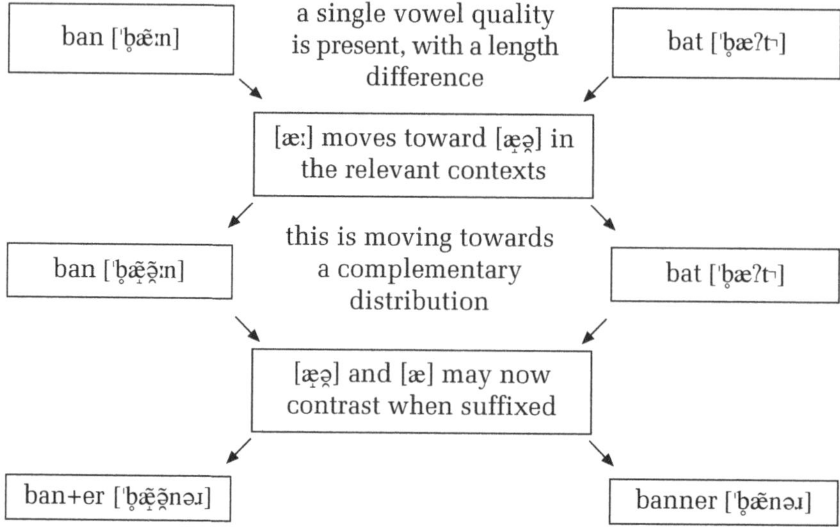

Figure 4.7 The diachrony of 'tense "a"'

English period, the low front lax vowel [æ] was long in certain contexts, and only in the most recent times is it being replaced by a raised and diphthongized form ([æ̝ə̝]) in various eastern American locales. Thus, for example, where 'ban' and 'bat' may have previously both possessed the lower *monophthong* with a length difference, the longer vowel in 'ban' has undergone tensing and diphthongization. Consequently, a word like 'banner' (['b̥æ̃nəɹ]) – containing only one morpheme – meaning 'pennant', possesses the lax vowel, while a bimorphemic word like 'banner' (ban+er ['b̥æ̝̃ə̝̃nəɹ]) meaning 'one who bans', retains its tense quality. The history of the tensing process is outlined in Figure 4.7.

Now comes the big question: is there any evidence that, despite the absence of alternation, [æ] and [æ̝ə̝] are functionally equivalent for New York speakers? Unlike Akan, New York does not have a reduplication process which would provide further testing ground for our hypothesis that these vowels are not functionally equivalent. However, it does have an unusual morphological process that is just as revealing as is reduplication in Akan, which provides us with another way to create words that minimally differ along the [æ]–[æ̝ə̝] dimension. Instead of adding morphemes to each other as in 'ban+er' and 'can+able', we can *subtract* part of a morpheme from itself. The remaining part of the morpheme may stand alone as a word, and since this subtraction process has (often subtle) consequences for word

Table 4.3 New York truncation exemplified

	shortens to	*contrasts with*
camera – c[æ̃]mera	(steady-)cam – c[æ̃]m	cam – c[æ̝̃ə̯̃]m (-engine)
Janice – J[æ̃]nice	Jan – J[æ̃]n	Jan (full name) – J[æ̝̃ə̯̃]n
Cabbott – C[æ]bbott	Cab-(Calloway) – C[æ]b	cab – c[æ̝ə̯]b

meaning, this shortened form is regarded as a separate morpheme in its own right. This subtraction process is known as *truncation*, and some examples follow: 'Nancy' N[æ̝̃ə̯̃]ncy – 'Nan-' N[æ̝̃ə̯̃]n-; 'Ashley' A[æ̝ə̯]shley – 'Ash-' [æ̝ə̯]sh-. These truncation patterns are straightforward. The vowels in question are in the context where we expect tensing – both in their full form and in their truncated form. But now consider a second group of examples: 'Janice' J[æ̃]nice – 'Jan-' J[æ̃]n-; 'cafeteria' c[æ]feteria – 'caf-' c[æ]f-; 'Massachusetts' M[æ]ssachusetts – 'Mass-' M[æ]ss-. Truncation does *not* induce alternations between [æ] and [æ̝ə̯], even though the [æ] vowel suddenly finds itself in the context where other morphemes have [æ̝ə̯]. This means that truncation can produce words that differ minimally in terms of the [æ]–[æ̝ə̯] distinction, just like our 'banner' – 'ban+er' cases, as the further examples in Table 4.3 show.

So, if 'camera' (with [æ]: [kʰæ̃mɹə]) is truncated to 'cam-', the vowel remains [æ], even though an [m] follows, and no vowel follows within the morpheme (no present-day English speaker says [kʰæ̃məɹə], with three syllables). What's especially interesting is that there are two different names in New York, 'J[æ̝̃ə̯̃]n' and 'J[æ̃]n'. The former is a full name, like 'Jan Brady' or 'Jan Murray'. The latter, however, is a shortened form of 'Janice' or 'Janet', where we have the expected [æ] in the full form, and so it is present in the truncated form as well. So truncation creates an exception to the generalization that [æ̝ə̯] is always found in this context. But again, the generalizations that I make as a phonologist of New York English are not the same generalizations that I make as a speaker of New York English. There is a generalization that [æ̝ə̯] and [æ] are in complementary distribution within morphemes. As in Akan, this generalization is over words, not individual sounds. So as a speaker of New York English, this distributional generalization has no bearing on the cognitive and functional arrangement of the sounds of my language, as the lack of alternation upon truncation shows so clearly.

There are some interesting exceptions to this pattern that, ultimately, prove the rule. Consider the word 'lab'. This word is pronounced [læ̝ə̯b], with the diphthong. However, 'lab' is related to the full form 'laboratory', which is pronounced l[æ]boratory, without the diphthong. In these related forms, then, it appears that the alternation is present when it 'shouldn't' be. I think the key to understanding this exception is found in the frequency of the word 'lab' in relation to the full form 'laboratory'. When a truncated form gets used often enough, it may lose its relationship to the full form, and become a fully-fledged word on its own, and come to conform to the phonological patterns that are characteristic of other full words in the language. So 'lab' has the diphthong, because it has become *lexicalised*: it has become an independent word. Consequently, it now behaves as any other word in the language does, and so we find the diphthong here.

Another interesting exception comes from Stevie Wonder's great song 'Master Blaster', from 1980. New Yorkers pronounce this title as a rhyme: m[æ]ster bl[æ]ster. Now, while 'master' is a single morpheme, and naturally has [æ], 'blaster' is built from two morphemes, blast+er, and is expected to have the diphthong [æ̝ə̯], and, indeed, whenever this word is encountered in other contexts, it is pronounced bl[æ̝ə̯]ster, just as expected. So why do New Yorkers treat this word exceptionally in this one single context? Why don't we say 'm[æ]ster bl[æ̝ə̯]ster'? Here's what I think is going on: these words rhyme for Stevie. After all, he's from Michigan, not New York. So I think New Yorkers are simply treating this term exceptionally because they unconsciously understand that a rhyme was intended by its creator.

By explaining away these (and a few other) potential counter-examples, we may now safely conclude that [æ] and [æ̝ə̯], despite their almost-perfect complementary distribution, are *not* related to each other in an allophonic fashion, and so they are not expected to alternate with each other upon truncation.

But how about a pair of sounds that are demonstrably allophonically related to each other? Do they substitute for each other upon truncation as they do in other situations? Let's go back to our [ɫ]–[l] alternation. Recall that dark l may be found whenever a vowel does not immediately follow. This is true both within morphemes, and across morphemes, thus accounting for alternations of the 'fill'–'filling' sort. What happens to a clear l when a following vowel sound is eliminated as a consequence of truncation? Here is our answer: 'Melanie' Me[l]anie and 'Philip' Phi[l]ip allophonically alternate with 'Mel-' Me[ɫ] and 'Phil-' Phi[ɫ], respectively. It seems, then, that sounds in complementary distribution that alternate everywhere else do so upon truncation as well, but sounds in complementary distribution elsewhere that don't alternate anywhere else don't alternate upon truncation either. So the unusual sequence of sounds that may arise in truncated words turns out to be fully expected when we analyse the *functional* relationships between sounds, and when we ignore the mere phonetic regularities that our preliminary phonological investigations reveal.

Summary

We've covered quite a bit of conceptual territory in this chapter on allophonic sound substitution. We began with two examples from English showing how sounds that are similar to each other, but different from all other sounds in the language, may behave as functionally equivalent, provided that they allophonically alternate with each other.

When we considered Corsican consonant allophony, we found we could eliminate the requirement that sounds in allophonic alternation must be different from all other sounds of the language. Recall that in Corsican, sounds that alternate with each other are in fact more similar to *other* sounds of the language than they are to each other. Yet still, due to the nature of the alternations, there is no neutralization, and so the alternation retains its allophonic character. By employing palaeophonetically plausible internal reconstructions, we may come to see that sounds which allophonically alternate in the present might come from a single historical value.

Finally, Taiwanese tone allophony showed us that sounds in alternation can be radically different from each other in terms of their phonetic characteristics. The alternants are not only very different from each other, but also, as in Corsican, they are largely identical to *other* tones of the language. Moreover, each pair of alternants differs from every other pair of alternants in terms of the phonetic nature of the alternation. It bears repeating: Taiwanese tone allophony is a phonetic mess. But the mess is *only* phonetic. In functional terms, the system does a remarkably good job of keeping forms distinct which differ in meaning.

The upshot is that physical similarity does not always correlate with functional identity, just as experimentally demonstrated in the work of Shepard, Hovland and Jenkins. Instead, what matters in the determination of allophonic relatedness is merely that sounds alternate with each other in a non-neutralizing way. This result shouldn't be surprising to us, given the assertions I've been making throughout the book. Learners of language are primarily concerned with pairing sound with meaning, not with extracting phonetic regularities from the speech signal. This point is driven home in our discussions of Akan and New York English. These patterns provided us with linguistic evidence for the necessity of alternation to the structuration of morphemes into smaller units. Recall that in Akan, [k] and [tç] never alternate with each other, despite their complementary distribution. So we find [tçi, tçɪ, tçe, tçɛ], and also [ku, kʊ, ko, kɔ, kɑ], but since there are never any alternations here, there is no motivation for learners to decompose these sound sequences into smaller units. That is, [k] and [tç] do not emerge from the phonetic background as elements of combination and recombination, just as our investigation of reduplicated forms showed us. This is not to say that language learners don't become aware of phonetic regularities in the speech stream – that [ku, kʊ, ko, kɔ, kɑ] are often found, as are [tçi, tçɪ, tçe, tçɛ] – but there is no evidence to learners that these phonetic complexes are decomposable into smaller bits, since there are no alternations which would set their component parts into high relief against a stable phonetic background.

By contrast, exactly because [ɫ] and [l] alternate in New York, and so function as re-combinatory units in their own right, they might emerge from the phonetic background of the morphemes to which they belong: 'filling' [fɪlɪŋ] but 'fill' [fɪɫ]; 'Philip' [fɪlɪp] but 'Phil' [fɪɫ]. In fact, we find this result in language after language: if two sounds don't alternate elsewhere, then they don't alternate upon truncation or reduplication either, even if they are phonetically similar. And if two sounds alternate elsewhere, then they always alternate upon truncation or reduplication too, even if they are phonetically *dis*similar.

Further reading

On Corsican allophony:

Dinnsen, Daniel and Eckman, Fred R. (1977). 'Some substantive universals in atomic phonology', *Lingua* 45: 1–14.

On Taiwanese tone behaviour:

Chen, Matthew Y. (2000). *Tone Sandhi: Patterns Across Chinese Dialects*. Cambridge: Cambridge University Press.

On classification and categorization:

Kruschke, John K. (1992). 'ALCOVE: an exemplar-based connectionist model of category learning', *Psychological Review* 99.1: 22–44.

Nosofsky, Robert M. (1986). 'Attention, similarity, and the identification–categorization relationship', *Journal of Experimental Psychology: General* 115: 39–57.

Nosofsky, Robert M. (1988). 'Exemplar-based accounts of relations between classification, recognition, and typicality', *Journal of Experimental Psychology: Learning, Memory, and Cognition* 14: 700–08.

Shepard, Roger, Hovland, Carl and Jenkins, Herbert (1961). 'Learning and memorization of classifications', *Psychological Monographs* 75(13): Whole No. 517.

The Hockett quotes ('Other things being equal ...', 'For a rarer irregular form ...'):

Hockett, Charles (1958). *A Course in Modern Linguistics*. New York: Macmillan, pp. 396–7.

On Akan:

Schachter, Paul and Fromkin, Victoria (1968). *A Phonology of Akan: Akuapem, Asante, and Fante* (Working Papers in Phonetics 9). Los Angeles: UCLA.

On the comparative method, internal reconstruction, and historical linguistics in general:

Anttila, Raimo (1972) [1989]). *Historical and Comparative Linguistics*. Amsterdam: John Benjamins.

Fox, Anthony (1995). *Linguistic Reconstruction*. Oxford: Oxford University Press.

Hoenigswald, Henry M. (1960). *Language Change and Linguistic Reconstruction*. Chicago: University of Chicago Press.

McMahon, April M. S. (1994). *Understanding Language Change*. Cambridge: Cambridge University Press.

On New York's 'tense "a"':

Trager, George L. (1930). 'The pronunciation of "short *a*" in American Standard English', *American Speech* V: 396–400.

Trager, George L. (1934). 'What conditions limit variants of a phoneme?', *American Speech* IX: 313–15.

Trager, George L. (1940). 'One phonemic entity becomes two: the case of "short a"', *American Speech* XV: 225–58.

Silverman, Daniel (2002). 'Dynamic versus static phonotactic conditions in prosodic morphology', *Linguistics* 40.1: 28–58.

5 Variation and probability

The existence of variation

When I first introduced set notation during our discussion of 'phone books' and 'foam books' in Chapter One, I wrote, 'Let's suppose for the moment that the word "foam" has only one pronunciation, whereas "phone" has ... three ... which are dependent on the context in which the word is found. While this is a simplification, for now, let's just suppose it's true'. We're now ready to discuss the nature of this simplification. Although I have not called your attention to it, perhaps you have realized that my phonetic transcriptions, intended as they are to capture the physical properties of a single particular instance – or *token* – of a word spoken by a particular speaker at a particular time, are actually highly idealized in the sense that I have not linked these transcriptions to a specific utterance by a specific speaker. In fact, in the history of the world, it is almost certainly the case that no two spoken utterances have ever been *exactly* alike. But the notation we have been employing up to now does not reflect this token-to-token variation at all. Instead, I have been using a single transcription that, at its very best, might represent either an average or an idealized pronunciation.

A far more representative display would involve a great number of transcriptions which all vary ever so slightly from one another in a manner that reflects the true variable nature of speech. Of course, even this sort of representation would not do genuine justice to reality, because we can never document the totality of realizations of any word. But we can, at least, employ a notational system that better approximates the true nature of speech. So look at the revised display in Figure 5.1.

The *clouds* or *pools* of tokens in this figure do a modicum of justice to the genuine variability of speech production by suggesting that every token differs slightly from every other token. The idea is that each token falls in its own location in some (as yet undefined) multi-dimensional articulatory/acoustic/auditory space. For example, the formant values of the vowel differ slightly from token to token; the tongue position of the nasal's oral closure is slightly different from token to token as well. Now, you'll immediately notice that I've transcribed every token within each pool in an identical way. So be it.

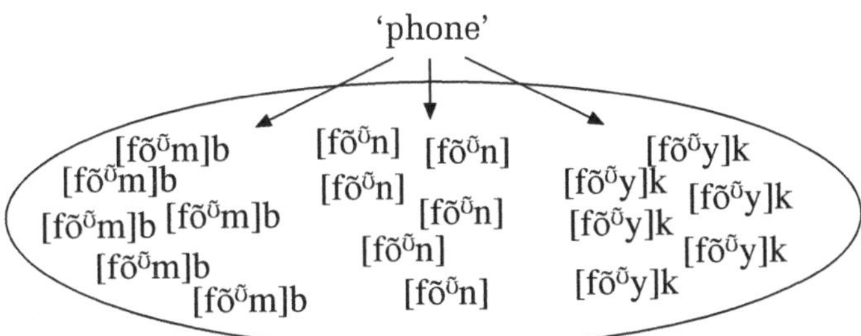

Figure 5.1 Variation within alternants

This is just an impressionistic display and is not intended to convey the actual properties of the variation. For now at any rate, this sort of display suffices.

So, in addition to the phonetic distinctions found among alternants such as [fõ^{õ}m]b, [fõ^{õ}n] and [fõ^{õ}ŋ]k, this other sort of phonetic variation shows that categories which are clearly defined phonologically are not so clearly defined phonetically. Phonological categories are clear-cut and discrete in that meaning is not *gradiently* affected by sound substitutions: sound substitutions either change meaning, eliminate meaning distinctions or maintain meaning distinctions, and that's it. By contrast, gradually lowering the tongue in going from 'bid' to 'bed' to 'bad' does not produce corresponding intermediate meanings such as 'biddish bed' or 'beddish bad'. That is, the phonetic variation that we may observe among speech tokens has no direct correlates in terms of the categories to which these tokens belong: the gradience is only phonetic, and never semantic. Indeed, as the linguist André Martinet remarked in 1975, 'Linguistic identity does not imply physical sameness ... Discreteness does not rule out infinite variety.' So, while all tokens within a category are identical in linguistic terms, they are nonetheless phonetically diverse. So look at Figure 5.2.

Here, the 'x's represent tokens, the phonetic distinctions of which are suggested by their various locations along the one-dimensional scalar display. Moving from left to right, these tokens gradually change in terms of some phonetic property. Nonetheless, the categories which learners come to impose on this gradient distribution are completely

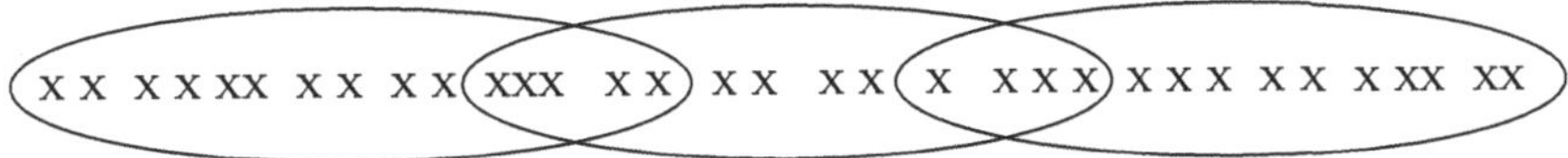

Figure 5.2 Variation on a single phonetic dimension

clear-cut and discrete. Despite the phonetic variation, some tokens fall into one category, others fall into the other categories.

But what about the intersecting regions of the sets? Certain tokens find themselves in two categories, or at the boundary between one category and another. These tokens are ambiguous between one discrete category and another. (Later in this chapter, these tokens will be argued to play a very important role in the sound system.) But still, phonetic gradience has no correlate in terms of category gradience. It's certainly *not* the case that these tokens combine semantic elements of the two words, producing a *meaning* somewhere in between one category and another: discreteness in meaning does not rule out infinite variety in sound, and infinite variety in sound does not rule out discrete categoricity in meaning.

Models of variation

What might be the origin of the phonetic variation that is always present in speech? One possibility is that phonetic constraints on speech are not so strictly imposed, and so speakers engage in an approximation of sorts. That is, their speech more or less resembles the speech around them, with a little deviation here, a little deviation there, that is somehow 'tolerated' at the cognitive level. We can refer to this approach as the *relaxed constraints model*.

Alternatively, there may indeed be strict cognitive constraints on speech. But if learners do have strict internalized constraints on their speech, then what accounts for the phonetic variation that is undeniably present? There are two common proposals for the cognitive organization of this variation, often referred to as the *prototype model* and the *exemplar model*, respectively. Both of these models (and also the relaxed constraint model) allow for the possibility that linguistic sound categories emerge through experience with individual examples or instances of perceptual events which come to self-organize themselves into distinct sets or categories. But these two approaches do have important differences between them. The prototype model of categorization proposes that speakers have very exact internalized phonetic 'targets' for their speech (be these targets articulatory, acoustic, auditory, or some combination of these) but they don't hit these targets each and every time. This would be something like an expert darts player who inevitably misses the bull's eye at least once in a while: the darts are clustered around the target, but even an expert can't hope to get it just right every time. Some version of the prototype model has been assumed by many linguists at least as far back as the nineteenth century. For example, in his book of 1880, Hermann

Paul wrote, 'However much ... movement may be the result of training ... it still remains left to chance whether the pronunciation be uttered with absolute exactness, or whether slight deviation from the correct path towards one side or the other manifests itself.' While Paul does not specifically propose an abstract prototype, he nonetheless assumes that there is a single articulatory 'target' that speakers aim for. In the prototype model then, there is an exact, abstract, category-defining value that emerges upon experience with individual tokens, and so any observed within-category variation is viewed as a deviation from this prototype.

What distinguishes the exemplar model is that perceptual categories are defined as the set of all experienced instances of the category, such that variation between tokens actually contributes to the categorical properties themselves. That is, a given category is the culmination of the variable forms themselves, in that the distribution of tokens is not viewed as a deviation, but is instead viewed as a defining aspect of the category. So, within-category variation is thus part and parcel of the category itself. But what about the *origin* of variation under the exemplar approach? One idea is that speech patterns are copied again and again by generation after generation, but inevitably with very slight inexactitudes once in a while. According to the exemplar model, one generation's variation – inexactitudes included – serves as the next generation's template for copy. So variation may be viewed as the accumulation of very minor inexactitudes both within and between generations of speakers: the long-term product of excellent-though-imperfect copying of ambient speech patterns. The result is that tokens within a category cluster around each other, with each generation's distribution of tokens differing ever so slightly from both the preceding and the following generation's tokens. As we'll see below, these slight differences may come to play a significant role in the way sounds change over a generation. If we further assume, as is reasonable, that more recently encountered tokens leave a stronger memory trace than do more remote tokens, then we can further account for the sound changes observable even across the lifetime of a single speaker.

This approach to linguistic categorization is hardly new, having been proposed in the nineteenth century by Mikołaj Kruszewski. Discussing a hypothetical case of a slightly fronted [k] (which he writes *k'*), with variants k'_1, k'_2, k'_3, etc., he wrote in 1883, 'Our characteristic, unconscious memory of the articulation of sound *k'* should be a complex recollection of all articulations of *k'* which we have performed. But not all of these articulations are arranged equally in the memory. For this reason, after performing the articulation of k'_3, the chances of performing k'_4 are much greater than they are for k'_1, etc'.

Herrmann Paul, although he does not seem to espouse an exemplar approach, nonetheless allows for his prototypes to evolve and change as a consequence of better remembering recent (versus remote) tokens:

> [V]ariability of production, which remains unnoticed because of the narrow limits in which it moves, gives the key to our comprehension of the otherwise incomprehensible fact that a change of usage in the sounds of a language sets in and comes to its fulfillment without the least suspicion on the part of those in whom this change is being carried out.
>
> If the motory sensation were to remain always unchanged as a memory-picture, the insignificant deviations would always centre round the same point with the same maximum of distance. In fact, however, this sensation is the product of all the earlier impressions received in the course of carrying out the movement in question, and, according to a common law, the impressions, not merely those which are absolutely identical, but also those that are imperceptibly different from each other, are fused into one. Correspondingly to their difference, the motory sensation must be somewhat modified with each new impression, to however insignificant an extent. It is, in this process, of importance that the later impressions always have a stronger always-influence than the earlier. It is thus impossible to co-ordinate the sensation with the average of all the impressions during the whole course of life; rather, the numerically-speaking inferior may, by the fact of their freshness, outbalance the weight of the more frequent ... There thus gradually arises, by adding together all the displacements (which we can hardly imagine small enough) a notable difference ...

The three approaches to speech variation are presented in the flowchart in Figure 5.3.

When we analyse the behaviour of an individual, it would seem extremely difficult to figure out which approach – relaxed constraint,

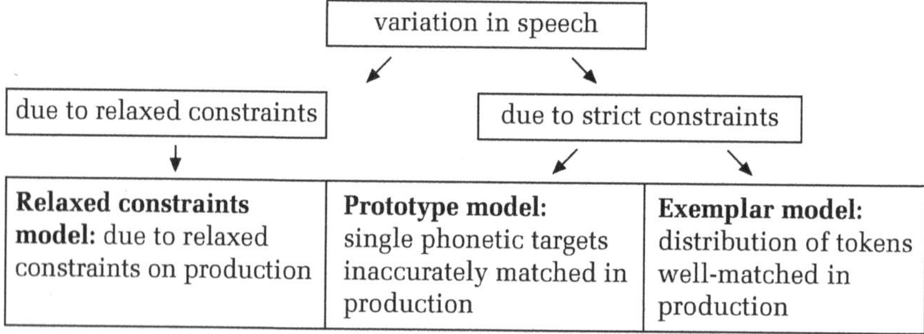

Figure 5.3 Three approaches to variation

prototype or exemplar – is best at characterizing the origin of variation and the nature of sound category formation. The category itself is largely observable, since we can, at least in theory, investigate the phonetic properties of individual tokens, and also observe whether or not the tokens we are looking at correspond to a particular meaning. We can't directly observe the meaning that is associated with a given token, of course, but we can probably determine if the speech signal was interpreted by a listener with the meaning intended by the speaker. In this way at least, meaning is observable. But since we are only dealing with the behaviour of the individual speaker, there is really no reliable way to tease apart the different approaches to variation and categorization. In short, all three approaches make untestable predictions about the categories and variation of individual speakers. In Figure 5.4, the distribution of elements is exactly the same within each set, and so there is no empirical evidence favouring any one approach over the others.

It now becomes apparent that, under the prototype model, *all* variation must be regarded as mistaken and unintended. And since virtually every token deviates from the abstract prototype in some way, this means that virtually *all* speech is to a certain extent *mistaken* speech. In this sense at least, both the relaxed constraint model and the exemplar model have a distinct philosophical advantage over the prototype model. However, in accounting for the variation itself, these latter two approaches are slightly different. The relaxed constraint

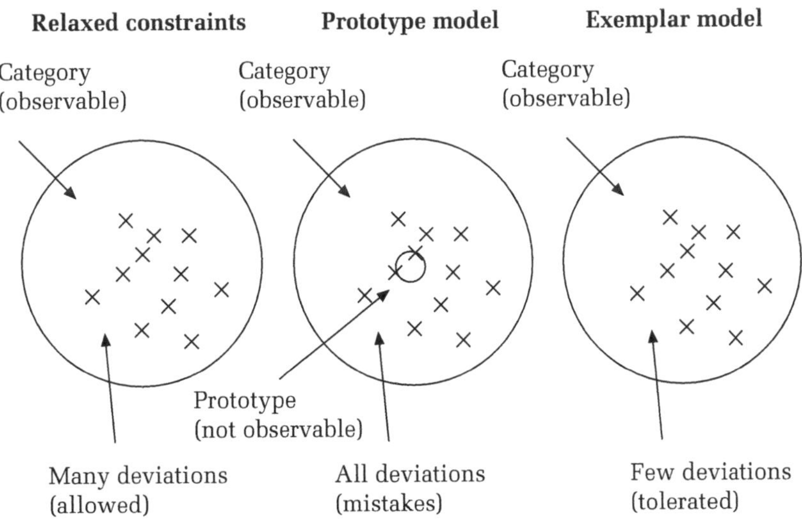

Figure 5.4 Again, three approaches to variation

model allows for some flexibility in the constraints on actual speech, and so all the variation is created anew by each speaker and each generation. The exemplar model assumes a particularly tight match-up between the cognitive constraints and actual speech, since most of the variation is copied intact.

Now let's talk about the individual as both a speaker and a listener. By doing so, we are incorporating the social context in which this categorization procedure takes place: listeners are listening to other speakers, and speakers are speaking to other listeners. Therefore, we can now *compare* the speech of various speakers in order to determine the similarities and differences of their within-category variation. This comparison could, in theory, open a window into how listeners' categories are similar to or different from the categories of those they are listening to. Moreover, the *extent* of their similarity or difference might help determine which approach – the relaxed constraint model, the prototype model or the exemplar model – is best at characterizing the sound categories and their variation. If variation is extremely well-matched from speaker to speaker and from generation to generation, this would favour the exemplar model. This is because the exemplar model predicts very little difference in the nature and extent of variation from speaker to speaker and from generation to generation. By contrast, the other approaches allow for the possibility that the nature and extent of variation may be quite different from one speaker to another, and from one generation to the next, since under these theories variation is created anew by each speaker. We turn to this issue now.

Probability matching

Both speaker-to-speaker and generation-to-generation comparisons are very important to our understanding of sound categorization. These are the areas of *variation* and *diachrony* respectively, and it is here – as opposed to the investigation of individual speakers – where we might better understand the cognitive organization of the linguistic system. To be sure, investigating variation and diachrony are indirect routes to understanding the nature of linguistic knowledge. But therein lie their greatest advantages. By analysing variation and diachrony, we make no presumptions about accessing the content of psychological states, which are inherently private and so unknowable to the outside world. Instead, we are comparing structural arrays of genuine physical objects – speech tokens – and so we harbour no illusions about the object of our inquiry. Although speaker-to-speaker variation is extremely important in this regard, our main focus here, and for the remainder of the book, is on generational comparisons: how sound categories remain stable, and how they change, as language passes from generation to generation. So the question we now turn to is this: what is the nature and extent of within-category *differences* in variation from generation to generation?

In order to answer this question, let's first talk a little bit about rats and ducks. It is well documented that animals appear to perform remarkably sophisticated statistical analyses as they navigate the world around them. For example, on the face of it, an animal foraging for food in the wild appears to be randomly searching high and low for a morsel here, a morsel there. However, it turns out that this behaviour is remarkably well-matched in terms of actual payoff. What I mean is, the animal actually recapitulates the likelihood of payoff in terms of its foraging behaviour, spending more time in a patch of ground that has a greater payoff, and less time in a patch of ground that has a lesser payoff. So, if two-thirds of the available food is in one region, and one-third is in another region, the animal very quickly comes to spend two-thirds of its foraging time in the one area, and only one-third of its foraging time in the other area. This phenomenon is known as *probability matching*.

A number of ingeniously simple experiments have been performed which show that animals indeed engage in probability matching. In one of the simplest studies, a rat placed in a T-maze is rewarded with food 75 per cent of the time at one end, 25 per cent of the time at the other. When provided with feedback, the rat's foraging behaviour quickly comes to match the probability of reward – running to the one end 75 per cent of the time, the other end 25 per cent of the time. What's especially interesting is that the rat does not maximize its payoff. If it ran to the 75 per cent-payoff end 100 per cent of the time, it would be rewarded with food 75 per cent of the time. But by distributing its foraging in a way that matches the probability of payoff, it actually reduces its food intake. So, 75 per cent of the time it searches at the location where 75 per cent of the food is found, and 25 per cent of the time it searches at the location where 25 per cent of the food is found. This means that it only receives 61.5 per cent ($.75 \times .75 + .25 \times .25$) of the total available food, as opposed to the maximum of 75 per cent.

As counter-intuitive as this result may seem, from a long-term, evolutionary perspective, the rat's behaviour makes very good sense indeed. Remember that this experiment only involved a single rat. But rats in the wild, of course, live in packs. If all rats were to forage only in the location with the greatest payoff, then fierce competition would result in a rapid depletion of resources. After these supplies run out, these rats might very well move on to the location with less food, and again compete fiercely for the rapidly diminishing resources. But consider a rat which bucks this strategy, and instead quickly matches its foraging behaviour to the probability of payoff. This rat would have less competition for resources at the location of lower payoff, guaranteeing itself a steadier intake of food. So those rats which engage in probability matching are in less competition for resources than those which forage exclusively in the locations of highest yield. Due to this reduced competition, these rats are more likely to survive, and so transmit their foraging proclivities to their offspring, who, in turn, are more likely to survive. So probability matching benefits the individual, and, as a by-product, enhances the long-term stability and survival of the population as a whole. This behaviour, then, is the long-term emergent result of variable feeding strategies among individual rats.

Experimental variations on the rat-in-a-T-maze theme have been employed, yielding similar results. For example, in a somewhat less controlled experimental setting, two experimenters, standing by a pond, set apart from each other some distance, throw food to ducks at two different rates. Very quickly, the ducks are able to calculate the distinct rates of feeding, and match their time near each experimenter accordingly, spending more time at the location of greater payoff, and switching to the location of lesser payoff for a percentage of time that matches the lower yield. I should point out that these ducks' behaviour is not merely a conditioned response to a reward schedule, since they do not necessarily receive any food before matching their behaviour to the probability of payoff. Rather, they are able to predict the payoff before it is received! So it's clear that animals are sensitive to the probability of reward, and quickly match their behaviour accordingly.

It turns out that similar statistical calculations underlie aspects of human linguistic behaviour, in that the nature and extent of variation in speech is indeed largely matched as listeners become speakers. So let's consider an example of probability matching in phonology, in particular how probabilities come to be matched during the course of language learning. Our focus is on the word-initial stops in English that we write 'b, d, g'. All along, I have been transcribing these as [b̥, d̥, g̥], the hollowed circles indicating that the stop closure is mostly voiceless, with voicing beginning just around the point when the closure is released into the next vowel. But now it won't surprise you to learn that these transcription conventions fail to capture the actual variation in these sounds' production. We find token-to-token variation, and also variation depending on the location of the stop closure itself. Typically, the farther forward in the mouth the stop closure is, the more often that tokens are genuinely voiced; the farther back in the mouth the closure, the less often that tokens are voiced.

(We'll go into the phonetic motivation for this variation in Chapter Six.) Research on young English-learning children shows that they initially produce all their word-initial stops – whether orthographic 'p, t, k' (sometimes called the 'fortis' category) or orthographic 'b, d, g' (sometimes called the 'lenis' category) – something like [p, t, k], with neither the aspiration ([p^h, t^h, k^h]) nor minimal voicing ([b̥, d̥, g̊]) that are characteristic of the adult fortis and lenis categories respectively. Such young children may still lack the articulatory prowess to match the patterns they hear. Through three years of age, the two stop categories for English begin to take shape, in that some word-initial fortis stops are aspirated, but, still, voicing during the stop closure is extremely infrequent in the lenis series, though less so for stops made at the lips. Even up to six years of age, children's lenis category involves fewer voiced tokens than adults'. Finally, only after six years of age do learners come to largely match the nuanced variability of their elders.

As with probability matching in lower animals, such behaviour betrays an extremely sophisticated statistical analytic ability on the part of language learners. Moreover, children's eventual productions betray evidence that they are able to implement their calculated probabilities in their own speech with startling, though imperfect, accuracy. While we can never know for sure, a rather straightforward account of probability matching in speech production might consist of speakers randomly choosing one out of their pool of stored tokens each time they speak a word. So token variants which they hear often are more likely to be chosen, and token variants that they hear less often are less likely to be chosen. In this way, the overall distribution of tokens will be well matched from speaker to speaker and from generation to generation. Speaking, then, is not like playing darts at all. Even expert darts players can't hope to accurately match the variation of their opponents.

Of course, every person's linguistic experience is different from every other person's. This is even true among individuals with very similar linguistic experience such as siblings. Consequently, if variation is largely a consequence of experience, each individual's variation will be different – in some cases ever-so-slightly different – from every other person's. But within a *speech community*, such differences – by definition – are never sufficiently great to adversely affect communicative success.

'It is not a hypothesis that children do probability matching [during language learning]. It is simply a description of the observed facts.' So writes William Labov in his 1994 book. The *fact* that children engage in probability matching during language learning fully supports the *hypothesis* that they engage in exemplar modelling of variation and categorization, and casts strong doubt on both the relaxed constraint approach and the prototype approach. Neither of these approaches is properly equipped to handle the fact that variation is largely matched from generation to generation. Both of these approaches view variation as created anew by each speaker, unconstrained by the extent and nature of variation to which these speakers are exposed. They therefore predict that speaker-to-speaker and generation-to-generation variation will not be probability-matched. Finally, I should point out that the facts of the exemplar-and-probability matching approach are consistent with the gradual nature of sound changes. Kruszewski's remarks, though not couched in the parlance of modern cognitive science, are perhaps all the more remarkable for exactly that reason.

> In the course of time, the sounds of a language undergo changes. The spontaneous changes of a sound depend on the gradual change of its articulation. We can pronounce a sound only when our memory retains an imprint of its articulation for us. If all our articulations of a given sound were reflected in this imprint in equal measure, and if the imprint represented an average of all these articulations, we, with this guidance, would always perform the articulation in question approximately the same way. But the most recent (in time) articulations, together with their fortuitous deviations, are retained by the memory far more forcefully than the earlier ones. Thus, negligible deviations acquire the capacity to grow progressively greater ...

In other words, a prototype model does not readily allow for the possibility of gradual sound changes, since prototypes are presumably fixed. But allowing for both variation and probability matching, and differential sensitivity to recent versus remote tokens, the gradual nature of sound change may be accounted for quite straightforwardly.

But before wholeheartedly embracing the exemplar-and-probability-matching approach, I'd like to address a possible objection to its account of variation. Isn't it possible that the cross-generation stability of variation is not rooted in the nature of categorization, but is instead purely physiological in origin? That is, since we all have comparable speech apparatus, mightn't the similar distribution of variants across the generations simply follow as a natural physical consequence? Well, yes, this is certainly a possibility, but there are a few good reasons why we should be sceptical of this explanation.

First, if variation in speech were solely a consequence of physiological forces, then we might expect the nature and extent of variation to be nearly identical across languages with similar sound systems.

For example, given two languages with similar vowel inventories, we might expect that the phonetic variation found in these languages' vowels should be extremely similar. But in fact, this doesn't seem to be the case. Both the extent and the nature of variation is different from language to language, even among those whose sound inventories are otherwise quite comparable. A similar result emerges when we investigate nasalization on vowels when followed by a nasal consonant. Every language investigated has a certain amount of variable vocalic nasalization in this context, but different languages vary in different ways. The nasalization will always be there, but to different extents in different languages. So variation itself seems to be *conventionalized* on a language-specific basis. This sort of language-specific conventionalization is readily understandable under the exemplar-and-probability-matching approach, but is difficult to reconcile with a purely physiological account of speech variation.

Second, probability matching in language is found in domains that are surely not explicable in physiological terms. Some studies have shown that the optional use of certain morphemes – for example, agreement markers in certain grammatical constructions in Caribbean Spanish – is probability-matched across speakers: the rate of these morphemes' presence versus absence is conventionalized. For example, the Spanish plural marker is used on both nouns and adjectives. We may imagine the plural marker being used 95 per cent of the time in the context where a plural meaning is intended, and so is not used 5 per cent of the time. It turns out that this usage pattern won't significantly vary from speaker to speaker, but instead will be conventionalized throughout the speech community.

These sorts of results have also been reproduced in the speech laboratory. In one such study, subjects were taught a contrived mini-language in which nouns were optionally marked with a definite article (a morpheme meaning 'the'). Subjects were divided into groups which differed in the extent to which the nouns they heard possessed this marker: one group was exposed to nouns, 75 per cent of which had the marker, and another group was exposed to nouns, 25 per cent of which had the marker. After sufficient exposure to the mini-language, subjects were asked to produce sentences in the taught language. Remarkably, subjects matched their usage to their exposure. That is, subjects in the 75 per cent group produced about 75 per cent of their nouns with the marker, and subjects in the 25 per cent group produced about 25 per cent of their nouns with the marker.

Since the exemplar-and-probability-matching approach offers a clear and satisfying account of conventionalized morphological variation – which cannot possibly be attributed to physiology – there would seem good motivation to propose a similar account of conventionalized phonetic variation as well. And after all, as William Labov wrote in 1994, in a discussion of probability matching in language learning, 'We should not be embarrassed if we find that systematic readjustments in ... language are governed by the same cognitive faculty that governs the social behavior of mallard ducks ... We are products of evolving history, not only our own but that of the animal kingdom as a whole, and our efforts to understand language will be informed by an understanding of this continuity with other populations of socially oriented animals.'

Probability matching promotes category separation and phonetic stability

Given the evidence for probability matching in language learning, it becomes quite understandable how phonological systems remain quite stable from generation to generation. Actually, I now want to argue that, in a seemingly paradoxical fashion, the excellent-though-imperfect matching of speech variation actually serves to *curtail* the very variation that is being matched! Let's consider how this can be so.

In Chapter Two I mentioned that front vowels are usually unrounded, like [i] and [e], and back vowels are usually rounded, like [u] and [o]. I wrote that this is probably because keeping the lips unrounded and keeping the tongue in a front position combine to create a very short oral cavity, while rounding the lips and backing the tongue combine to create a longer oral cavity. The difference in the lengths of the oral cavities corresponds to a difference in the acoustic qualities of front and back vowels. The second formant is significantly higher for front unrounded vowels, and is significantly lower for back rounded vowels. These differences, I suggested, are good from a functional standpoint, because they render the different vowel qualities less confusable with each other. Of course, there are languages that do have front rounded vowels, as our discussions of Finnish and Hungarian vowel harmony have shown us, for example. But the overwhelming tendency is that if a language has front rounded vowels, then the language has front unrounded vowels as well. So Hungarian has [y], but it also has [i]; [y]'s acoustic properties are somewhat intermediate between [i] and [u], since it involves lip-rounding (serving to lower F2) and tongue-fronting (serving to raise F2). The idea I'm getting at here is that the vowel qualities in any given language tend to be *dispersed* in terms of their acoustic qualities. The fewer the vowels, the more distinct from each other they tend to be. Consequently, as the vowel system gets more crowded, the acoustic distinctions between

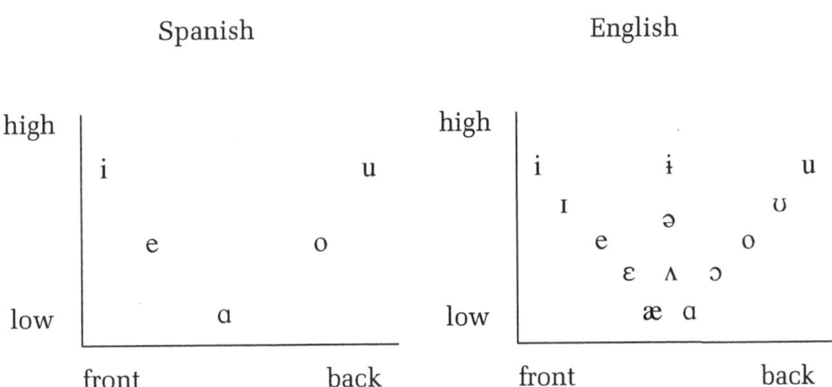

Figure 5.5 The dispersed symmetry of the Spanish and English vowel systems

the vowel qualities necessarily decreases. Compare, for example, the Spanish vowel system – quite a common one in that it contains only five members – with that of many American English dialects. These are shown in Figure 5.5.

In a five-vowel system like Spanish, the vowels are symmetrically dispersed quite widely in terms of their acoustic qualities, which for our purposes includes the first two formants (though there are many other phonetic differences as well). Since English has so many more vowel qualities than Spanish does, the vowel space is more tightly packed, but still the vowels are symmetrically dispersed, and avail themselves of a comparable overall acoustic space. In fact, we can see that the Spanish system is merely a subset of the English system in that all the Spanish vowels have acoustically similar correlates in the English system: [i, e, ɑ, o, u] are present in both languages.

The particular subset relation isn't the only conceivable one, however. We could imagine that Spanish or another language might have one of the subsets of the English system shown in Figure 5.6.

In fact, no language has anything remotely approximating these lopsided distributions. In all likelihood, it is neither by design, by

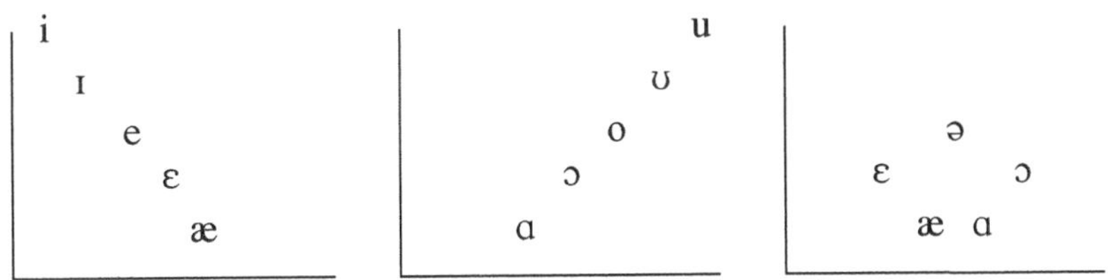

Figure 5.6 Nonexistent asymmetries in vowel systems

intention, nor by chance that vowels systems take the dispersed forms that they do. Rather, it is most likely due to a form of *evolution*, specifically, of *natural selection*. Vowels systems take the forms they do exactly because there are *selectional pressures* to keep vowel categories dispersed, so that words are rendered distinct from one another.

Before going even one step further, there are important aspects of the arguments I will be developing that require clarification. Specifically, when I say 'natural selection', what exactly do I mean, or, more to the point, what exactly do I *not* mean? First, I expressly do not mean that vowel systems, or any other structural properties of language, are genetically transmitted from generation to generation, and as such are subject to the genuinely evolutionary pressures which genetic mutations allow. I don't mean this *at all*. Second, I am *not* proposing that the dispersion we observe in vowel systems today historically derives from vowel systems that did *not* have this quality of dispersion. There is no reason to believe that the general characteristics of vowel systems have ever been significantly different from what they are today. Third, I am not proposing a theory of evolution that allows for goal-directed behaviour on the part of the individual speaker. Indeed, the theory of natural selection does not admit this possibility. Probability matching suggests that speakers are primarily engaged with copying the speech patterns that they hear around them, and not with actively modifying their speech patterns so that one sound is rendered more distinct from another.

So what *do* I mean then? If vowel systems are not genetically endowed, and if they are not a consequence of design, intention or chance, then what is the nature of this 'natural selection' that I propose is influencing their symmetrical shape? Well, we now know that there is inherent variation in speech, such that no token is ever identical to any other token. Inevitably, tokens deviate from each other in terms of their articulatory, acoustic and auditory properties. Nonetheless, tokens of particular vowels do cluster together – and *away* from other vowels – so that the speech signal is transmitted quite effectively to listeners, and so variation in production is well-matched from generation to generation. I said 'well-matched', but not 'perfectly matched'; *any* system of reproduction – genetic or otherwise – is subject to imperfect copy.

Where is the locus of this imperfection? In fact, both language perception and language production are demonstrably imperfect. Most tokens, of course, are perceived accurately, in the sense that the meaning intended by speakers is recovered by listeners, because the tokens sound remarkably similar to previous tokens of the same word. These correctly perceived tokens are also usually produced as accurate copies. However, once in a while, the production of one vowel might

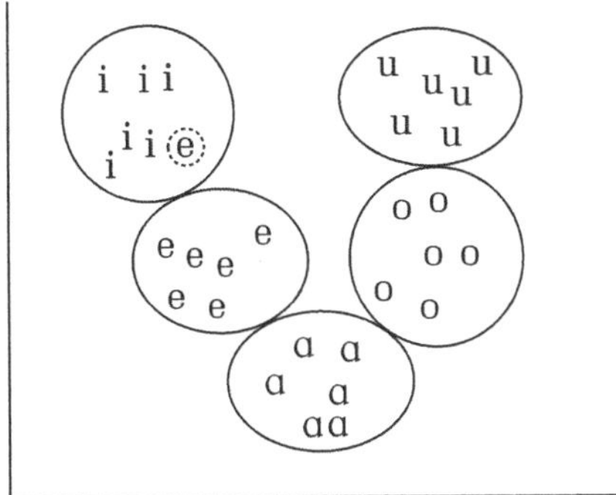

Figure 5.7 Vowel production

stray a little too close to the phonetic quality of some other vowel. For example, every once in a while, a Spanish word which usually has [e] might be made with a somewhat higher tongue position, and end up sounding like [i]. Such stray tokens are inevitable: systems of reproduction are *never* perfect.

With this in mind, let's reconsider the vowel inventory of Spanish, this time employing the 'cloud of tokens' notation I introduced at the beginning of this chapter, but allowing for the presence of these stray tokens, as in Figure 5.7.

Tokens situated well within a given cloud keep a safe distance from all the other vowel qualities, and so are sufficiently distinct from vowels in the other clouds that misinterpretation is not a problem. In all likelihood, these will be unambiguously communicated to listeners, and quite accurately reproduced. The pooling together of these variable tokens into a single category is indicated, as always, by the circles. (Of course, learners do not come pre-equipped with these categories, these circles. Rather, they emerge from experience with pairing sound and meaning.) However, once in a while there will be tokens that should be grouped with one vowel quality, but stray into the region of another vowel quality. Look at the stray token of [e] in the dashed circle. Although the word with which this token is associated almost always has a mid front vowel, this particular token was made with a slightly higher tongue position, so that it is largely indistinguishable from words that usually have [i]. As we know, listeners are usually able to overcome any ambiguities in the speech signal, because the context – real-world or grammatical – will serve to clarify meaning. So, if listeners encounter such a stray token, the chances are fairly good that they nonetheless supply the word with the meaning intended by the speaker. (More on these correctly interpreted strays in the next section.) But learners, who are still getting the hang of pairing sound with meaning, are still developing their knowledge of the real world and their knowledge of grammar. Consequently, they are less able to recover the intended meaning of these stray tokens. It's been shown that adults are also found to misinterpret these stray tokens, more often than you might imagine, in fact. By my reckoning, there are at least three different ways that learners might misinterpret this confusing token: (1) if the stray vowel quality results in another word of the language (for example, if *mella* [meɟɑ] 'notch' is produced as *milla* [miɟɑ] 'mile'), they could conceivably pair the token with the wrong meaning; (2) they might assign the token to more than one meaning; (3) if the stray token results in a meaningless word, the token might remain uninterpreted. Each of these sorts of misinterpretation has the potential to induce confusion on the part of the listener, since the meaning intended by the speaker is not recovered by the listener. So, almost all tokens will be unambiguous, but *some* tokens will be confusing to listeners, and will remain uninterpreted or assigned to the wrong meaning.

How do stray tokens affect the probabilities which learners come to match in their own speech? Consider the pool over which learners determine the phonetic distribution of tokens. Within-pool variants are clustered together, but stray tokens – those that fall within the phonetic space of some other value, and also ambiguous tokens that are at the outer reaches of the cluster – might be ignored, since they may not have been categorized properly. Consequently, these confusing tokens will not be pooled with the vowel quality which is normally employed for that particular word. Since these will not be pooled with other tokens of these vowels, this results in categories consisting of distinct pools of tokens with fairly sizeable phonetic buffer regions separating them. And since listeners can only match probabilities to their *perceptions* of speakers' productions, and not to speakers' productions directly, they might conclude that the variation in the speech signal is *not as extensive* as it actually is. That is, they *overestimate* the percentage of speakers' non-stray tokens, and match this estimate in their own speech.

So now let's consider how a learner might perceive the array of tokens that were produced by our Spanish speaker. Look at Figure 5.8.

The token of the [e] word which had strayed into [i]'s territory has not been perceived as such by the listener. So, as these listeners become speakers, their productions – which largely match the distribution of variation that they perceive – also consist of pools of tokens with fairly sizeable buffer regions separating them (with, of course, new strays now and again). So, the uninterpretability of stray tokens actually serves to reinforce the distinctions between the categories

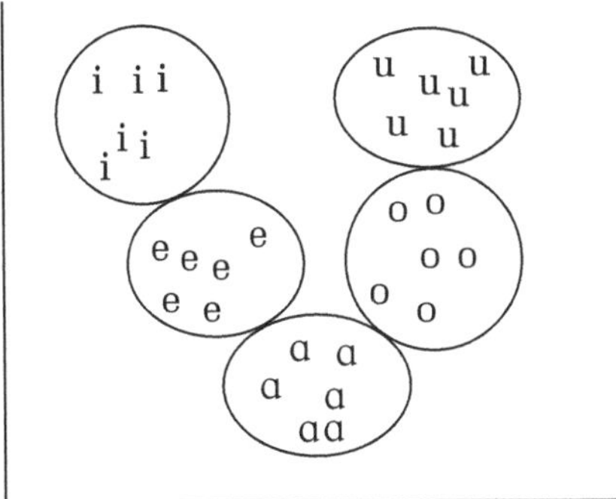

Figure 5.8 Vowel perception

themselves, driving one category farther away from others, and thus rendering the linguistic system more effective in fulfilling its communicative function. These uninterpreted tokens also serve to promote the long-term stability of the phonetic qualities of the vowel system, since usually only tokens that are similar to the norm will be perceived, and, in turn, produced. So, under the exemplar-and-probability-matching account, production errors *create* variation in speech, but consequent perception errors *curtail* variation in speech.

Now, before going on, it's important to keep something in mind. The confusions induced by stray tokens are *not* comparable to the ambiguities of standard neutralizations. Neutralized forms are part of a regular linguistic pattern, and so listeners encounter them all the time, and rather easily come to master their distribution. By contrast, stray tokens are not regular or patterned in their occurrence; they are genuinely aberrant, and so listeners are not equipped to deal with them in a comparable way.

Let's revisit the figure I provided at the beginning of this chapter. We can see now that the array of tokens in that display was not a realistic one, in that the tokens were dispersed very uniformly across the acoustic space. But we now know that, due to the uninterpretability of strays, tokens in the border regions may very well be eliminated, and probability matching will maintain the separation of categories. The revised display in Figure 5.9 reflects this more realistic distribution of tokens.

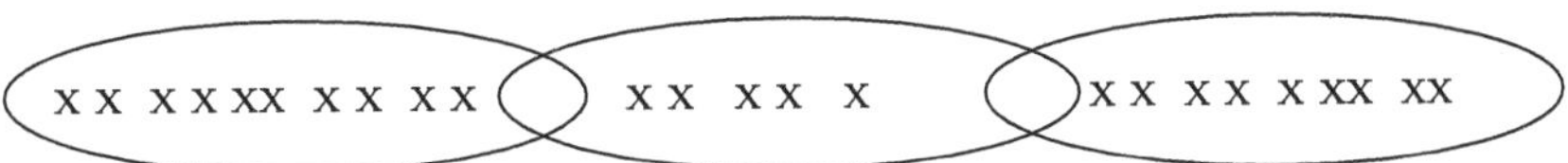

Figure 5.9 Separation of categories along a single phonetic dimension

Of course, we will inevitably find a few strays located in the border regions, but, still, the distribution of tokens across the acoustic space is probably far less regular than our first figure indicated, with most tokens falling into well-separated pools.

To summarize, in general speakers do a remarkable job of matching the variation that is present in the speech signal, and listeners do a remarkable job of perceiving this variation. However, the system isn't perfect: there are both stray tokens and consequent perception errors that influence the categorization procedure. The passive filtering out of these strays enhances the phonetic distinction between tokens belonging to different sound categories. The result is that vowel systems tend to avail themselves quite well of the phonetic space, dispersing their members into well-defined, well-separated regions. So the dispersion of vowel qualities in the phonetic space, and the buffer regions between them, may be seen as the natural, passive consequence of the miscommunication of stray tokens. The idea, then, is that our excellent-though-imperfect ability to engage in probability matching both *causes* and *inhibits* variation in speech. And the phonetic separation and stabilization of categories is as much a *consequence* of effective communication as it is a *cause* of effective communication.

We can now see how imperfect copy may lead to the symmetrical distributions that we observe time and time again in vowel systems. Contrary to the assertion of some linguists, I don't think this derived symmetry should be viewed as some sort of cognitive pressure in the minds of individual language users that favours the symmetrical distribution of elements. I don't think the symmetry of the system is seen as relevant at any psychological level by language users; it's only appreciated by linguists. Indeed, these processes are extremely slow-acting and so cannot be attributed to individual speakers – speakers are excellent in mimicking what they hear, and so changes are very gradual. Rather, the symmetry evolves passively, as a function of language use within a community of speakers.

This sort of system may be viewed as both self-organizing and self-sustaining. It is self-organizing because its structural properties are a consequence of its use, requiring no outside monitor, guide or force to affect its organization. It is self-sustaining because, by its very use, it repairs and maintains itself. So once again, language form is inseparably intertwined with language use and language function.

Probability matching promotes category separation and phonetic *change*

We've just seen how imperfect copy might contribute to the phonetic separation and phonetic stability of sound categories. However, sounds *do* change, and these changes are embodied in the slightly different distribution of tokens which are observable as the generations proceed. We'll now consider a rather different effect: imperfect copy might lead not to stabilization, but to an *increased* separation of sound categories. This mechanism, in fact, is already built into the system as we have characterized it. Since tokens of one category which are more distinct from tokens of other categories are more likely to be perceived correctly, then sound categories may drift farther apart over the generations, but only provided that this drift does not come to encroach on the phonetic character of yet *another* category.

Given the enormously complex interaction of forces that come into play in phonological systems, asymmetric subsystems are bound to develop, at least temporarily. So let's imagine a situation in which contrastive categories, for one reason or another, are not fully dispersed in the perceptual space. Under these circumstances, one category may increase its phonetic distance from another, and no third category is present to provide a limiting counterforce. For example, we might imagine a hypothetical language like Spanish, except that it lacks a high front vowel (an admittedly unlikely system).

A wildly stray [i]-like token of a word that usually possesses [e] may well induce confusion on the part of listeners, since it is so different from the vowel qualities that they are used to (Figure 5.10).

Such tokens will probably be thrown away – filtered out – regarded as mere speech errors. If noticed, they might be laughed at by both speaker and listener (Figure 5.11).

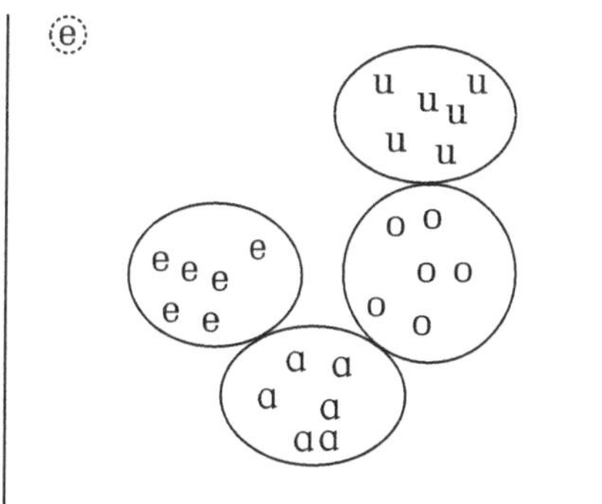

Figure 5.10 Vowel production

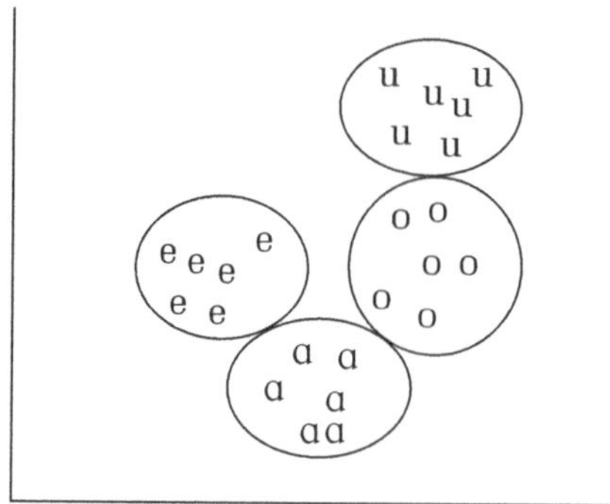

Figure 5.11 Vowel perception

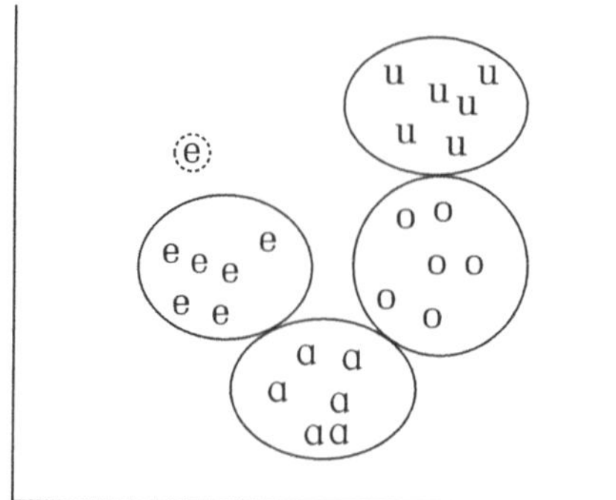

Figure 5.12 Vowel production

However, a token of an [e]-word that is only marginally [i]-like might not induce confusion at all, but on the contrary might be better at communicating the intended message to listeners, since this token is actually further dispersed from the other vowels of the system ([ɑ, o, u]), though not outlandishly distinct from other [e]s (Figure 5.12).

In this language, since the tokens that marginally drift farther and farther away from other categories are *not* encroaching on a third category, then it's these tokens that are most effective in conveying the meaning intended by speakers (Figure 5.13).

Over time, the whole pool of tokens may gradually drift farther and farther away from the other categories, and a more symmetrical four-vowel system might emerge; other values may now spread out to exploit the entirety of the available acoustic space. The result is that the system will evolve towards a symmetrical dispersion of its categories (Figure 5.14).

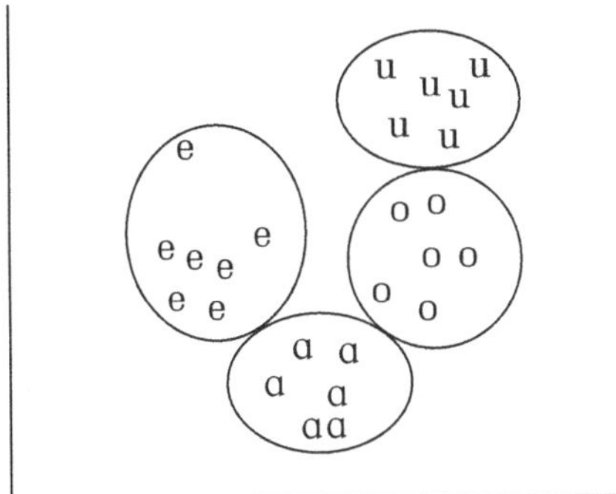

Figure 5.13 Vowel perception

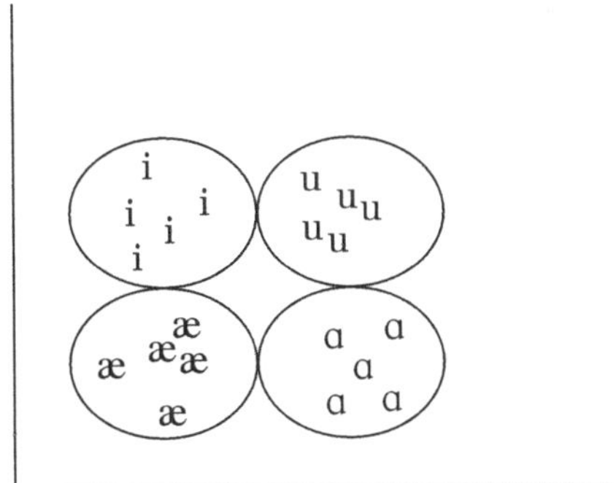

Figure 5.14 Newly evolved system

So let's move away from the hypothetical realm, and consider a real-world example of this sort of dispersion effect.

Trique

Trique (pronounced ['t̥ɹike͜ɪ], though the Spanish spelling Triqui is often seen, pronounced ['tɾiki]), is a language spoken in the southern regions of Mexico. It is a member of the Otomanguean language family. In Trique, whenever a round vowel precedes a tongue-body consonant ([k, g]), it is immediately followed by [w]. So look at the examples; I've underlined the relevant sounds ([ʒ] as in 'azure').

[nukwɑh]	strong	[dukwɑ]	possessed house
[dugwɑh]	to twist	[zugwi]	(name)
[ʒugwɑ]	to be twisted	[dugwe]	to weep
[dugwɑne]	to bathe (someone)	[rugwi]	peach
[rugwɑh]	hearth stones	[dugwi]	together with, companion

You'll notice that when we have [u] followed by either [k] or [g], there is [w] immediately following: the language does not have sequences such as [uka] or [uga]. You can readily see how the [w] is merely a continuation of the [u], such that the lip-rounding gesture is realized both immediately before and immediately after the consonant. The pattern, then, can be conceived of as a minor form of vowel harmony.

It wasn't always this way, however. Employing the comparative method, when we investigate other languages that are closely related to Trique we do *not* observe the 'unhingeing' of round vowels. Related languages usually have [uka] and [uga] in words for which Trique has [ukwa] and [ugwa]. And since less common patterns among closely related languages often reflect more recent changes, Trique was probably innovative in this sense. Evidence from the internal reconstruction method also suggests that the Trique pattern is an innovative one, as these [w]s are completely predictable in their presence such that we can 'undo' their present distribution and recover an earlier stage of the sound pattern. Consequently, both the comparative and the internal reconstruction methods converge on the same conclusion about the history of Trique. At an earlier stage of the language, the round vowel was *not* realized on both sides of the tongue-body consonants. Instead, there was *uka and *uga, the patterns that are completely absent today. (Reconstructed forms are traditionally indicated by an asterisk preceding them.) But at some point in the language's history, round vowels began to 'unhinge' from their position and continue across [k] and [g] – the tongue-body consonants – eventually turning these into [kw] and [gw], respectively.

But now look at the next set of words. Here – when the consonant which follows the round vowel is made with the tongue tip – the [w] is not present. In fact, it's *never* present here. So, we never find [utwa] or [udwa], for example.

[rune]	large black beans	[utah]	to anoint
[utʃe]	to get wet	[utʃi]	to nurse
[uta]	to gather	[duna]	to leave something
[gunah]	to run	[rudaʔa]	stone rolling pin
[ʒutʃe]	hens, domestic fowl	[guni]	to hear

The question that a phonologist must now ask is, why did the Trique pattern arise? Why did [u] harmonize across [k, g], but not across [t, d]? The answer I'd like to pursue is that this minor form of vowel harmony *enhances* the acoustic distinction between the tongue-body and tongue-tip consonants. Perhaps you recall that tongue-tip consonants like [d] bring F2 toward about 1800Hz as the closure is being released. By contrast, when releasing a tongue-body consonant like [g] into a vowel, F2 begins at about 1600Hz. (We'll just be discussing [d] and [g] from here on, but all arguments apply to [t] and [k] as well.) This means that the difference in F2 between, say, [da] and [ga] is about 200Hz at consonantal release. (There are several other acoustic differences between these two sounds, and so they are not terribly likely to be confused with one another.) Now, if the tongue-body consonant is altered such that a [w] is superimposed onto its release, the oral cavity becomes longer, and so F2 lowers. In fact, F2 lowers rather significantly, to about 900Hz. This means that the difference in F2 between [da] and [gwa] is about 900Hz (1800Hz minus 900Hz). Clearly, the superimposition of the [w] increases the acoustic distance between the release quality of tongue-tip and tongue-body consonants. Importantly, since [gw] and [kw] sequences were elsewhere absent in the earlier stage of the language, harmonizing lip-rounding across [g] increased the acoustic distinction between these consonants and the tongue-tip consonants without encroaching on another sound category. So [uga] could become [ugwa], and there were no other words in the language like [ugwa], and so there was no functional counter-pressure acting to inhibit the sound change.

Harmonizing across the tongue-tip consonants, by contrast, would serve to diminish the tongue body–tongue tip acoustic distinction. Why is this so? Superimposing a [w] onto the release of a tongue-tip consonant would change the F2 onset from about 1800Hz to about 1500Hz, decreasing the difference in F2s to a mere 100Hz (1600Hz minus 1500Hz). So, an accompanying change from [uda] to [udwa] would have undone the functional benefits of the [uga] to [ugwa] change, as portrayed in Figure 5.15.

Of course, this [w] didn't just pop out of the ether in order to help increase the acoustic distinction between [uda] and [uga]. For example, we wouldn't expect an [s] or an [m] to arise in order to enhance the perceptual distinctness in the [uga] context. Instead, these sorts of

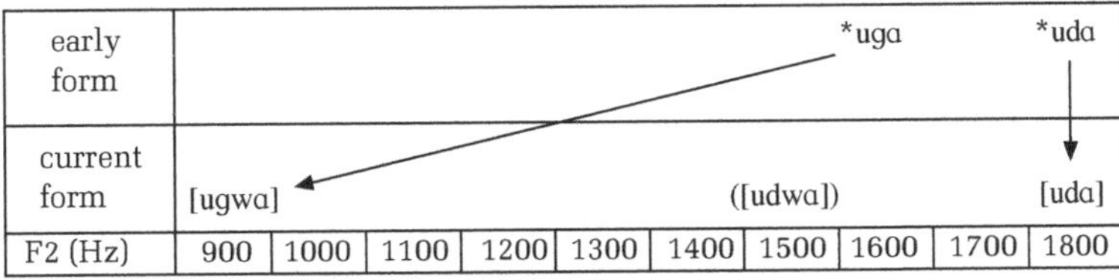

Figure 5.15 In Trique, the diachronic harmonizing of lip-rounding onto the release of the tongue body consonants ([ugwa]) increased their F2 distinctions from the tongue tip consonants ([uda]), and didn't encroach on the perceptual space of another category. Harmonizing lip-rounding onto the release of the tongue tip consonants ([udwa]) woud have had counter-functional consequences.

changes exploit the sounds that are already loitering in the neighbourhood, so to speak, their properties harnessed, co-opted, or, in the parlance of Stephen Jay Gould and modern evolutionary biologists, *exapted* to fulfil new functional roles: [ga] and [da] are not especially confusable with each other, but since [u] was right next door, and since its harmonizing across [g] served only to increase the acoustic separation of the elements without jeopardizing another contrast, there was nothing to inhibit the beneficial change. So [u] served a contrastive role on its own, and was passively recruited to assist in distinguishing another, neighbouring sound. Over time, the number of [ugwa] variants was likely to increase, since these forms increased the acoustic distance from [uda], and so were more likely communicated correctly to listeners. Meanwhile, [uda] remained largely stable over time: [udwa]-like variants were confusable with both [uga] and the increasing number of [ugwa] tokens, and so were not likely to take hold. The proposal, then, is that due to the acoustic and consequent functional advantages of harmonizing lip-rounding across the tongue-body consonants, and the disadvantages of harmonizing across tongue-tip consonants, the Trique system evolved towards its present state.

Consider how the exemplar-and-probability-matching approach may account for sound changes like this. There is inherent gradience and variation in speech production, and so [uga...ug̹a...ugwa] and [uda...ud̹a...udwa] are among the possible variants that any speaker might produce. (The subscripted hook indicates partial rounding.) In the earlier stages of the language, productions and subsequent probabilities leaned heavily toward [uga] and [uda], just as they still do in the languages related to Trique. However, stray [ugwa]-like variants rendered these words more distinct from their [uda] counterparts. This is especially true since words with [ugwa] were *not* previously present in the language. Consequently, there was no counterforce inhibiting a change toward [ugwa]. Therefore, those variants with [w] were more likely communicated unambiguously to listeners. Ambiguous tokens were sometimes confusing to listeners. Specifically, [udwa]-like variants of words that usually had [uda] may be confused with [ugwa], and so weren't added to the pool of tokens over which probabilities were calculated. They were 'repelled' due to the presence of [ugwa] forms. Consequently, as the generations proceeded, listeners were more likely to perceive [ugwa] and [uda] as unambiguously belonging to different categories, and so they were more likely to produce [ugwa] and [uda] in their own speech, as a consequence of probability matching.

So, the variation engaged in by elders was largely matched by learners, but nonetheless, due to the greater likelihood of unambiguous

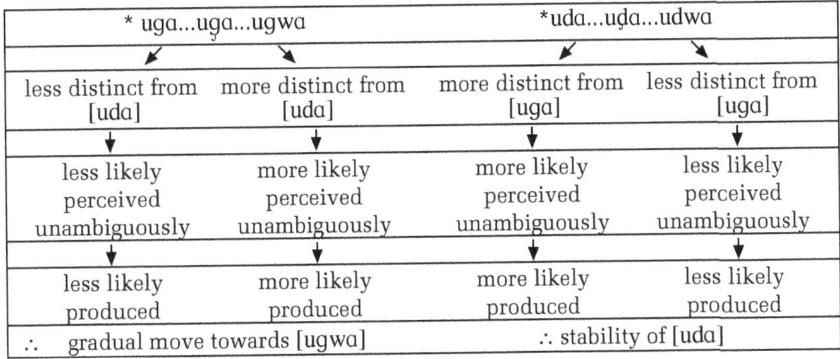

* uga...uga...ugwa
*uda...uda...udwa
less distinct from [uda]
more distinct from [uda]
more distinct from [uga]
less distinct from [uga]
less likely perceived unambiguously
more likely perceived unambiguously
more likely perceived unambiguously
less likely perceived unambiguously
less likely produced
more likely produced
more likely produced
less likely produced
∴ gradual move towards [ugwa]
∴ stability of [uda]

Figure 5.16 The fates of *uga and *uda

perception of certain variants over others – [ugwa] over [uga]; [uda] over [udwa]) – learners' calculated probabilities may have differed slightly from their elders', in that the variants which were more dispersed from the opposing value were more often perceived correctly, and so, in turn, more often produced. In essence, the presence of ambiguous tokens may result in listeners *overestimating* the prevalence of more distinct tokens. This overestimation, in turn, may result in more distinct tokens being produced, and, eventually, the better separation of phonological categories.

These proposals are summarized in Figure 5.16, which demonstrates how very minor phonetic tendencies, coupled with the confusion they might induce or eschew, may eventually have far-reaching consequences for the sound system.

Let's consider this in a bit more detail. Look at Figure 5.17. Entering the sound change midstream, we might take a 1000 token sample from one generation of speakers. Let's call them Generation W. Of these tokens, 750 are [uga], while 250 are [ugwa]. Most of these tokens are produced as a consequence of learners' matching their probability of occurrence to the productions of Generation V. In turn, Generation X perceives *all* [ugwa] tokens unambiguously. Among [uga] tokens, however, let's suppose that a full 5 per cent of these 750 tokens (38 in all) are confusing to listeners, since their acoustic separation from [uda] is not as sharp. These 38 misperceived tokens will not be pooled with those over which Generation X-ers calculate their probabilities. Now we iterate the process: if we take a random sample of 1000 of Generation X's *productions*, we should observe that they largely match the probabilities that they *perceive* their elders to have produced. Generation X perceived 712 out of 962 tokens as [uga] (38 tokens were misperceived); this constitutes a rate of 74 per cent.

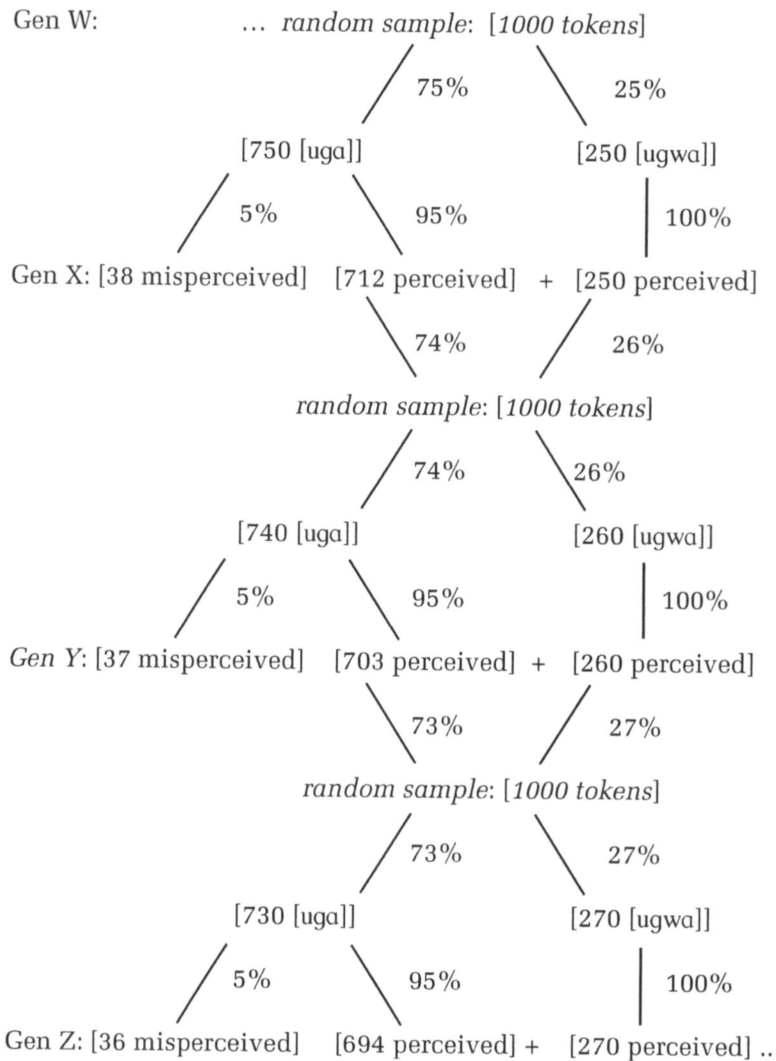

Figure 5.17 Schematic diachrony of [uga]-to-[ugwa]

So, out of 1000 tokens produced by Generation X, 740 will be [uga], and 260 will be [ugwa]. And again assuming that 5 per cent of the [uga] tokens will be misperceived by Generation *Y*, *these* children will perceive only 73 per cent tokens as [uga] (703 of 963 tokens), and so on down the generations. We may now see, given the small tendency to better perceive [ugwa] tokens, how, over the course of time, the conventions of the language may change.

A model like this does not perfectly or exhaustively predict specific language patterns. As already noted, we can no better predict the future direction of a sound than we can the future direction of a species. Indeed, one of the best advantages of this account is that it effectively captures the *probabilistic* nature of sound change. Trique's relations did not undergo the sound change that Trique did. There simply exists some level of likelihood that any given sound change will take hold in any given language. Probabilities may be affected by, among many other factors, the language-specific system of contrasts: in Trique the introduction of labio-velars was contrast-enhancing, since harmonizing did not induce homophony. In some other language, a prevalence of contrastive labialized velars might very well passively induce the curtailment of such a sound change.

These sorts of proposals for the origin and development of sound changes may actually be reproduced in a laboratory setting. A laboratory condition may serve to recapitulate elements of the hypothesized historical scenario in 'speeded-up' form if we find a way of inducing a high rate of perception errors on the part of listeners. How might we do this? I had subjects listen to [uda], [udwa], [uga] and [ugwa] in various levels of 'white noise' (computer-generated noise across a broad frequency range which decreases the signal-to-noise ratio, making the signal harder to decipher). Noise introduced into the speech signal might induce a 'speeded-up' rate of misperception in certain contexts, and thus reflect one origin of real-world sound change. I found, indeed, that listeners were far more likely to hear [uda] as [uga] than they were [uda] as [ugwa]. Among the four forms presented, these latter two forms ([uda] and [ugwa]) were the least often confused with each other.

Now, this sort of result doesn't immediately translate into a real-world context that unfolds over generations of speakers, but nonetheless, it is noteworthy – and consistent with my proposed explanation – that in my experiment, the least confusable forms ([uda] and [ugwa]) are exactly those which actually seem to have evolved in Trique from more confusable forms ([uda] and [uga]). So, given that language learners largely (though imperfectly) match the variation they perceive, the sorts of perceptual errors induced in my experiment might only reflect the culmination of a slow, generation-to-generation accretion of such errors, rather than offering any major insights into the online processing of natural speech. Nonetheless, the results are consistent with the hypothesis that the gradience and variation inherent in speech production may be the fodder for these sorts of sound changes: the more distinct the variant from an acoustically similar word, the more likely that it will be interpreted correctly, and so the more likely the system will wend towards this value.

The past is not only reflected in extant phonological alternations; the same sorts of forces that gave rise to the present state of the system may, at least in theory, be brought to the fore under the proper laboratory conditions, not necessarily by modifying the natural speech *signal*, but instead by modifying the *noise* that accompanies this signal. As remarked by Baudouin de Courtenay in 1910, 'I must emphasize the importance of errors in hearing (*lapsis auris*) when one word is mistaken for another, as a factor of change at any given moment of linguistic intercourse and in the history of language as a social phenomenon. Experimental methods can help to define the types and directions of these errors.'

Before concluding our discussion of Trique, there is an important point to consider. In both my discussion of the actual Trique system and in the experiment I performed, I have been operating under the assumption that [uga] and [uda] constituted the critical distinction between the words that drove the sound change. However, it's simply not the case that a huge inventory of Trique words were originally differentiated *solely* in terms of whether they had [uda] or [uga]. Usually, words with these sequences had additional elements that rendered them distinct, such as the presence of word-initial consonants (for example [utah] 'to gather' versus [nukwah] 'strong', which have the voiceless stop counterparts of [d] and [g]), and/or different tones (I haven't been indicating tones, but Trique is a tonal language). Moreover, if some words were indeed solely differentiated by [uda] versus [uga], couldn't Trique have evolved the [ugwa] pattern only in those specific cases in which homophony might otherwise be the result?

Indeed, it may be that [ugwa] in Trique first arose in those very [uga] words that were minimally distinct from [uda] words, that is, in those words that were identical except for their [g] versus [d]. But these few pioneering [uga] words that evolved toward [ugwa] may have opened the floodgates of change: as *some* words were now implemented with [ugwa], more and more words may have quickly fallen in line with the emerging pattern. Why might this have happened? Due to the pioneering [ugwa] words, the language now possessed three relevant patterns: [uda], [uga] and [ugwa]. Of these three patterns, [uda] and [uga] are phonetically much more similar to each other than either is to [ugwa]. At this point, when an [uga] word was now heard, it was more likely to be confused with [uda] than with the newly-developed [ugwa] words; since [ugwa] has now entered the language, new stray [ugwa] variants were more likely to be recognized, and so were communicated more effectively to listeners. We might even say that the presence of new [ugwa] words *attracted* [uga] words toward them,

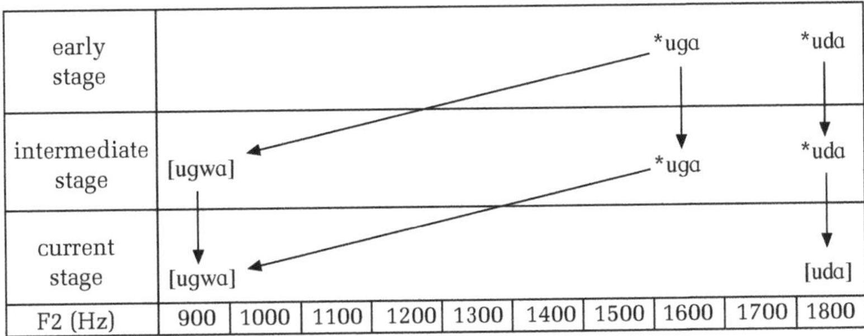

Figure 5.18 The proposed Trique change: the first words to become *ugwa may have been *uga words that minimally contrasted with *uda words. With these *ugwa forms now in place, the pattern was more likely to generalize, changing all *uga words to [ugwa]. Meanwhile, *uda remained stable.

though I want to emphasize again that any such attraction was not due to the intentions – conscious or otherwise – on the part of speakers.

In sum, functional pressures may have induced the change to [ugwa] in some words. But now that [ugwa] was present in the system, it was far more likely that additional [uga] words would fall in line with the new pattern, since [uga] is far more confusable with [uda] than it is with [ugwa] (Figure 5.18).

We actually observe this sort of scenario time and time again in phonology. The linguist Joan Bybee has demonstrated that sound changes often begin in a word here, a word there, but eventually come to permeate the language. Inspired by the proposals of nineteenth-century scholar Hugo Schuchardt, Bybee observes that it is the most frequently used words that might change first (more on this in Chapter Seven), but what I'm suggesting here is that passive pressures for ambiguity avoidance may also trigger individual words to undergo pioneering changes.

To summarize, the conventions established by speech communities betray a nuanced mastery of the phonetic variation internalized by individual speakers that is demonstrably a part of these speakers' linguistic knowledge. The exquisite articulatory control that speakers display in their productions is best evidenced by the fact that they are able to largely match the variation present in the ambient pattern. On this view, learners' articulatory talents may be harnessed largely in service to copying or imitating, not modifying (improving upon or otherwise) the ambient speech pattern: the target of phonological acquisition may be the gradience and variation itself. But still, speakers' mimetic talents are not perfect. Stray tokens are inevitable, and it is the functional benefit of certain of these strays which might ultimately take hold in a system and come to permeate the language.

Comaltepec Chinantec

Like a classical Darwinian approach to evolution, I've just suggested that the origin of lip-rounding harmony in Trique is rooted in two related phenomena. First, random, minor inexactitudes of speech production slowly amass over generations of speakers, such that one generation's inexactitudes serve as the next generation's template for copy. The result is that variation is largely – though imperfectly – matched over generations of speakers. Second, beneficial variants are more likely to be perceived correctly by listeners, and so it's these variants that are more likely to survive and propagate as listeners become speakers. These beneficial phonetic variants may come to be generalized throughout the language.

In Trique, change was initiated by purely random, directionless, phonetically *isotropic* chance, since variation potentially proceeds in a radially symmetrical fashion. Variation may have proceeded in any direction, but *some* tokens just happen to have better functional success over others, and so the sound change moved in that direction. Maintaining rounded lips through a tongue-body consonant is no more phonetically natural than *not* maintaining this lip rounding. Rather, it is due to the functional advantages of lip-rounding harmony that the Trique sound system began its new trajectory.

In this section, I'd like to consider a slight variation on the theme exemplified by Trique. Some sound changes, although also subject to the sorts of functional pressures discussed for the Trique pattern, are actually 'helped along' by certain natural phonetic tendencies. What I mean is, certain variants may be more likely than others due to purely phonetic pressures. And if these variants are *functionally* beneficial as well, then a sound change is more likely to be channelled in that direction. The variation which leads to sound change in this scenario is not phonetically *isotropic*, but is instead phonetically *anisotropic*.

Chinantec, like Trique, is a member of the Otomanguean language group. The dialect we are interested in is spoken in the beautiful mountainside village of Santiago Comaltepec ([koˌmɑlteˈpɛk], a four-hour bus ride north of the city of Oaxaca, Mexico. The Comaltepec dialect of Chinantec, like all Otomanguean languages, is tonal. Comaltepec Chinantec words may have a low tone (L), mid tone (M), high tone (H), low-to-mid tone (LM), or low-to-high tone (LH), along with a few allophonic alternants which we'll discuss shortly. I'll now try once again to get you to love – and not fear – tones. It might help to use the music scale as a guide. Let's translate these five tones into a do-re-mi notation: L = do, M = re, H = mi, LM = do-re, and LH

= do-mi. For the contour tones, don't just sing one note followed by the next. Instead, glide your pitch from the first note to the second. It might help if we use more iconic symbols to represent the tone values. Simply hum along to the non-vertical line of the following symbols: ˩ = L, ˧ = M, ˥ = H, ˩˧ = LM, ˩˥ = LH. These represent relative pitch values, whereas the vertical line itself represents the entirety of the pitch range, from L at the bottom, to H at the top. Now, to complete the picture, let's attach these five tonal melodies to some consonants and vowels, say, 'la': la˩, la˧, la˥, la˩˧, la˩˥.

In Comaltepec Chinantec, there is a rather complicated tone substitution pattern, aspects of which we'll be considering now. First, when a LH word precedes a word that otherwise has a L-tone, then HL (˥˩) is found instead of L.

[toː˩]	banana	[kwɑ˩˥ toː˥˩]	give a banana
[ŋɨh˩]	chayote	[kwɑ˩˥ ŋɨh˥˩]	give a chayote

Second, when a LH word precedes a word that otherwise has M, then HM (˥˧) is found instead of M.

[kuː˧]	money	[kwɑ˩˥ kuː˥˧]	give money
[dʒuː˧]	jug	[kwɑ˩˥ dʒuː˥˧]	give a jug

Finally, when a LH word follows another LH word, this latter LH changes to MH (˧˥).

[ʔŋɑ˩˥]	forest	[heːh˩˥ ʔŋɑ˧˥]	in the forest
[bʌʔ˩˥]	ball	[kwɑ˩˥ bʌʔ˧˥]	give the ball

Now, there are two interesting generalizations we can make about these sound substitutions, one generalization about their phonetic character and one about their functional character. Phonetically, we can characterize the sound substitution in much the same way we did the lip-rounding harmony process of Trique. Specifically, the H component of the HL and HM contour tones may be viewed as being a mere extension of the preceding H tone, moving across the intervening consonant, and continuing into the first part of the next vowel. So the substitution of HL for L and HM for M is a consequence of the preceding H tone being implemented both before and after the intervening consonant. The MH tone may be viewed in similar terms, the preceding H tone serving to at least partially raise the first portion of the following LH tone.

The second interesting generalization is a functional one. Recall that I've listed five tone values for Comaltepec Chinantec – L, M, H, LM, LH. These five tones may occur on words that do *not* follow words with LH tones. However, we've just discussed three more tones that

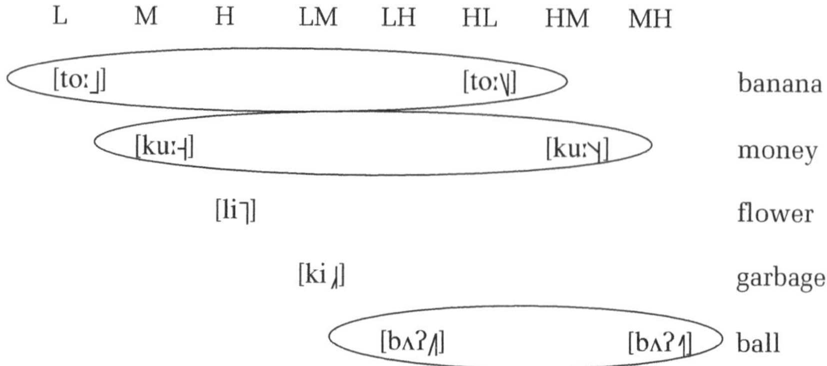

Figure 5.19 The allophonic nature of Comaltepec Chinantec tone substitution

may *only* occur on words that follow LH tones: HL, HM and MH (H and LM may occur here as well, but L, M and LH do not). In other words, L allophonically alternates with HL, M allophonically alternates with HM, and LH allophonically alternates with MH; this is a non-neutralizing sound substitution. Set notation is provided in Figure 5.19.

Given these two generalizations, we're now in a position to understand the origins – the *explanation* – of this aspect of the Comaltepec Chinantec sound system. The first point to consider is a phonetic one. It's been shown experimentally that pitch rises take longer to implement than do pitch falls. This is schematically portrayed in Figure 5.20.

Given the sluggishness of pitch rises in comparison to pitch falls, a consonant may already be made *before* a pitch rise is fully achieved: upon the release of this subsequent consonant, finally, maximum pitch height is achieved on the next vowel. The idea then, is that rising tones are more likely than falling tones to spill their high component

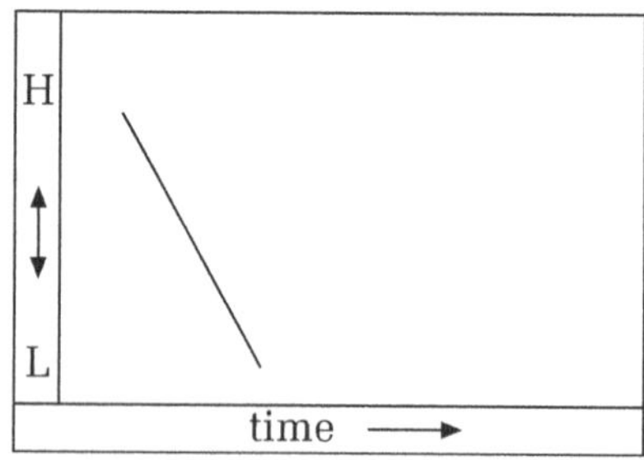

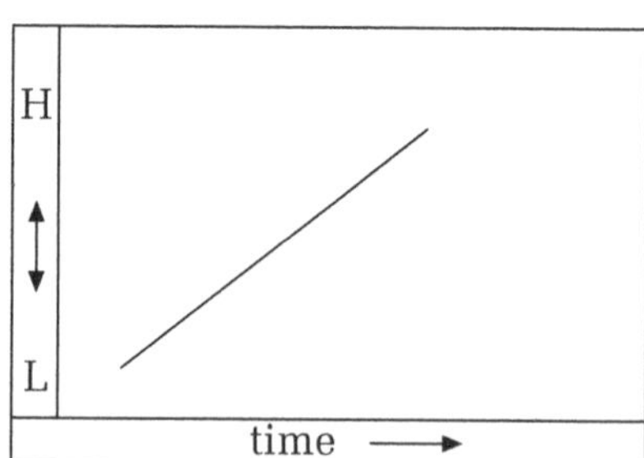

Figure 5.20 Pitch rises take longer to implement than pitch falls

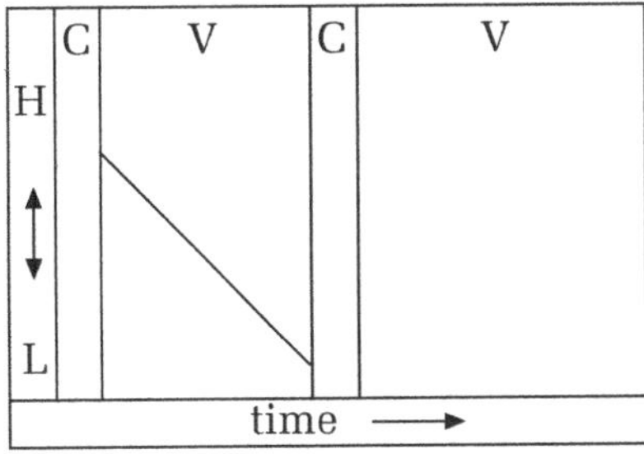

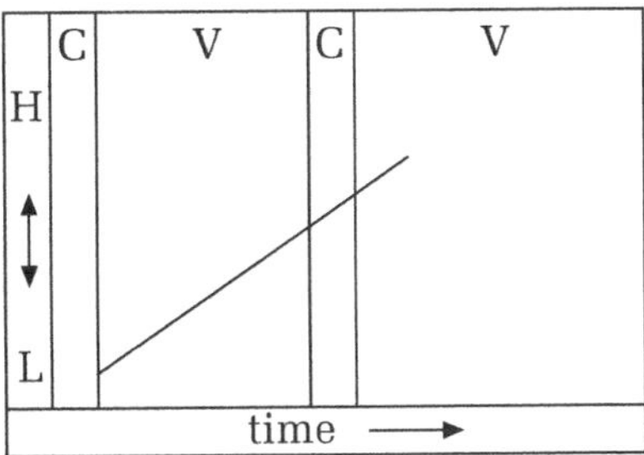

Figure 5.21 High tone 'spill-over' from rising tones

on to a following vowel. Since falling tones can be produced faster than rising tones, they might be less likely to spill over onto the next vowel. In Figure 5.21 I've superimposed consonants ('C') and vowels ('V') on the pitch patterns. The potential for H 'spill-over' should be clear.

Comaltepec Chinantec has conventionalized this phonetic tendency in a way that fairly hugs the physical limitations of the speech apparatus. The H component of LH contour tones is implemented both at the end of the first vowel and into the beginning of the second vowel.

But just because speakers' physiological limits might be encountered in an experimental context doesn't mean that these limits will play a role in natural linguistic contexts. Indeed, only if it can be shown that speech patterns *exactly match* experimentally-determined physical limitations can we establish a direct link between phonetic limitations and phonological patterning. In fact, as far as I know, an *exact* match between physiological constraints and linguistic conventions has *never* been established in linguistic research. For example, it's been found that women can raise their pitch more quickly than can men, but no language is sensitive to such sex-based differences. Nonetheless, physiological constraints might come to constrain phonological patterning at a historic distance. That is, the conventions of sound systems might not push the absolute limits of physiology, but might nonetheless come to be palaeophonetically shaped by them.

This is where functional forces on the system become relevant, which may, over generations of speakers, crucially interact with phonetic pressures. If H tones did not spill over in Comaltepec Chinantec, then they might be misperceived by the listener as belonging to the LM tone category, due to the only limited temporal domain in which the pitch rise is implemented. The pitch rise may be cut off as

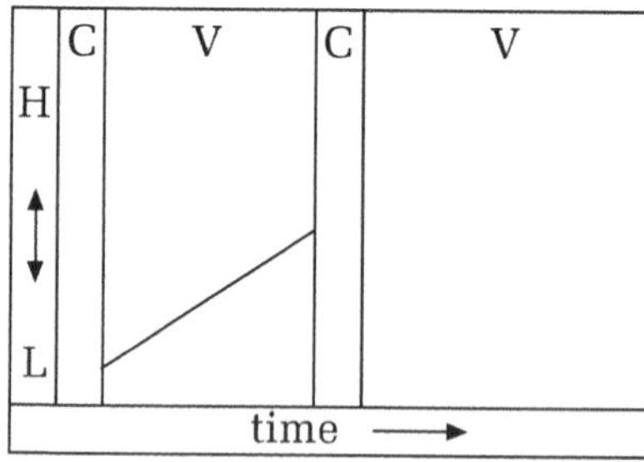

Figure 5.22 Early cut-off of a low–high tone may be confusable with a low–mid tone

the second consonant is beginning, and so does not achieve nearly as high a value. With its lower ending point, the tone might be confusable with LM tones. This scenario is schematized in Figure 5.22.

As greater pitch increases can be effected *after* the following consonant, and since there is a natural tendency for pitch rises to 'spill over' anyway, the LH tone may be better cued when it spills over. Also, since HL, HM and MH are elsewhere absent in the language, high-tone spill-over better conveys the high tone value without the possibility of neutralization. So, variant forms in which the H component of LH forms spills over on to a following vowel are functionally advantageous in two ways: (1) the LH tone is now less likely to be confusable with LM tones (and maybe L tones too), and (2) the spilled-over component can never neutralize distinctions, since HL, HM and MH are purely allophonic sound substitutions.

What I am suggesting is that H tone spill-over has its origins in phonetically anisotropic variation: there is an intrinsic phonetic influence on high tone spill-over in Comaltepec Chinantec, and exactly because the high tone spill-over has functional value – meaning that distinct words are more readily conveyed to listeners – this tone value has been conventionalized in its present form.

There are complications, however. M tones on syllables which lack post-vocalic [h] or [ʔ] induce the same tone substitutions on following syllables as LH tones do.

[hi˩]	book	[mɨː˧ hi˥˩]	I ask for a book
[mohʔ˩]	squash	[mɨː˧ mohʔ˥˩]	I ask for squash
[kuː˧]	money	[mɨː˧ kuː˥˧]	I ask for money
[ʔoː˧]	papaya	[mɨː˧ ʔoː˥˧]	I ask for papaya
[ŋi˩˥]	salt	[mɨː˧ ŋi˦˥]	I ask for salt
[loh˩˥]	cactus	[mɨː˧ loh˦˥]	I ask for a cactus

Also, these allophonic MH and HM tones may themselves induce tone changes on following syllables! Since they induce the tone change when they are LH and M, they also do so even when they have been substituted by MH and HM, respectively. That is, the tone substitution pattern may iterate itself across a string of words. In theory, then, certain words may possess nice smooth M tones in most contexts, but suddenly encounter a very bumpy road if they end up next to each other: [˧], [˧], [˧], [˧], but [˧ ˥˧ ˥˧ ˥˧]!

This unusual pattern calls out for an explanation. Why should an H tone suddenly pop up after an M tone? Clearly, the proposed explanation cannot offer an immediate account of this pattern. Indeed, I'm really at a loss to offer any sort of proximate, phonetically-rooted account here. But, of course, proximate phonetic forces are only of limited help when trying to fully understand synchronic phonological patterns. Instead the answer may be recoverable from an investigation of language history, where phonetic factors interact with cognitive and functional factors.

As in Trique, both the comparative and internal reconstruction methods converge to offer a compelling account of the present-day pattern. Forgoing the details, the linguist Calvin Rensch has reconstructed an earlier stage of Chinantec, and suggests that the M tones which induce an H tone on following syllables are historically derived from H tones.

Present-day Comaltepec Chinantec	Historic Chinantec	
[kuː˧]	*kuː˥	money
[ⁿdʒœː˧]	*dʒuː˥	earthen jar/jug
[ʔwɨːŋ˧]	*ʔwɨː˥	Ojitlán (a large Chinantec village)

Historic H tones which were immediately followed by [h] or [ʔ] have remained H, according to Rensch.

Present-day Comaltepec Chinantec	Historic Chinantec	
[lih˥]	*lih˥	flower
[huːh˥]	*huːh˥	word
[huːhʔ˥]	*huːʔ˥	pineapple

If this is so, the origins of this superficially strange pattern can be suggested. We have established that the high component of LH tones naturally spills onto a following vowel. Over time, this pattern may have *generalized* to include other tones which ended on a high pitch. In particular, H tones on vowels that were not immediately followed by a laryngeal sound ([h] or [ʔ]) were the most likely tones to be recruited into the pattern.

Why should this be so? Glottal opening ([h]) and glottal closing ([ʔ]) typically make demands on the vocal folds that are in conflict with tone production. If a laryngeal sound immediately follows the H tone, the vocal folds are not likely to maintain the posture necessary for the production of this tone. *Without* a following laryngeal sound however, a pitch may be prolonged into the following vowel without interference. So, *level* H tones also came to be associated with the appearance of an H tone on the first portion of a following vowel, provided no [h] or [ʔ] immediately followed. But then, these H tones lowered to M, and so all these historic H tone forms disappeared from the language. There are reasonable aerodynamic reasons for this sort of pitch differential, since both shutting down and opening up the glottis may both – for rather different reasons – be accompanied by pitch raising: [h] involves increased airflow, which might raise pitch, and [ʔ] involves tensed vocal folds, which also might raise pitch. (Both these patterns are found in other languages, by the way.) In Comaltepec Chinantec, these historic H tones are lower today, but the following H tone remains, as a relic or vestige of the past pattern. So whenever one of these former H tones (which has now become M) comes up against a following L, M or LH tone, these following tones are still substituted with HL, HM and MH, respectively: the preceding H tone has lowered to M, but the substitution pattern on the following vowel remains solidly in place.

As a result of all this, former H tone words which *lacked* a post-vocalic laryngeal are now M tone words, and they induce the presence of an H tone on a following vowel. But the H tones which *possessed* a post-vocalic laryngeal remained H, yet these do *not* spill their H on to the following vowel! The timeline in Figure 5.23 summarizes the proposed sequence of changes.

A final complication involves LM tones, which are never substituted with other tones when LH or M immediately precedes. Why not? Well, if, in the history of Comaltepec Chinantec, H tones were to slowly 'spill over' on to LM tones, then LM might be substituted with HM. The problem is that HM tones are already found in this context, as alternants of M tones. In other words, if LM were to alternate with HM here, it would run the risk of neutralizing with M tones that alternate with HM here. Although we really don't know the historical sequence of events that led to this fortuitous 'blocking' of a potentially neutralizing alternation, suffice it to say for now, the present-day pattern may be remarkably well-motivated when considering the functional pressures that result in communicative success.

Some readers may feel a sense of dissatisfaction at my liberal use of these sorts of conjectures, and, indeed, it would be very nice if linguists could state with certainty the evolution of present-day

Time 1	Time 2	Time 3	
What H spreads rightward from LH syllables.	**What** H spreads rightward from H-final vowels which lack postvocalic [h] or [ʔ].	**What** Level H without postvocalic [h] or [ʔ] lowers to M; the H tone on the following vowel remains.	**What** Level H with postvocalic [h] or [ʔ] remain H; there is no H tone spread.
Why Functionally beneficial anisotropic variation leads to the conventional-ization of H-tone spill-over in this context.	**Why** The pattern is generalized to include those H-final vowels most susceptible to spill-over: those lacking [h] or [ʔ].	**Why** Lack of post-vocalic laryngeals leads to a phonetically natural pitch split, while the allophonic substitution remains unchanged.	**Why** Presence of post-vocalic laryngeals ([h] and [ʔ])make demands on the vocal folds that may be in conflict with tone production.
Example toː˩ banana kwɑ˩˥ toː˥˩ give a banana	**Example** hi˩ book mɨː˥ hi˥˩ I ask for a book	**Example** kuː˧ money mɨː˧ kuː˥˧ I ask for money	**Example** ʔneh˥ need ʔneh˥ ni˩ kih˧ We need to pay

Figure 5.23 Proposed timeline of Comaltepec Chinantec tonal allophony

phonological patterns. But, of course, we don't have phonetic data across centuries of language use. Nonetheless, I do hope to have demonstrated that linguists, even with their limited data and limited tools, might arrive at reasonable – if not necessarily confirmable – conclusions about a language's previous state.

To summarize, the present-day tone patterning Comaltepec Chinantec, as superficially strange as it is, can be understood as the culmination of a series of small, local, and emphatically *natural* incremental changes. First, phonetically anisotropic variation of LH tones may have become conventionalized, since those LH tones which, quite naturally, spilled over onto a following vowel were better at keeping words distinct from each other that differed in meaning. These variants were naturally selected, and the spill-over came to be conventionalized.

The pattern seems to have generalized to include level H tones as well, but only those that lacked post-vocalic laryngeals. Without conflicting demands placed on the vocal folds (due to the absence of a following [h] or [ʔ]), it was these tones that were most naturally incorporated into the pattern. And although these tones subsequently lowered to M for rather well-understood aerodynamic reasons, the tone-change process had been fully conventionalized by this time, and so we still observe – up to today – an H tone on the first portion of the following vowel. The result is that this pattern has neither functional nor phonetic motivation, at least for present-day speakers of Comaltepec Chinantec.

The appearance of H tones following M tones in Comaltepec Chinantec exemplifies something quite remarkable about the nature of sound substitution. Even when a phonological pattern seems to be downright bizarre, lacking any reasonable phonetic or functional motivation at all, there will be perfectly natural, incremental processes that have unfolded over time that may account for the pattern. A series of small, local interactions of phonetic, functional and cognitive pressures may, over generations of speakers, render alternants quite distinct from each other: *alternations in the present – even when phonetically unnatural and superficially counter-functional – are the long-term product of small, local, and perfectly natural processes that play themselves out over generations of speakers.*

Still, phonological systems tend to remain remarkably natural and phonetically plausible, even though the ravages of time logically allow for bizarre patterns to slowly emerge. This disparity between reality and logical possibility can be reconciled quite intuitively, however: with every utterance by every speaker in every language, phonetic pressures exert force on the system. As unnatural patterns slowly emerge (always, of course, as a consequence of slow, natural and local steps), phonetic pressures will always be exerting themselves, due to the simple fact that each speech utterance is an actual physical event that unfolds in real time, and so is subject to genuine physical forces. In time, irregular, unusual patterns may once again be slowly shaped by raw physiology. Consequently, phonetically implausible patterns are constantly under pressure to fall back in line, and so those that do survive are not only phonetic oddities but are statistical oddities as well.

In the case of Comaltepec Chinantec, at least, we may have uncovered some of the major pressures on the system that have led to its present state. But even in those cases when the present state of the system is hopelessly obscured by long-forgotten, undocumented (pre)historical changes, we should not just throw up our hands and give up the notion that *all* patterns are explainable by real-world forces that are known to act locally in any number of natural circumstances. The optimistic nature of scientific pursuit demands us to operate under the assumption that broadly applicable, locally active principles go far in explaining the complex world around us, in phonology and elsewhere.

Summary

In this chapter we've explored in some detail how variation in speech can sometimes lead to confusion for listeners, and how this confusion may lead to the better separation of phonological categories. We've seen how, under some circumstances, variation may promote the phonetic stability of categories, but under other circumstances, variation may promote sound change. Under both sets of circumstances, however, I attributed the variation inherent in speech production to the accumulation of minor, chance errors over generations of speakers. *Sounds in alternation in the present, which undergo quantum leaps of change in phonetic quality as they shift from context to context, have evolved in the absence of the users who come to possess them.* Allophonic alternants can now be viewed as the culmination of a series of small, natural changes to the system that take place over generations of speakers. Even when a pattern does not lend itself to a compelling explanation in the present, we should not abandon the idea that phonetic, functional and cognitive pressures are ultimately responsible for its linguistic comportment. *Present-day alternations have no present-day causes; they only have present-day effects.*

Although many linguists believe otherwise, the regularities we observe in sound change and in alternations are not a consequence of linguistic laws or principles that *constrain* or, in the limiting case, *determine* linguistic patterns. Instead, these alternations are merely the most easily observed consequences of the *true* laws and principles that underlie linguistic sound patterns, laws and principles that cannot be readily observed, since they do not have overt, isomorphic analogues in linguistic patterns. As Baudouin de Courtenay wrote in 1910,

> Many scholars, who are either undemanding or incapable of critical thinking, confuse law, that is, functional interdependence, with statistical statements of fact or with plain coincidence. Others posit logical, methodological, and epistemological axioms, set up conditions sine qua non for each scientific proposition, and formulate subjective laws for any theoretical ideas in place of objective laws that account for the relationships of observable facts.

Baudouin de Courtenay wrote that the *genuine* law-governed primitives that operate on linguistic patterns derive from four main sources: (1) 'the psychological world of the individual', (2) 'the biological and physiological world of a given organism', (3) 'the external, physical world' and (4) 'the social world (the transmission of linguistically expressed ideas from one individual to another)'. Operating under the incorrect assumption that the emergent outputs of these interacting systems are directly law-governed elements themselves, Baudouin de Courtenay wrote,

> ... can be compared to such 'laws' as meteorological generalizations or to various kinds of statistical generalizations; in fact, they are only statements of what occurs on the surface of phenomena. Genuine 'laws,' the laws of causality, are hidden in the depth, the intricate combination of the most diverse elements. 'Laws' do exist, but not where they are being sought ... Between the starting and ending point of historical change ... there is no relationship that could be interpreted as a law of evolution.

Further reading

The Martinet quote ('Linguistic identity ...'):

Martinet, André (1975 [1988]). 'The internal conditioning of phonological changes', *La Linguistique* 24.2: 17–26. Quote on page 25.

The Paul quotes ('However much ... movement ...', '[V]ariability of production ...'):

Paul, Hermann (1880 [1970]). *Principles of the History of Language.* College Park, MD: McGrath, pp. 43 and 44–5.

The Kruszewski quotes ('Our characteristic, unconscious memory ...', 'In the course of time ...'):

Kruszewski, Mikołaj (1883 [1995]). 'An outline of linguistic science', in Konrad Koerner (ed.), *Writings in General Linguistics* (Amsterdam Classics in Linguistics 11). Amsterdam: John Benjamins Publishing Company, pp. 66 and 85.

On rats and ducks:

Gallistel, Randy (1990). *The Organization of Learning.* Cambridge, MA: MIT Press.

Harper, D. G. C. (1982). 'Comparative foraging in mallards: ideal free ducks', *Animal Behaviour* 30: 575–84.

The Labov quotes ('*It is not a hypothesis ...*', '*We should not be embarrassed ...*'):

Labov, William (1994). *Principles of Linguistic Change, Vol. 1: Internal Factors.* Oxford: Blackwell, pp. 583 and 598–9.

On cross-linguistic patterns of vowel nasalization:

Clumeck, Harold (1976). 'Patterns of soft palate movements in six languages', *Journal of Phonetics* 4: 337–51.

Probability matching in Caribbean Spanish:

Poplack, Shana (1980). 'The notion of the plural in Puerto Rican Spanish: competing constraints on (s) deletion', in William Labov (ed.), *Locating Language in Time and Space.* New York: Academic Press, pp. 55–67.

Poplack, Shana (1980). 'Deletion and disambiguation in Puerto Rican Spanish', *Language* 56.2: 371–85.

Probability matching in the laboratory:

Hudson, Carla L. and Newport, Elissa L. (1999). 'Creolization: could adults really have done it all?', in Annabel Greenhill, Heather Littlefield and Cheryl Tano (eds), *Proceedings of the Boston University Conference on Language Development, 23.* Somerville, MA: Cascadilla Press, pp. 265–76.

On the acquisition of English stop consonants:

Preston, M. S. and Yeni-Komshian, G. (1967). 'Studies on the development of stop consonants produced during the second year of life', *Annual Report, Neurocommunications Laboratory.* Baltimore: Johns Hopkins University School of Medicine 3: 211–22.

On speech variation, exemplar modelling, etc.:

Johnson, Keith (1997). 'Speech perception without speaker normalization: an exemplar model', in Keith Johnson and John W. Mullennix (eds), *Talker Variability in Speech Processing.* New York: Academic Press, pp. 143–65.

Gluck, Mark A. and Bower, Gordon H. (1988). 'Evaluating an adaptive network model of human learning', *Journal of Memory and Language* 27: 166–95.

Goldinger, Stephen D. (1997). 'Words and voices: perception and production in an episodic lexicon', in Keith Johnson and John W. Mullennix (eds), *Talker Variability in Speech Processing.* New York: Academic Press, pp. 33–56.

Goldinger, Stephen D. (1998). 'Echoes of echoes? An episodic theory of lexical access', *Psychological Review* 105.2: 251–71.

Janda, Richard D. and Joseph, Brian D. (2001). 'Reconsidering the canons of sound change: towards a Big Bang theory', manuscript of paper presented at the International Conference on Historical Linguistics, Melbourne.

Liberman, Mark (2002). 'Simple models for emergence of a shared vocabulary', paper presented at *Laboratory Phonology VIII.* New Haven, CT.

Lotto, Andrew (2000). 'Language acquisition as complex category formation', *Phonetica* 57: 189–96.

Nosofsky, Robert M. (1988). 'Exemplar-based accounts of relations between classification, recognition, and typicality', *Journal of Experimental Psychology: Learning, Memory and Cognition* 14: 700–08.

Ohala, John J. (1981). 'The listener as a source of sound change', papers from a parasession on Language and Behavior, Chicago Linguistics Society, 178–203.

Ohala, John J. (1989). 'Sound change is drawn from a pool of synchronic variation', in Leiv E. Breivik and Ernst H. Jahr (eds), *Language Change: Contributions to the Study of its Causes.* Berlin: Mouton de Gruyter, pp. 173–98.

Steels, Luc (2000). 'Language as a complex adaptive system', in Marc Schoenauer, Kalyanmoy Deb, Guenter Rudolph, Xin Yao, Evelyne Lutton, Juan Julian Merelo and Hans-Paul Schwefel (eds), *Lecture Notes on Computer Science. Parallel Problem Solving from Nature.* PPSN–VI, 17–26.

On Trique:

Hollenbach, Barbara E. (1977). 'Phonetic versus phonemic correspondence in two Trique dialects', in William R. Merrifield (ed.), *Studies in Otomanguean Phonology*. Dallas: Summer Institute of Linguistics.

Longacre, Robert E. (1957). 'Proto-Mixtecan', *International Journal of American Linguistics* 23.4.III. Bloomington: Indiana University Research Center in Anthropology, Folklore and Linguistics.

Longacre, Robert E. (1962). 'Amplification of Gudschinsky's Proto-Popolocan-Mixtecan', *International Journal of American Linguistics* 28: 227–42.

Longacre, Robert E. and Millon, René (1961). 'Proto-Mixtecan and Proto-Amuzgo-Mixtecan Vocabularies: A Preliminary Cultural Analysis', *Anthropological Linguistics* 4.3: 1–44.

Silverman, Daniel (2006). 'The diachrony of labiality in Trique, and the functional relevance of gradience and variation', in Stephen Anderson, Louis Goldstein and Catherine Best (eds), *Papers in Laboratory Phonology VIII*. Berlin: Mouton de Gruyter.

The Baudouin de Courtenay quotes ('I must emphasize the importance ...', 'Many scholars ...'; '... can be compared ...'):

Baudouin de Courtenay, Jan (1910 [1972]). 'Phonetic laws', in Edward Stankiewicz (ed.), *A Baudouin de Courtenay Reader*. Bloomington: Indiana University Press, pp. 267, 272 and 276.

On sound patterns suggesting the passive curtailment of potentially homophone-inducing sound changes:

Manuel, Sharon (1990). 'The role of contrast in limiting vowel-to-vowel coarticulation in different languages', *Journal of the Acoustical Society of America*, 88: 1286–98.

Manuel, Sharon (1999). 'Cross-language studies: relating language-particular coarticulation patterns to other language-particular facts', in William J. Hardcastle and Nigel Hewlett (eds), *Coarticulation: Theory, Data and Techniques*. Cambridge, UK: Cambridge University Press, pp. 179–98.

Öhman, Sven E. G. (1966). 'Coarticulation in VCV utterances: spectrographic measurements', *Journal of the Acoustical Society of America* 39: 151–68.

On homophone avoidance:

Casenhiser, Devin (2005). 'Children's resistance to homophony: an experimental study of pseudohomonyms', *Journal of Child Language* 32: 1–25.

Charles-Luce, Jan (1993). 'The effects of semantic content on voicing neutralization', *Phonetica* 50: 28–43.

Kiparsky, Paul (1972). 'Explanation in phonology', in S. Peters (ed.), *Goals of Linguistic Theory*. Englewood Cliffs, NJ: Prentice-Hall, pp. 189–227.

On Chinantec:

Anderson, Judi L. (1989). *Comaltepec Chinantec Syntax* (Studies in Chinantec Languages v. 3). Dallas: Summer Institute of Linguistics.

Anderson, Judi L., Martinez, Isaac H. and Pace, Wanda (1990). 'Comaltepec Chinantec tone', in William R. Merrifield and Calvin. R. Rensch (eds),

Syllables, Tone, and Verb Paradigms (Studies in Chinantec languages v.4). Dallas: Summer Institute of Linguistics, pp. 3–20.

Pace, Wanda J. (1990). 'Comaltepec Chinantec verb inflection', in William R. Merrifield and Calvin. R. Rensch (eds), *Syllables, Tone, and Verb Paradigms* (Studies in Chinantec languages v.4). Dallas: Summer Institute of Linguistics, pp. 21–62.

Rensch, Calvin R. (1968). *Proto Chinantec Phonology* (Papeles de la Chinantla VI. Serie Científica 10). Mexico City: Museo Nacional de Antropologia.

Rensch, Calvin R. (1976). *Comparative Otomanguean Phonology*. Bloomington: Indiana University.

Silverman, Daniel (1997). 'Laryngeal complexity in Otomanguean vowels', *Phonology* 14.2: 235–61.

Silverman, Daniel (1997). 'Tone sandhi in Comaltepec Chinantec', *Language* 73.3: 473–92.

On the sluggishness of pitch rises in comparison to pitch falls:

Ohala, John J. and Ewan, William G. (1973). 'Speed of pitch change', abstract, *Journal of the Acoustical Society of America* 53: 345.

Sundberg, Johan (1979). 'Maximum speed of pitch changes in singers and untrained subjects', *Journal of Phonetics* 7.2: 71–9.

6 The pull of phonetics; the push of phonology

In Chapter Five we considered two ways that token-to-token variation may lead to sound change. The first type, exemplified by Trique lip-rounding harmony, was potentially radially symmetrical or phonetically *isotropic*: variation among tokens is not pushed in a particular direction due to any intrinsic phonetic force. Instead, variation may potentially proceed in *any* direction, but it just so happens that certain variants over others are more successful in rendering forms distinct which differ in meaning, and thus are more successfully communicated to listeners, and so come to take hold in the system. The second type of variation, exemplified by the behaviour of Comaltepec Chinantec high tones, was radially asymmetrical, or phonetically *anisotropic*: certain variants over others are favoured due to intrinsic phonetic factors. Under the proper phonological conditions, these phonetically-favoured variants are more successful than others at rendering words phonetically distinct that differ in meaning; it is these variants that are ultimately conventionalized. In this chapter, we see how phonetically isotropic and phonetically anisotropic variation may interact within a single phonological system. As phonetic pressures may influence a particular phonetically anisotropic change in one sound, functional pressures may seize upon certain variants of another sound of the language, sending otherwise chance, phonetically isotropic variation on a specific trajectory of change.

Specifically, certain intrinsic articulatory or aerodynamic conditions may favour some sorts of deviations over others. Now, in and of themselves, these sorts of phonetically favoured variants might not induce sound changes, for, as we saw in the previous chapter, a change in the phonetic quality of one sound might be inhibited by the presence of another sound which already occupies the neighbouring acoustic space. So a sound with phonetic properties x might vary toward y in some context c, but since y is already present in c, a change from x to y is inhibited, and so x and y may remain largely stable and well-separated over time. However, under different conditions, there is another possible outcome to this sort of scenario: x may indeed slowly become more like y in c, but only because y has an 'escape hatch'. That is, the change of x to y is accompanied by a change of y to z, where z is a new phonetic value that was previously absent in c. The change from y to z may not have any intrinsic phonetic motivation. Rather, tokens of y that just happen to be more z-like were better at keeping themselves distinct from the increasingly y-like tokens of x. So x moves toward y for phonetic reasons, and y moves toward z for functional reasons. The result is that contrastive sounds remain dispersed from each other in the phonetic space. We'll thus see that conditions in one part of the phonological system may effect changes in another, seemingly unrelated part of the system.

A change from x to y, and from y to z, is usually known as a *chain shift* in phonological parlance, and it is this phenomenon that we explore in this chapter.

Our primary language of investigation in this chapter is a remarkably complex pattern from American English. In general, one must proceed with an especial caution when investigating one's own language. As I have been emphasizing throughout, it is frightfully easy to fall back upon one's intuitions and schooling under such circumstances. Many an otherwise careful scholar has been caught in the embarrassing situation of making errors of analysis of their native language, simply because their objectivity was thwarted by appeals to their feelings rather than appeals to the objective facts of sound patterning.

Before jumping headlong into American English though, we first revisit Corsican, which displays a much simpler, though ultimately similar pattern.

Corsican again

Perhaps you recall from Chapter Four that in Corsican, certain forms of phonologically contrastive sounds bear more resemblance to each other than they bear to their respective alternants. So word-initial voiceless stops (#[p, t, k]) alternate with voiced stops intervocalically (V[b, d, g]V), for example [teŋgu] 'I have', versus [u deŋgu] 'I have it'. (We'll use 'V' as a variable for any vowel. Recall that '#' indicates a word boundary.) Meanwhile, word-initial voiced stops (#[b, d, g]) alternate with voiced fricatives intervocalically (V[β, ð, ɣ]V), for example [dente] 'tooth' but [u ðente] 'the tooth'. Although both series have voiced stops, learners never mistakenly group the two sorts of voiced stops together into a single phonological category, simply because they never alternate with each other. Instead, they group the dissimilar sounds together (#[p, t, k] and V[b, d, g]V; #[b, d, g] and V[β, ð, ɣ]V) as a consequence of their alternation. (Incidently, [v] is found in Corsican as an alternant of word-initial [f]: [fele] 'faithful', but [u vele] ‘the faithful one’. Meanwhile, word-initial [v] alternates with [w] in this same context: [veni] ‘come’, but [ajju ða wena] ‘shall I come’; there is no potential for neutralization!)

In Chapter Four, we merely observed this behaviour, without offering any phonetic or functional motivation for it. In Chapter Five, we offered a functional explanation for the evolution of such patterns (though not for Corsican specifically), rooted in the phonetic variation intrinsic to speech production and in probability matching and the exemplar approach: minor variants which are more successful at keeping words phonetically distinct from other words are more likely communicated successfully to listeners, and hence are more likely to be produced as these listeners become speakers. Slowly, then, minor beneficial variants become the new norm. Now, in Chapter Six, we identify the specific phonetic trajectory that the Corsican sound change has taken. In particular, we consider the phonetic and functional origins of the two alternating sound pairs, #[t]–V[d]V and #[d]–V[ð]V. (For ease of exposition, we'll just concentrate on the tongue-tip consonants from now on, but all arguments apply equally well to the labial and tongue-body consonants.)

Phonetically anisotropic variation: word-initial voiceless stops and the voicing mechanism

We first focus on Corsican's word-initial voiceless stops (for example, [t̪eŋgu]). It turns out that voicelessness among word-initial stops makes good aerodynamic sense, and for this reason is the cross-linguistic norm. Let's consider why this is so. In order to induce the regular vibration of the vocal folds that is characteristic of voicing, two conditions must be met. First, the vocal folds – two pieces of flesh that reside in the larynx – must be postured in a way that promotes their vibration. They cannot be spread too far apart, and they cannot be pressed too tightly together. If they are spread too far apart, then they will not be able to slap together and come apart at regular intervals; among other problems, they won't even be able to reach each other across the gap between them, which is called the glottis. (The glottis is the *space* between the vocal folds; it is not the vocal folds, nor is it the larynx. It is only present when the vocal folds are not pressed together.) If the vocal folds are pressed together too strongly, also, voicing cannot ensue, because their necessary back-and-forth vibration is inhibited. Although vocal fold tenseness and glottal aperture are controlled by the laryngeal muscles, their actual vibration is not controlled at the intrinsic level. What I mean is, neither the vocal folds nor their surrounding laryngeal mechanisms engage in any sort of active muscular activity which induces their back-and-forth movement. Rather, the control mechanism is extrinsic to the vocal folds themselves. We can view the larynx (which, recall, houses the vocal folds) as dividing the aerodynamic system into two chambers: beneath the larynx (the lungs), and above the larynx (the vocal tract). Vocal fold vibration is a consequence of the aerodynamic conditions in these two chambers. Basically, when the air pressure ratio between the sub-laryngeal and supra-laryngeal chambers is sufficiently positive, then air will flow from the lungs, across the glottis, and into the vocal tract. After inhalation, the chest muscles may apply pressure on the lungs to decrease their size, and thus the sub-laryngeal air pressure increases, forcing air's escape across the glottis. Trans-glottal airflow thus induces the vocal fold vibration necessary for voicing.

The pressure differential necessary for vocal fold vibration is best maintained when making a vowel sound, since air can be freely shunted out of the vocal tract, thus maintaining a positive sub-laryngeal–supra-laryngeal pressure ratio. The maintenance of a sufficiently positive sub-laryngeal–supra-laryngeal pressure ratio, then, is the second condition necessary for vocal fold vibration. So, it is this trans-glottal airflow which is responsible for vocal fold vibration, but only, of course, if the vocal folds are postured correctly in the first place. Again, if they are spread too far apart, then no amount of trans-glottal airflow will be able to induce the proper vibratory motion for voicing; if they are pressed too tightly together, then air will not be able to cross the glottis anyway, and so again no voicing will be generated.

The periodic vocal fold vibration itself is a consequence of cyclic changes in air pressure in the glottis. When air rushes through the glottis from the lungs into the vocal tract, the air pressure in the glottis lowers. Anything that is situated next to the air current will consequently be sucked inward with a significant force. We've all experienced this effect when sitting in a train in the station. When an express zooms by on the next track, your train is suddenly sucked toward the moving train. This phenomenon is called the Bernoulli Effect, named after Daniel Bernoulli, the scientist who first documented it. Under these conditions then, the vocal folds will be sucked toward each other, and the glottis will close.

Now, when the vocal folds are sucked together due to the pressure drop in the glottis, they slam shut against each other. At this point, air is still being pushed up from the lungs, but is halted at the sealed vocal folds. Consequently, the sub-laryngeal pressure quickly becomes so great that now the vocal folds are blown apart. Now, again, due to the pressure differential, air rushes through the glottis, pressure in the glottis drops, and the folds get sucked together once again. This is the glottal cycle, and as it is repeated and repeated, voicing is generated. The periodic slamming action of the vocal folds disrupts the distribution of air particles in the region of the glottis. These regularly-timed disruptions propagate outward, eventually impinging on the ear of the listener, culminating in what we perceive as voicing. The faster the rate of the glottal cycle, the higher the perceived pitch of the consequent sound; the lower the rate, the lower the pitch.

Now let's get back to Corsican. Remember I said that in word-initial position, the Corsican voiceless stops are aerodynamically natural. Why should this be so? Remember that, unlike vowels, stops are made by completely sealing off the vocal tract, thus providing no escape for any air that may rush up from the lungs. Since air cannot escape the mouth, then, very quickly, the positive sub-laryngeal–supra-laryngeal pressure ratio disappears. So if the chest muscles are pressing down on the inflated lungs while a stop is being made in the mouth, air pressure both below and above the glottis becomes the same, and so no more air is able to cross the glottis, and so voicing cannot be generated. For word-initial stops, then, the natural aerodynamic state is one which is not conducive to voicing. It's only when the stop is released into the following vowel that air can once again escape the mouth, that the sub-laryngeal–supra-laryngeal pressure ratio becomes sufficiently positive, and that voicing may naturally begin.

It's no coincidence, then, that *every* language has words that begin with voiceless stops. Indeed, we can establish a strong correlation between phonetic naturalness and linguistic prevalence, and moreover establish a *direction* of causation: it is due to facts about the physical world that some sound patterns are more common than others. Voicelessness for word-initial stops is common exactly because it is aerodynamically natural.

Phonetically anisotropic variation: intervocalic stops and the voicing mechanism

If voicelessness is aerodynamically natural for word-initial stops, is there a change in aerodynamic conditions that naturally induces these stops to voice when they end up between vowels (recall, [t̠eŋgu] but [u d̠eŋgu], [p̠ɛðɛ] but [u b̠eðe])? Yes, there is! When a stop finds itself between vowels, there is voicing immediately before the stop (during the preceding vowel), and immediately after the stop as well (during the following vowel). Because the vocal folds are already in a state of vibration as the stop is being implemented, and, just as importantly, because the stop closure itself is of a short overall duration, the sub-laryngeal–supra-laryngeal pressure ratio remains sufficiently positive that trans-glottal airflow may be maintained straight through the stop closure, and right into the following vowel. The result is *intervocalic* (between-vowel) voicing, as in Corsican, and as in a huge number of other languages as well. Once again, the prevalence of a sound pattern can be explained by appeals to independent, real-world facts. In the absence of constant real-world fact-checking, the prevalence or rarity of phonological patterns becomes a deeply unsatisfying mystery. Fortunately for us phonologists, and just as we should expect, *all* common phonological patterns lend themselves to these sorts of external explanations.

Of course, both the articulatory and acoustic qualities of the word-initial alternant (#[t]) and the intervocalic alternant (V[d]V) are different from each other. But their physical difference may now be viewed as a mere accommodation to the phonetically natural state of aerodynamic affairs. Therefore, we may now reconstruct the possible historic origin of the present-day alternation. The token-to-token variation that was historically responsible for the present-day #[t]–V[d]V alternation of Corsican was phonetically anisotropic in nature: there are well-motivated aerodynamic reasons why the word-initial stops naturally gravitate to a voiceless state, and why the intervocalic stops naturally gravitate to a voiced state.

Phonetically isotropic variation: word-initial voiced stops and the voicing mechanism

This is all well and good, but what about the word-initial voiced stops of Corsican? Obviously, these can't *also* be natural in word-initial position. Instead, what we find time and time again in languages is that *less* natural sounds are found in some position only when *more* natural sounds are found in that position. In every language investigated, the existence of words with initial *voiced* stops implies the existence of words with initial *voiceless* stops. Why should this be so? To induce voicing of word-initial stops, various articulatory postures are implemented so that the sub-laryngeal–supra-laryngeal pressure ratio remains positive during the oral closure: the entire larynx may lower, the throat may widen, the soft palate may be raised, and the cheeks may puff out (at least for [b], for which cheek-puffing actually has aerodynamic consequences). All these actions may conspire to increase the size of the sealed oral cavity, which, in turn, allows air to cross the glottis for a longer period of time, which increases the likelihood that voicing may be maintained during the stop closure (because labial stops have a larger supra-laryngeal chamber, trans-glottal airflow is more likely to persist even during oral closure, and so labial stops tend to be voiced more often than stops made farther back in the mouth). So voicing may be present in word-initial stops, but its maintenance requires a less natural articulatory configuration. It sounds rather complicated, and indeed it is. It is probably exactly for this reason that children are able to produce word-initial voiceless stops earlier than word-initial voiced stops (though they may produce voiced labial stops somewhat earlier than other voiced stops).

Phonetically isotropic variation: intervocalic spirantization

In Corsican, as in quite a number of languages, word-initial voiced stops alternate with voiced fricatives in intervocalic position. Fricatives form a salient contrast with voiced stops in the intervocalic context, which, recall, are the intervocalic alternants of word-initial *voiceless* stops. We might consequently characterize the variation ultimately responsible for the #[d]–V[ð]V alternation as phonetically isotropic in nature. Let's consider why. When words with an initial [d] find themselves in intervocalic position, the phonetically natural thing to do is to simply remain [d]; remember, voicing is natural here. The problem is, if they were to remain [d], then they run the risk of becoming homophonous with otherwise identical words that have [d] here as a consequence of the #[t]–V[d]V alternation. Instead, those sporadic variants that just happened to be somewhat more fricative-like – made without a complete seal in the vocal tract – are more successful at keeping such words distinct from those V[t]V words that began to move toward V[d]V, and so it is these particular variants that are communicated more successfully to listeners, and ultimately come to hold sway in the system. (It's important to realize that these fricatives ran no risk of inducing homophony. Remember: just as intervocalic fricatives were taking hold, fricatives previously present in this context were changing as well: [v̠eni] versus [ajju ða w̠ena].)

Variation from the stop toward the fricative here is phonetically isotropic in origin, because no variant is phonetically favoured over any other. Rather, certain variants just happen to be more successful than most others at keeping words distinct that differ in meaning.

Now, it's uncontroversial that voiceless stops are aerodynamically more natural than voiced stops in word-initial position (#[t]), and that voiced stops are aerodynamically more natural than voiceless stops between vowels ([VdV]). However, not all linguists agree that voiced stops are more natural than voiced fricatives between vowels ([VðV]). Some say that it's natural for voiced stops to become fricatives here, because it supposedly requires a lesser expenditure of effort *not* to seal the mouth than it does to seal it shut. Unfortunately, these linguists are unable to offer a quantitative measurement of effort expenditure, and this renders their hypothesis difficult to evaluate. Despite this, a few have gone so far as to incorporate 'laziness' as an important principle in explaining phonological patterns (more on 'laziness' in Chapter Seven). Others, including me, suspect differently: forming an oral seal may be quite a bit easier than positioning the articulators in exactly the right posture to generate the correct amount of air turbulence which characterizes a fricative. As the great phonetician Peter Ladefoged has remarked, it's probably easier (though, admittedly, more painful) to run smack into a brick wall than it is to suddenly stop just before impact! Nonetheless, although it might be phonetically less natural to produce an intervocalic voiced stop than an intervocalic voiced fricative, the voicing itself is surely natural: we would certainly *not* expect voiceless stop variants to evolve in this context. That is, we do not expect an alternation of the form #[d]–V[t]V.

Although phonetic arguments based on 'ease' and 'difficulty' are difficult to evaluate no matter which side of the issue one supports, there is actually some indirect, purely linguistic support for the claim that voiced stops are more natural than voiced fricatives between vowels: it is *extremely* common for languages to possess an alternation of the Corsican type (#[t]–V[d]V), but is very hard to find a language that has further allowed the voiced alternant to spirantize, which would result in a #[t]–V[ð]V alternation. (*Spirantize* is derived from *spirant*, another word for a fricative; it is usually preferred to the unwieldy 'fricativize'.) If fricatives were so natural in this context, this sort of alternation should be rather common. In fact, the linguist Naomi Gurevich has shown that spirantization usually involves an alternation with a voiced stop – not a voicless stop – and it usually is found in languages that *also* have a #[t]–V[d]V alternation as well. Indeed, Gurevich shows that spirantization is almost never neutralizing. All this may be viewed as circumstantial, indirect support for the hypothesis that intervocalic voiced fricatives are less natural than intervocalic voiced stops, and are the product of phonetically isotropic variation that has functional value.

The idea, then, is that intervocalic spirantization arises *in functional response* to the phonetically natural #[t]–V[d]V alternation. Just as [t] naturally moves towards [d] intervocalically largely for *phonetic* reasons, the *other* [d] here will *not* be pushed in any particular direction for phonetic reasons, but instead will gradually be pushed toward [ð] largely for *functional* reasons, since tokens with fricative variants were communicated more successfully to listeners, while variants that remain [d]-like will be more confusable with those intervocalic [d]s that alternate with word-initial [t]. Due to their communicative success, minor, fortuitous deviations in the direction of a more fricative-like sound may accrete over time, though wildly distinct variants will surely be discarded, due to their unrecognizability. Slowly, then, a voiced fricative may evolve in place of the voiced stop. And, just as discussed in Chapter Five, it might be that V[ð]V first arose in those very words that ran the risk of neutralizing with words that were shifting from V[t]V to V[d]V. But there is an overwhelmingly strong tendency for phonological patterns to generalize. And as there was certainly no functional *loss* if intervocalic voiced stops spirantized, the sound change came to permeate the language. Indeed, *pattern generalization* is found in virtually every other domain of human learning (and animal learning too), and since there is every reason to believe that the organizing principles of phonological knowledge are indistinct from those operating in other domains of learning, we should expect some form of pattern generalization to be active in phonology as well.

One more point before going on: although I have been discussing the links in this chain shift in terms of a genuine chain of sequenced events, this is *not* how they should be conceived. It is almost assuredly *not* the case that first the intervocalic voiceless stops began to voice, and subsequent to this voicing the contrastive voiced stops began to spirantize. Just imagine if first #[t] went to V[d]V, with nothing happening to the other series. Poor Corsican would end up with the merger of its two stop series in intervocalic position. So how could the language then 'know' which intervocalic stops should become fricatives, and which should remain stops? How did the language get it just right so that exactly those words with #[t] remained V[d]V, and those words with #[d] then moved on to V[ð]V? Obviously, it couldn't. So although we speak of chain shifts, causes and effects, and functional responses, the only reasonable way of envisioning chain shifts is if all links in the chain are shifting simultaneously. Of course, the shift plays out over time, but all links shift in coordinated tandem: just when tokens with the voiceless stops began to voice, tokens of the other series began to spirantize. There is really no other way it could be.

To summarize, the example of Corsican reveals something very important about the inter-relatedness of contrastive sounds that each has its own set of allophonic alternants: while phonetic pressures may pull one sound towards a context-specific *more* natural state, functional pressures may, in response, push an opposing sound to a context-specific *less* natural state. The result is that the sounds of any given language naturally and passively disperse themselves, thus fulfilling their primary function of keeping words phonetically distinct from each other. The idea, then, which should now be familiar to you, is that the voiced fricatives may be the result of slow, passive, functional pressures acting on the sound system over generations of speakers. Just as [t]-initial words are naturally prone to voicing when the [t] ends up between vowels, those tokens of [d]-initial words which happen to vary toward [ð] when between vowels were better at keeping themselves acoustically distinct, and so were communicated more successfully to listeners, who, in turn, might overestimate their prevalence and produce more of them in their own speech as a consequence of probability matching. So the sound system would slowly evolve toward a new, better-adapted state. This aspect of the chain shift may not have been *phonetically* natural, but in *functional* terms it makes perfect sense.

American English

The case of Corsican is a comparatively simple one, involving two contrastive sounds that each possesses only two major context-dependent alternants. Although the American English pattern we now turn to also involves only two contrastive sounds, each of these two categories possesses *four* major (and several more minor) context-dependent alternants. But despite its overwhelming complexity, the American English stop system has evolved so that almost all alternants are allophonic; homophony is rarely if ever encountered. But just like Corsican, however, we will see that the first stop series, the so-called lenis series (orthographic ‘b, d, g’) – regardless of the context in which it is found – is always realized in the phonetically natural way. The second series – the so-called fortis series (orthographic ‘p, t, k’) – is realized in a phonetically less-natural way. In those rare contexts when the two values might be rendered in a near-identical fashion, their shared value is the phonetically natural one.

So let’s take a systematic look at some examples of the alternants. Tabulated examples are shown in Table 6.1. Though we will concentrate on only the tongue-tip consonants – orthographic ‘t’ and ‘d’ – the story largely holds for the labial and tongue-body stops as well. Some alternants have more than one major realization, and these are indicated as appropriate. When the length of the preceding vowel is relevant to the nature of the contrast, this is indicated, although the particular vowel quality is irrelevant for this purpose; I have merely indicated the vowel that is present in the example used. Also, when stress is relevant, this too is indicated. Unfamiliar symbols are explained below.

Some examples of alternations are provided in Table 6.2.

Table 6.1 Examples of the lenis and fortis alveolar stops in American English

	lenis			*fortis*		
	form	*example*		*form*	*example*	
(A) word-initial	t d̥	tăk d̥ăk	dock	tʰ	tʰak	tock
(B) before a consonant, or word-final	at ad̥	nat nad̥	nod	ăt˺ ăˀt˺ ăʔ	năt˺ năˀt˺ năʔ	knot
(C) word-internal before a stressless vowel	eɪ̯ɾ ĕɪ̯ɾ	ˈfeɪ̯ɾɨd̥ ˈfĕɪ̯ɾɨd̥	faded (neutralized)	ĕɪ̯ɾ	ˈfĕɪ̯ɾɨd̥	fated
(D) word-internal before a stressed vowel	d	əˈdɪkʃɛn	addiction	tʰ	əˈtʰăp	atop
(E) following [s]	form: t example: stap˺ stop (non-contrastive)					

Table 6.2 American English alveolar stop alternation

Lenis	(A)–(C)	determined	pre-determined
	(A)–(D)	do	redo
	(B)–(C)	nod	nodding
	(D)–(C)	addiction	addict
Fortis	(B)–(C)	yacht	yachting
	(B)–(D)	dictate	dictatorial
	(D)–(C)	atomic	atom

The phonetically anisotropic origin of the lenis series

Let's consider the lenis series first (orthographic 'b, d, g'). In word-initial position (A), these are realized quite similarly to the voiceless series in Corsican, although the vocal folds tend to begin vibrating slightly earlier in English, usually just around the interval of stop release. As I've mentioned, these are usually referred to as 'devoiced' stops, being indicated with subscripted hollowed circles ([b̥, d̥, g̊]): 'dock' [d̥ak] (sometimes [tak]).

Before consonants, and also in word-final position (B), also, the lenis value is typically devoiced, as in 'nod' ([nad̥], sometimes [nat]). When stop consonants are not released into vowels, and instead are immediately followed by another stop or fricative – recall, these are the obstruent consonants – or are word-final (recall that a word-final consonant will usually be followed by a word-initial one), airflow cannot be naturally maintained for the duration of their closure. This is due to the extended duration of the oral obstructions which, we know, inhibits the continuation of trans-glottal airflow. Consequently, vocal fold vibration is likely to peter out, resulting in a stop that may start out with vocal fold vibration, but quickly shifts to a voiceless state. Languages typically evolve such that these sorts of natural phonetic tendencies become generalized and conventionalized: stops in these contexts may devoice even when a word-initial vowel or *any* sort of consonant, either obstruent or resonant, immediately follows.

Now, let's take the word 'nod' and turn it into 'nodding'. What happens when we add the vowel-initial suffix? Although we spell the resulting word with the 'd' doubled, suggesting that it is lengthened, the consonant actually *shortens* rather significantly. Whenever the lenis tongue-tip consonant occurs between vowels and – this is important – the second of these vowels is not stressed (C), the consonant is considerably shorter than in other contexts. It ends up as nothing more than a tap of the tongue against the roof of the mouth, as we discussed in Chapter One. The tap, recall, is transcribed [ɾ], and so 'nodding' can be transcribed [ˈnɑɾɪŋ], where the diacritic indicates that the following vowel is stressed. Since the obstruction in the mouth is so short in duration in the context of a following stressless vowel, a tap is always voiced: the closure is much shorter than the intervocalic [d] of Corsican, and so is obviously not long enough to allow the oral cavity to fill up with air. Consequently, air may continue to cross the vocal folds, and so their vibratory motion can continue through the tap and into the following vowel.

The word 'addict' also has a tap, because the lenis value finds itself between vowels, the second of which is stressless: [ˈæɾɪkt]. However, when we change 'addict' to 'addiction', something new happens (D). Here, the following vowel is *stressed*, and the stop is quite a bit longer than the tap found in 'addict'. Nonetheless, it is usually fully voiced, emerging as a fully-fledged [d]: [əˈdɪkʃən].

And finally, after [s], we only find a [t]-like sound, as in [stɑp˺] (E); there is no lenis–fortis contrast in this context.

There is an important – and, due to our discussion of Corsican, now familiar – generalization we can make about the phonetic properties of the lenis stop. No matter what context it finds itself in, its voicing value is conventionalized in a largely *natural* aerodynamic way, in the sense that it seems to passively conform to the aerodynamic conditions of its surrounding context. So the lenis stop is typically voiceless when the aerodynamic conditions are *not* conducive to vocal fold vibration, and it is typically voiced when the aerodynamic conditions *are* conducive to vocal fold vibration.

The phonetic isotropy of the fortis series

Let's now consider the phonetic properties of the fortis tongue-tip stop, orthographic 't'. We'll see, in fact, that this value is realized in an aerodynamically *un*natural way, in that it does not seem to passively conform to the aerodynamic context in which it is found, but instead opposes itself to the lenis value.

Regarding the fortis value in initial position (A), the glottis is open during the stop, and remains open beyond the stop release. Then, the vocal folds are brought closer together, and voicing begins for the vowel. The result is *aspiration* for the interval between stop release and vowel voicing, as in 'tock', [tʰɑk]. Aspiration may thus be properly characterized as a mere delay – until well after the release of the stop – of vocal fold vibration. That is, instead of the vocal folds immediately coming together for vibration at stop release (which would produce a plain, voiceless stop [t]), their vibration is delayed by keeping them well apart from each other, producing a puff of air, that is, aspiration ([tʰ]).

When the fortis stop occurs before most consonants, and also word-finally (B), it usually takes one of two forms. First, as we discussed way back in Chapter One, this stop may be glottalized and unreleased. It is also usually accompanied by a slightly shortened vowel, as in 'knot'. You might *feel* that the phonetic difference between, say, the words 'nod' and 'knot' is in a voicing distinction between the last consonants ([d]–[t]), because that's what we are taught when we learn to spell. But in actuality, the difference is, to a great extent, in the preceding vowel: the vowel in 'nod' is quite a bit longer than the vowel in 'knot'. So, while a fairly faithful transcription of a typical token of 'nod' might be [nɑd̥], a fairly faithful transcription of 'knot' might be [nɑ̆ˀt̚], the breve indicating a short vowel. If you reflect on your own pronunciation of these words, I think you'll agree that there is a clear contrast in vowel length. This shorter vowel is actually an extremely common concomitant of such voiceless stops, although different languages have different degrees of shortening; the American English case is comparatively pronounced. Some phonologists have suggested that the vowel length difference in this context is a consequence of rhythmic considerations: since voiceless stops are usually longer than voiced stops, their preceding vowel may concomitantly shorten, so that the overall duration of the 'beat' (syllable) is more or less equivalent for both configurations, [ɑd̥] and [ɑ̆ˀt̚]. At any rate, the vowel length distinction surely works *in tandem* with the stop distinction, thus keeping categories phonetically distinct from each other; one cannot be said to *cause* the other.

Alternatively in this context, a glottal stop can take the place of the oral occlusion, also with a shorter vowel, [ɑ̆ʔ]. Now, you might be wondering why two such different articulatory gestures – an oral stop and a glottal stop (for which there is no oral closure at all) – have come to vary with each other. Well, despite their articulatory differences, it turns out that glottal stops and [t] are actually quite similar in acoustic terms, especially when the [t] remains unreleased. When a tongue-tip stop is unreleased, there are no formant transitions into a following sound. Instead, information about the location of the stop resides exclusively in the formant transitions into the stop closure itself. Now, the tongue tip – unlike the tongue body or the lips – is not significantly involved in the formation of vowel sounds, which necessarily involve specific tongue body and lip positions. Consequently, in the context of a vowel which precedes a [t], the tongue tip itself can almost achieve the correct posture for the ensuing stop well before it actually makes contact behind the upper teeth, without having a significant effect on vowel quality. The result is only a very minor change in the shape of the vocal tract as the closure is finally implemented. This means that the formant transitions from the vowel into this oral closure – which, recall, are the only cues to the consonant's place of articulation – are not very pronounced at all. (Certainly, they are far less pronounced than those for tongue body and labial stops. Since both of these articulators are necessarily otherwise engaged during the formation of a preceding vowel, they must markedly shift position during the vowel-to-stop transition, thus inducing more prominent formant transitions.) Because the tongue-tip stops have very minor formant transitions in this context, their acoustic quality mimics those of a glottal stop. Since glottal stops don't make any demands on the lips or tongue at all, they have negligible influence on the formant structure of any neighbouring vowels. So, a [t˺] may be misperceived as a glottal stop, and the two may vary with one another.

Intervocalically before a *stressless* vowel (C) is a particularly poor context for voicing contrasts to be maintained. Stressless domains tend to be quieter and shorter in duration than their stressed counterparts, and also, articulatory gestures tend to be less extreme. Consequently, contrastive configurations have less opportunity to be rendered acoustically distinct from one another, and thus the tendency toward the elimination of phonological distinctions is increased. In most dialects (including mine), the contrast here survives primarily in terms of the preceding vowel length. The fortis-derived tap is preceded by a slightly shorter vowel; the lenis-derived tap a slightly longer one. So we find [ˈfe͡ɪɾɨd̥] 'faded' (from 'fade' [ˈfe͡ɪd̥]) versus [ˈfĕ͡ɪɾɨd̥] 'fated' (from 'fate' [ˈfĕ͡ɪˀt˺]). Indeed, it's no coincidence that the contrastive cues reside away

Table 6.3 Naturalness and unnaturalness in American English alveolar stop alternation

Context	*(A) word-initially*	*(B) before a consonant and word-finally*	*(C) word-internal before an unstressed vowel*	*(D) word-internal before a stressed vowel*	*(E) following [s]*
Lenis 'd'	d̥ / t (natural)	d̥ / t (natural)	ɑ̆ɾ / ɑɾ (natural)	ˈd (natural)	t (natural)
Fortis 't'	t^h (less natural)	ɑ̆^{ʔ}t / ɑ̆ʔ (less natural)	ɑ̆ɾ (natural)	ˈt^h (less natural)	

from the stressless domain, and instead reside in a stressed domain, for, as noted, the loudness and increased duration of stressed elements allows them to encode a greater number of contrastive phonetic cues.

Before a stressed vowel (D), we have what might be regarded as an 'embarrassment of riches' scenario: stressed domains, with their increased energy, duration and articulatory force, allow for maximally distinct values to be readily implemented. So we find a voicing versus aspiration contrast, [dɑ] versus [t^{h}ɑ], as in 'addiction' versus 'atop'.

As already noted, after [s] (E), the fortis–lenis distinction does not exist.

The upshot here is that the American English fortis stop consonants are always implemented in a less natural way than their context-dependent lenis counterparts. But in contexts where it is less likely that contrastive values may be maintained, it may, just like the lenis series, be realized as the tap. Here, neutralization is possible. These results are summarized in Table 6.3.

On the evolution of change

So where has the American English stop system come from, and how has it evolved towards its present-day shape? Alas, we will almost assuredly never know for sure. The existing historical record is frustratingly scanty regarding phonetic descriptions of the stop alternants. Most scholars of English, Germanic (the group of European languages of which English is a member) and Indo-European (the huge family of languages stretching into the Indian sub-continent, of which Germanic is a member) have neglected even to address the paucity of evidence – textual, comparative, or even internal reconstructive – and so the issue remains, perhaps forevermore, unresolved. Nonetheless, internal reconstructive hypotheses might be able to illuminate the issue somewhat.

Before moving on, a warning: it is tempting to assume perfect symmetry in an idealized linguistic past which has been distorted over time into the asymmetries of today. But just as today's asymmetries will be the future's imperfect past, today's past was probably just as imperfect. Although I will assume a degree of symmetry in the distant past, the proposed reconstruction should be construed as an idealized abstraction, and not a solid proposal about the state of the system at a particular point in time. The various context-specific sound changes I will be proposing have probably had their own unique timelines, such that at any given point in history the system was in as much phonetic disarray as it's in today, and as it will be in the future.

(A) Word-initial position

Consider first the word-initial alternants. In this context, at least, the comparative method suggests that the devoiced stop–aspirated stop contrast in English ([d̥]–[t^h]) historically derives from a voiced-voiceless contrast in Germanic (*d–*t; recall that reconstructed historical forms are indicated by an asterisk), which in turn derives from an earlier Indo-European *$d^ɦ$–*d contrast ([$d^ɦ$] is a voiced aspirated stop). So, as phonetically anisotropic forces effected a pull of these word-initial Germanic voiced stops (*d) to a more voiceless realization, then exactly those variant tokens of the Germanic *voiceless* stops (*t) which possessed a slight delay in the onset of voicing were rendered phonetically distinct. In time, the phonetically isotropic variation that allows for a slight degree of aspiration here may have been pushed and pushed towards the conventionalized aspiration that we observe today. Under this proposed scenario, then, the slight voicing that we find in present-day lenis stops (recall, [b̥, d̥, g̊]) may be seen as a relic, or vestige, of the earlier, historical voiced form (*b,*d,*g).

Earlier in this chapter I wrote that *all* common phonological patterns lend themselves to external, real-world explanations which are often rooted in phonetic theory (acoustics, aerodynamics, physiology). But if this is the case, how can we reconcile the phonetic distinction between, say, the Corsican word-initial voiceless stop [t] and the American English devoiced version [d̥]. If all common phonological patterns lend themselves to phonetic explanation, why don't we see, over and over, in language after language, identical phonetic forces creating identical phonetic realizations? Actually, we already have an answer to this question: phonetics is *necessary* but *insufficient* to explain phonological patterns. Recall that speech is conventionalized on a language-specific basis, which is readily understandable under an exemplar-and-probability-matching approach to language structure and language change, but is difficult to reconcile under a purely physiological account of speech variation. Given this, we can never hope to establish a one-to-one mapping between phonetics and phonological patterning. There are always slight mismatches between a pure phonetics and the conventions of phonology, and it is quite remarkable that only rarely are these mismatches striking in their degree. Most phonological patterns do indeed hug quite closely to a realization that a purely phonetic account would predict, and only rarely do we encounter a pattern that has been transmogrified into a genuine phonological curiosity. Any linguist can multiply the number of truly bizarre sound patterns many times, but never will they reach a significant trend: most patterns are naturally adapted to their phonetic conditions, or are a consequence of functional responses to natural phonetic developments affecting another sound, and are mediated by a bewildering array of forces which interact over the ages, some of which we understand, but many of which have yet to be isolated. Indeed, the negligible voicing we observe in the word-initial lenis stop of American English is just that: negligible.

(B) Before a consonant and word-final position

Now consider stops which precede a consonant or are word-final. We have already discussed the fact that the fortis value here is accompanied by a significantly shorter preceding vowel (recall 'nod' [nɑd̥], 'knot' [nɑ̆ˀt̚]), and that such vowel length distinctions are exceedingly common when following stops differ in terms of their voicing value. The problem with this account as applied to American English is that the lenis value is itself largely voiceless! So, if there really *isn't* a voicing distinction in the final consonants, then where does the vowel length distinction come from? I propose, again, that this length contrast is a consequence of the historical forces that have shaped the present-day system: at some point, the present-day lenis stop may have been truly voiced in this position, accompanied by a moderate preceding vowel length distinction between it and its fortis counterpart. Upon phonetically anisotropic diachronic de-voicing of the lenis value, its phonetic quality risked becoming increasingly similar to the voiceless fortis value. Where then might the fortis value be pushed, so as to maintain a healthy phonetic distance from the devoicing lenis value? What may have happened is that the preceding vowel length distinction may have been exapted to serve a more prominent contrastive role: just as devoicing was naturally taking hold among tokens possessing the lenis stop, those tokens of the fortis value that had a slightly shorter preceding vowel duration were more effective at keeping the forms distinct, and came to be conventionalized.

(C) Word-internal before an unstressed vowel

Recall that some dialects maintain a vowel length contrast in the context of a following tap. All the mechanisms are now in place to understand the possible origin of this context-dependent realization. If *t and *d were previously present, the vowel length distinction may have played only a minor role in cueing the contrast. But as the voicing contrast began to yield to tapping, those tokens which maintained (and increased) the vowel length distinction were more readily perceived by listeners as belonging to distinct categories, and so were more readily produced. Perhaps the tapping of both the lenis and fortis stops was tolerated here exactly because the contrast was displaced onto the preceding vowel: the loss of the distinction between the stops themselves was not met with any counterforce, since the contrast was safely shifted to the preceding vowel, and so the two values are now realized in an aerodynamically natural way. As this vowel is stressed – recall, longer and louder than unstressed domains – it is a logical and natural site for the maintenance of contrastive information. Nonetheless, some dialects have lost the contrast altogether, and so words like 'faded' and 'fated' have become homophones. The potential for neutralization is far greater when phonetic conditions do not permit sufficient variation between tokens of phonetically similar contrastive sounds.

(D) Word-internal before a stressed vowel

As already suggested, the increased energy and duration of stressed domains make it more likely that contrasts will disperse themselves more widely in the available acoustic space, and/or may allow for a greater number of contrasts. This is especially true for consonants which are immediately followed by vowels, because consonant releases, as we know, provide increases in acoustic energy which are auditorily salient. In this context then, we find perfectly natural voicing for the lenis value and quite unnatural aspiration for the fortis value, which are actually at opposite extremes of the voicing continuum: voiced stops have very early voicing onset, while aspirated stops have very late voicing onset. So, in stressed domains, before vowels, there is ample opportunity for beneficial variants of distinct contrastive sounds to be produced, and, in turn, be perceived by listeners. In other words, exactly because these consonants are in stressed domains, and because they are released into vowels, we find both a greater phonetic divergence between contrastive sounds, and also far less of a tendency toward sound substitutions that are potentially neutralizing.

(E) Following [s]

After [s], the fortis–lenis distinction does not exist. It is certainly not impossible for an aspiration contrast to exist after s-stop sequences. Two lines of linguistic evidence prove this. First, a few languages indeed have an [st]–[stʰ] contrast, Sanskrit having been an example. Second, English speakers may produce [stʰ] across word boundaries, or, rarely, when certain morphemes come together, for example 'mistook' may readily be pronounced [mɪstʰʊk]. So why is this pattern never found *contrastively* in English?

First, recall from Chapter One that morpheme-internal articulatory routines are the most common, across-morpheme boundary routines are less common, and across-*word* boundary routines are less common again. Some phonologists have proposed that articulatory routines which are more frequent may be more susceptible to simplification over time. So, even if a language somehow evolved words with initial [s]-aspirated stop sequences (for example, #[stʰ]), these may more readily succumb to the loss of aspiration than those [s]-aspirated stop clusters which are divided by morpheme boundaries ([s]+[tʰ]), which, in turn, may be more susceptible to the loss of aspiration than those [s]-aspirated stop clusters which are divided by *word* boundaries ([s]#[tʰ]). In time, no aspiration contrast may remain in the word-internal condition. These proposals are summarized and exemplified in Table 6.4. (We explore the motivation for these sorts of articulatory simplifications due to frequency of usage in Chapter Seven.)

Second, [s] requires a wide-open glottis so that a strong flow of air can generate sufficient turbulence at the constriction sites. The noise that is characteristic of [s] is actually rather similar to that which

Table 6.4 Frequency and simplification in English

Across a word boundary	*Across a word-internal morpheme boundary*	*Within a morpheme*
Least common; least likely to lose aspiration Always [stʰ] ('miss Tom') [mɪs'tʰɑm]	More common; more likely to lose aspiration Usually [st]; occasionally [stʰ] ('mistook') [mɪstʊk] [mɪs'tʰʊk]	Most common; most likely to lose aspiration Always [st] ('mysterious') [mɪs'tiɹijɨs]

accompanies aspiration, which, of course, also involves a wide-open glottis. Consequently it is probably not so easy to reliably distinguish [st] from [st^h] in running speech, and languages may tend to eliminate this contrast should it arise, especially when within a word, rather than between words.

An exemplar-and-probability-matching approach to word-initial tongue-tip stops in American English

I've so far suggested that phonetically natural aerodynamic forces may have effected changes in the realization of the lenis value, from a historic *voiced value to the present-day devoiced realization. But how might these phonetic and cognitive forces have diachronically interacted to produce the proposed sound changes?

In the past, younger generations may have largely matched the *voiced category variations present in preceding generations, although all the while there existed phonetically anisotropic variation in the direction of an increased number of devoiced productions. So, probabilities may have been largely matched, but still, devoicing was gaining ground. Specifically, among elders' *voiced category tokens (see (a) in Figure 6.1), phonetically voiced tokens are communicated as such to learners, and thus learners add them to their pool of *voiced tokens, reinforcing the voicing of this category. Devoiced tokens fall into two subcategories. One subcategory consists of what the linguist William Labov calls *supported* tokens, which, despite consisting of phonetically devoiced tokens, are nonetheless disambiguated with grammatical or real-world information; this provides 'support' in conveying the semantic intentions of the speaker. These tokens are thus pooled with the *voiced category (b). As learners' productions match their calculated probabilities, these devoiced *voiced tokens serve to tug the *voiced category towards an increasingly devoiced state. The other subcategory of devoiced tokens leaves learners in the dark: without 'support', such tokens cannot be added to the pool of *voiced tokens (c). All these tokens may be factored out of the pool over which voicing probabilities are matched within the *voiced category. Even though there is a naturally-induced devoicing in progress, the effect of these factored-out tokens is to slow the rate of change toward the voiceless state. The pool of reliably interpreted *voiced tokens is smaller for learners than for elders, and so the percentage of phonetically voiced *voiced tokens is greater for learners than for elders. In the flowchart, bold cells highlight those token types which effect the *change* toward a devoiced state, whereas the non-bold cells contain those forces that serve to maintain voicing.

Consider how such a gradual devoicing of the proposed historical English word-initial *voiced series may have affected the proposed

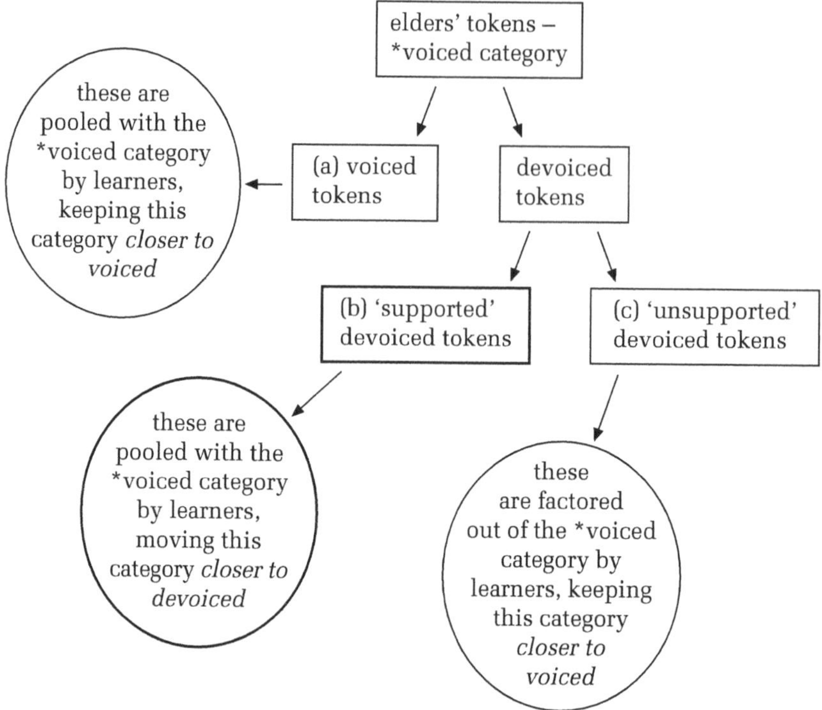

Figure 6.1 Phonetically anisotropic variation in American English word-initial *voiced stops may have led to this series' devoicing

historical word-initial *devoiced series. As the *devoiced series also engaged in variations that were largely matched from generation to generation, we might first conjecture that the end result would be a sound merger: as *voiced stops devoiced, they would ultimately merge with the other series. But this is not what we find, of course. Instead, just as phonetically isotropic variation may have led to devoicing in the *voiced series, selectional pressures on certain phonetically anisotropic variants within the *devoiced series may have led to an overall movement toward aspiration. Specifically, those *devoiced variants in which the onset of vocal fold vibration was slightly delayed came to be functionally beneficial as the *voiced series began to creep towards voicelessness: exactly those stray variant tokens that were more distinct from the increasingly devoiced *voiced series were successful in cueing lexical distinctions to learners. Learners, interpreting the signal unambiguously in such contexts, were more likely to reproduce these forms in their own speech. Consequently, such stray tokens served to promote the shift toward the aspirated state.

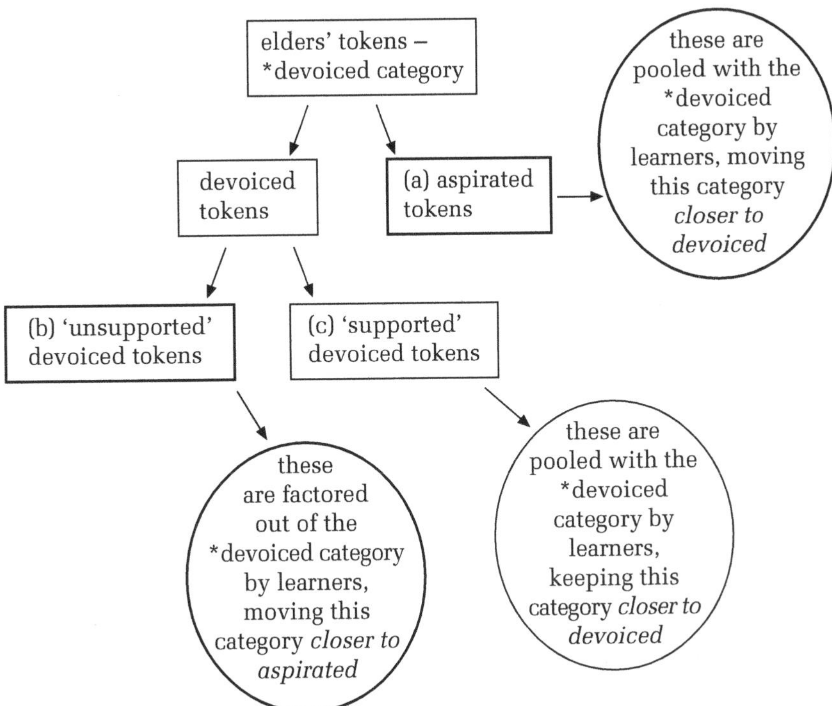

Figure 6.2 Phonetically isotropic variation in American English word-initial *devoiced stops: selectional pressures may have led this series toward an aspirated state

That is, because phonetically *in*distinct forms – being more likely misinterpreted by listeners – were factored out of the pool of relevant tokens, then those token variants that provided a clear phonetic contrast between phonologically distinct forms – due to the higher estimated probability of their occurrence – were produced more often as these listeners became speakers. In short, it is the communicative success of unambiguous tokens that might have pushed the *devoiced series toward its present-day aspirated state. In Figure 6.2, again, bold cells highlight the direction of change.

Phonetically aspirated tokens (a) will be communicated successfully to listeners, since these are robustly distinct from *voiced words. Some devoiced tokens (b) will be unsupported, and possibly thrown out of the overall pool of *devoiced tokens. This results in an overestimation of aspirated forms, so these tokens too will assist the change to the aspirated state. Finally, supported devoiced tokens (c) will be interpreted as *devoiced. These tokens serve to inhibit the change towards aspiration. In time, the speech conventions of the language may have changed such that previously devoiced word-initial stops have evolved toward an aspirated state.

The theory of internal reconstruction is based on an extremely bold yet compelling assertion: the present holds the key to the past. Sounds in alternation in the present, which undergo quantum leaps of change in phonetic quality as they shift from context to context, have evolved in the absence of the user who comes to possess them. Instead, they may be seen as the long-term result of a gradual, token-to-token, generation-to-generation creep: *Natura non facit saltum*, 'nature makes no leaps'. Keeping this dictum in mind, we can now consider a hypothetical schematic timetable which captures the main forces argued to be at work in the diachrony of American English word-initial stops. For the sake of simplicity, I ignore many sorts of intermediate variants, wild strays, and so on; Figure 6.3 is just a schematic.

As in our scenario for Trique in Chapter Five, let's keep the numbers simple. Let's first say that the word-initial *voiced value is slowly creeping toward a devoiced state at a rate of 3 per cent per generation, due to natural aerodynamic forces. Entering the sound change midstream, we take a 1000 token sample from Generation W's *voiced

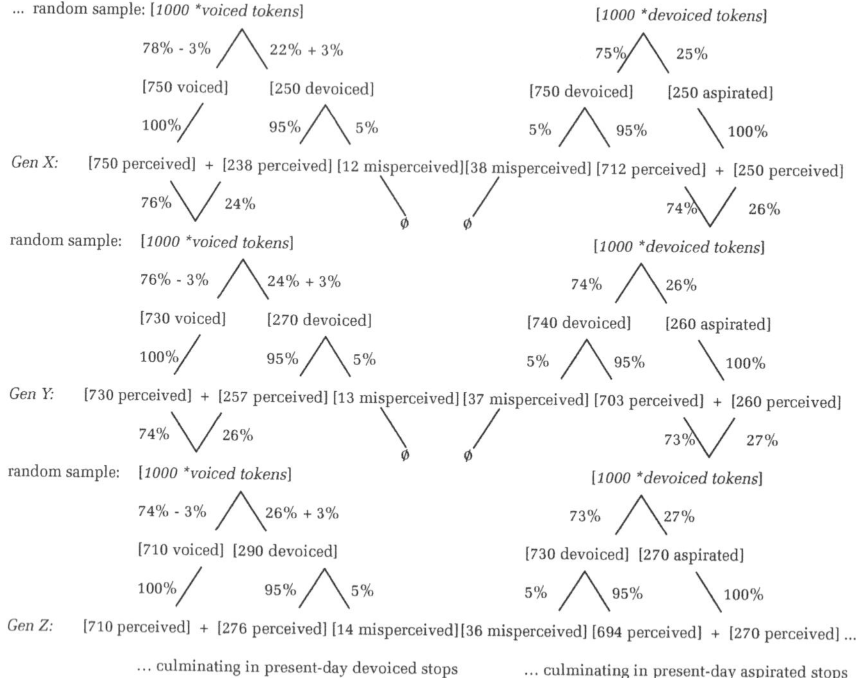

Figure 6.3 Hypothetical diachrony of the lenis and fortis values

tokens. Of these tokens, 750 are phonetically voiced, while 250 are phonetically devoiced. All the voiced tokens are transmitted successfully to the listeners of Generation X, because they are robustly distinct from the contrastive *devoiced stop. Of the phonetically devoiced tokens, let's assume that 95 per cent of them (238) are 'supported', and thus pooled with the lenis category; 5 per cent (12 tokens) are misperceived, and not pooled (some of these may be misperceived as belonging to the fortis category, but for simplicity's sake, let's assume that they are all thrown out). Combining the 750 phonetically voiced tokens and the 238 supported phonetically devoiced tokens gives us 988 *voiced tokens, 76 per cent of which are phonetically voiced, and 24 per cent of which are phonetically devoiced. These are the probabilities that Generation X will match in their own productions.

Now we iterate the process with another random sample of 1000 tokens. Again allowing for a 3 per cent drift towards devoicing in the *voiced series, Generation X produces 730 phonetically voiced tokens, and 270 phonetically devoiced tokens, 5 per cent of which are unsupported. This yields 987 tokens perceived as *voiced, 74 per cent of which are voiced. As the generations proceed, slowly, slowly, the *voiced category may undergo a sound change from voiced to devoiced.

But while all this is going on with the *voiced stop, what is happening to the *devoiced stop? For the sake of argument, let's suppose that this stop is also at a stage in which 75 per cent of the tokens are phonetically devoiced (750 out of a random sample of 1000), and 25 per cent are phonetically aspirated. All these aspirated tokens will be transmitted successfully to Generation X listeners, because they are robustly distinct from the contrastive *voiced stop. Let's again suppose that 5 per cent (38) of the phonetically devoiced tokens are 'unsupported', and so thrown out of the *devoiced category. This leaves 712 phonetically devoiced tokens, pooled with the 250 phonetically aspirated tokens, perceived by Generation X as belonging to the *devoiced category. Now Generation X matches the probability of perceived occurrence, producing 74 per cent (deriving from 712 perceived out of 967) phonetically devoiced realizations, and 26 per cent (deriving from 250 perceived out of 967) phonetically aspirated realizations. And so the process continues.

So, once again, just as with Trique, this scenario demonstrates how very minor phonetic tendencies, coupled with the ambiguities they might induce or eschew, may eventually have far-reaching consequences for the phonological system. In word-initial position, where stop releases allow for a wide array of phonetic modifications, there is ample opportunity for the two categories to maintain a healthy acoustic distance from each other. The lenis–fortis contrast survives, but has taken on new phonetic characteristics.

Concluding discussion

Due to the inherent variability of speech production, and selectional pressures acting upon this variation, phonological systems evolve in fulfilment of their communicative function. It is the adaptation of a contrastive value to its context, and its subsequent survival as a functionally beneficial component of the communicative system, which is responsible for allophonic patterns, both in American English today and throughout the languages of the world. In contexts where the extent of phonetic variation is limited – that is, in stressless domains which are shorter and quieter than stressed domains, or when a consonant precedes another consonant and so lacks an audible release, or after [s], which necessarily possesses spread vocal folds – it is more likely that overall similar sounds will succumb to a loss of their distinctive properties and potentially neutralize or merge.

I want to emphasize that I have only presented in any detail a simplified analysis of a single, tiny corner of the sound system of American English: stops made with the tongue tip that appear in word-initial position. But there are more stops, more contexts, and more consonants, and more vowels to consider as well, each appearing in a variety of contexts, and each subject to a hugely complicated array of phonetic, functional, cognitive and social pressures that interact over generations of speakers for any given speech community. To say that we have only scratched the surface of the problem is a gross understatement indeed!

In Chapter One I argued that no phonological system should be significantly more difficult to master than any other, regardless of its complexity. And indeed, phonology is acquired at more or less the same rate by all children, regardless of the language(s) to which they are exposed. The more complex the system, the more *evidence* of this complexity the learner is exposed to. I have also argued, in Chapter Four, that phonetic similarity plays very little role in the determination of allophonic relatedness. Instead, what counts is the *functional* identity or non-identity of phonetically distinct values, due to the presence or absence of alternations. When sounds alternate with each other, regardless of their phonetic qualities, this constitutes evidence to learners that they are allophonically related. Alternating elements are set into high relief against their stable phonetic backgrounds. It is these components of the sound system that might come to be individuated by learners, such that they can be recycled as necessary to comprehend and produce novel forms. When sounds do not alternate with each other, again, regardless of their phonetic similarities, learners have no evidence that they are allophonically related, and the assumption that such non-alternating components of the speech stream are individuated by learners is unwarranted. The sizes and shapes of the individuated linguistic elements, then, are not necessarily cross-linguistically regular, but are instead based on the size and shape of the alternating components themselves. In Chapter Five I proposed that variants of words which are more distinct from other words have a greater tendency to be perceived with the meaning intended by the speaker, and so have a greater tendency to be produced as listeners become speakers. Consequently, allophonic alternants arise as a consequence of speakers matching the variation they perceive in the speech signal. I also suggested that variants that are sufficiently similar to each other have the opportunity to be interpreted correctly; grossly outlandish strays may be regarded as speech errors, to be ignored or laughed at as mere mistakes. In part for these reasons – and also because phonetic pressures may continually, though slowly, exert pressure on patterns to conform with phonetic naturalness – even as allophonic values slowly evolve over generations of speakers, they tend to maintain a fair degree of phonetic similarity to each other. We may consequently assert that any phonetic similarity between alternants is mostly an accident of history, and has no principled standing in either our theories of phonology or in the minds of language learners: phonetically similar alternants are not highly valued at the cognitive level. Rather, they are simply the emergent consequence of the incidental – though overwhelmingly powerful – pressures affecting the way sounds change over time.

So consider a set-theoretic display of the allophones we have been considering in this section on American English, provided in Figure 6.4. For ease of exposition, I'll present the pattern from those dialects which do not maintain the 'faded'–'fated' vowel length distinction; 'V' refers to any vowel quality.

Now consider a hypothetical system with the exact same relations between elements, except that the elements themselves are completely unrelated to one another in phonetic terms, as shown in Figure 6.5. I'll just use the alphabet to suggest the phonetic unrelatedness between the elements.

This second system is an improbable sound system *not* because of anything intrinsic to the phonetic unrelatedness of its alternating forms, but primarily because of the extrinsic factors that have given rise to them: the system does not make palaeophonetic sense. These sorts of systems should be only rarely encountered, as indeed they are.

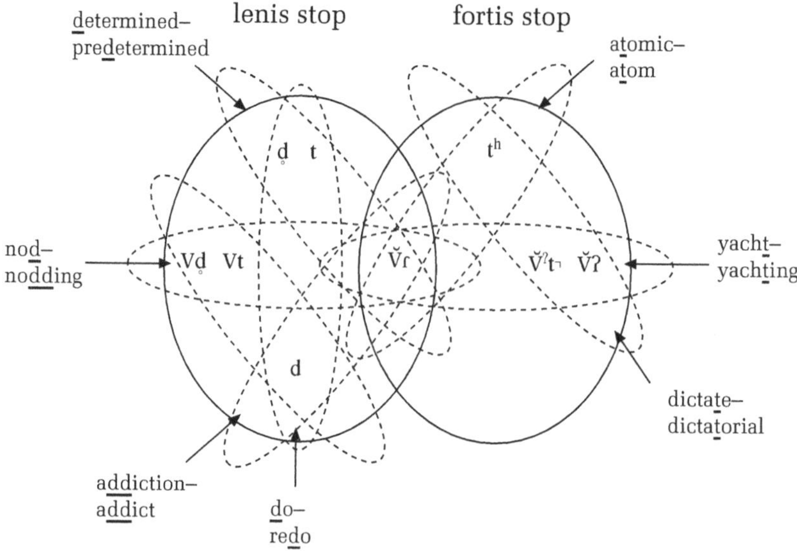

Figure 6.4 Set-theoretic display of alveolar stop alternation in American English

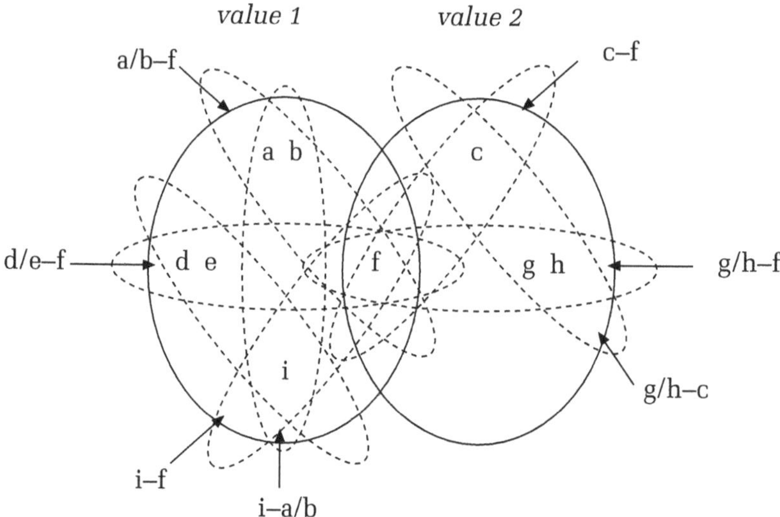

Figure 6.5 Hypothetical system with the exact same relations between elements, except that the elements themselves are phonetically dissimilar

In contrast to the richly articulated data array which provides learners with sufficient information to master allophonic relations within the stop system, consider finally the New York English [æ̝ə̯]–[æ] contrast in Figure 6.6, which we discussed at length in Chapter Four.

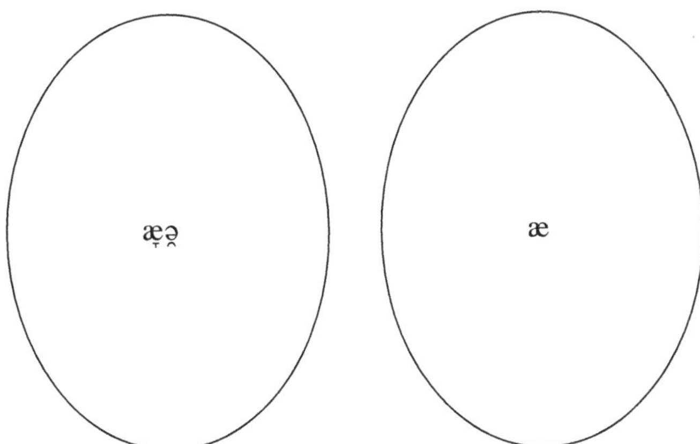

Figure 6.6 The complementary distribution of [æ̝ə̝] and [æ]: neat, simple, but functionally inert

Despite the simplicity of this subsystem, despite the phonetic similarity of its members, and despite the fact that these two elements happen to be in complementary distribution, there is no evidence that any sort of allophonic relationship exists here, since the two sounds do not alternate with each other.

And what of the future of English? This cannot be predicted, of course. But who knows? Perhaps, soon enough, it will be the fortis series' turn to succumb to phonetic pressures, and, for example, the word-initial fortis value will begin a creep back to an unaspirated state while the lenis value gets pushed back towards a voiced state. The linguist Charles Hockett entertained the first component of such a future scenario in his 1958 book:

> [If] some speaker of English, over a period of years, were to hear a relatively large number of initial /t/'s with unusually inconspicuous aspiration ... the location of the frequency maximum would drift, and his own speech would undergo the same modification. We would not, of course, expect any *single* speaker of English to have such an experience. In general, individuals who are in constant communication with each other will experience essentially parallel changes in their ... articulatory habits. It is just this sort of slow drifting about of ... distributions, shared by people who are in constant communication, that we mean to subsume under the term 'sound change'.

Language is not moving towards a perfected state; cyclic changes, due to ever-changing conditions of language use and disuse – some of which we understand, some of which we don't – are always well within the realm of possibility. As Leonard Bloomfield wrote in 1933, 'The favoring of variants which lead to sound change is a historical occurrence; once it is past, we have no guarantee of its happening again. A later process may end by favoring the very same acoustic types as were eliminated by an earlier change.'

Just as Charles Darwin's theory of evolution explores the circumstances under which variation leads either to species' survival (through individual organisms' adaptation to environmental conditions) or species' extinction (through individual organisms' failure to compete successfully for environmental resources), so too do the contrastive sounds in phonology survive or disappear as a consequence of their success at maintaining their contrastive status in varying contexts, and through their continued use. Either a contrastive value survives in a particular context (through individual tokens being successfully communicated from speaker to listener), or it is extinguished in a particular context (through individual tokens failing to be successfully communicated from speaker to listener). Expressed in this fashion, I have argued that phonological patterns are the emergent, self-organized consequence of phonetic and cognitive pressures that diachronically interact. I have shown why an alternation is either allophonic or neutralizing, and moreover I have shown that there are principled reasons for the phonetic direction toward which a given alternant will be drawn. Even when phonetically unnatural and superficially counter-functional, alternations may still be seen as the long-term product of small, local and perfectly natural processes that play themselves out over generations of speakers.

And how new are these ideas to the field of linguistics? Well, in 1895 Baudouin de Courtenay compiled a list of characteristic features of phonological alternations. I quote three of them here, prefaced by a succinct summary (italics are in the original). The terminology is a tad ornate at times, but the ideas shine through brightly.

> The complexity and causes accounting for the emergence and preservation of alternations must ultimately be ascribed to communal life and the physical (anatomico-physiological) and psychological make-up of the members of a speech community.
>
> –*At any given stage of a language, the cause of the phonetic alternation lies only in tradition (transmission), in social intercourse, in usage.* We have learned to speak in a certain way from our environment and our ancestors; such an explanation is completely sufficient.
> –*The anthropophonic causes of an alternation, its anthropophonic causal connections, lie in the history of the language and can be established only through historical-linguistic studies.* At one

time an anthropophonic cause was at work, but later it ceased to operate, and is now absent.
–*The degree of phonetic similarity of the alternating phonemes in such cases is completely immaterial*. It is only necessary that there be a psychophonetic association of the representations of particular anthropophonetic activities with the corresponding psychological distinctions.

Further reading

On spirantization and allophony:
Gurevich, Naomi (2004). *Lenition and Contrast: The Functional Consequences of Certain Phonetically Conditioned Sound Changes*. New York: Routledge.

The Hockett quote ('*[If] some speaker of English* ...'):
Hockett, Charles (1958). *A Course in Modern Linguistics*. New York: Macmillan, p. 443.

The Bloomfield quote ('*The favoring of variants* ...'):
Bloomfield, Leonard (1933). *Language*. London: George Allen and Unwin, p. 308.

The Baudouin de Courtenay quote ('*The complexity and causes* ...'):
Baudouin de Courtenay, Jan (1895 [1972]). 'An attempt at a theory of phonetic alternations', in Edward Stankiewicz (ed.), *A Baudouin de Courtenay Reader*. Bloomington: Indiana University Press, pp. 160 and 180–81.

Part 3
I speak therefore you are

7 *Parlo ergo es*

In a paper published in 1911, Etienne Lombard reported on a series of experiments in which he found that subjects increase the volume of their voice when the ambient noise level increases. This result has come to be known in some circles as the *Lombard Effect*. There have been a number of ways that the Lombard Effect has been interpreted. One straightforward interpretation is that the effect is an inherently *social* phenomenon: speakers maintain a speech-to-noise ratio that is favourable to communication, because if they don't, listeners might not hear them accurately. This can be interpreted as a form of *altruism* on the part of speakers, in that they want to ease the burden of their interlocutors. However, it can just as readily be interpreted as *selfish* in motivation: speakers want to effectively get their ideas across so that their own needs might be satisfied. Either way, however, this *social* interpretation of the Lombard Effect assumes that speakers are making use of a *public* feedback loop, requiring feedback from *listeners* in order to adjust their own speaking volume.

But Lombard also found that when speakers' ability to monitor their *own* speech is diminished (by, say, wearing earplugs), they also raise their voices. This suggests that the sound of one's own voice (called the *sidetone*) might be necessary in order to properly regulate its volume, and so there is not necessarily an inherent social dimension to the voice adjustment. Instead, the feedback loop may be wholly internal, or *private*, which is consistent with a *solipsistic* interpretation of the Lombard Effect. That is, speakers are not solely responding to feedback from the outside world, but instead their behaviour is a consequence of self-monitoring. These three interpretations are tabulated in Figure 7.1.

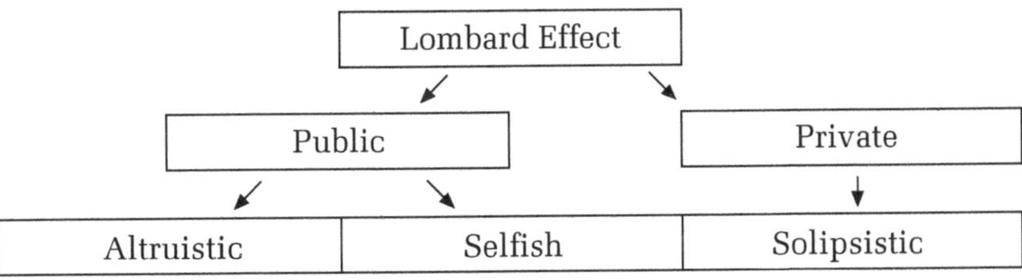

Figure 7.1 Three interpretations of the Lombard Effect

Altruism, selfishness and, more generally, speakers' *intentions* have sometimes been invoked to account not only for the Lombard Effect, but also for phonological patterns in general. In this chapter I investigate only one example each of 'altruistic' and 'selfish' approaches to phonology that have been explored in the literature, which are indeed characteristic – or, rather, symptomatic – of broad schools of linguistic thought. Unlike the Lombard Effect though, these effects aren't presumed to hold only under abnormal conditions. Instead, they are assumed to be fully active under normal conditions, in the sense that our mastery of language is claimed to be due to active mental processes of a broadly 'altruistic' and/or 'selfish' nature; an assumption I reject. I will suggest that any approach to phonological structure which makes reference to speakers' supposed *intentions* should be regarded with suspicion.

Most of these approaches, indeed most current phonological models in general, have their origins in Sapir's highly influential paper of 1933 on the supposed 'psychological reality of the phoneme'. (Recall from Chapter One that John Whitney's 'feeling a "t"' supposedly reflected an abstract element for which there was no phonetic evidence: the phoneme.) For adherents of Sapir's approach (fleshed out most fully by the linguists Noam Chomsky and Morris Halle in their book from 1968), alternants *derive* from a *single* underlying element, or phoneme. The underlying (or 'input') value *turns into* another value (or 'output value') as a consequence of a system of phonological rules or constraints. To take an example, adherents to this school of thought assume – arbitrarily, by most standards – that in cases of spirantization it is the stop that is underlyingly present (by convention, surrounded by slashes, as in Figure 7.2), and that this stop becomes a fricative in the relevant context, but stays a stop in others. For adherents to the Sapir/Chomsky and Halle approach, then, the various alternants derive from a single psychological entity – the phoneme – which takes on new phonetic characteristics depending on its context.

This approach is very different from the one presented in this book. The difference hinges on my contention that *functional non-distinctness is not the same as identity of mental origin.* In the present approach, I have been capturing the functional non-distinctness of

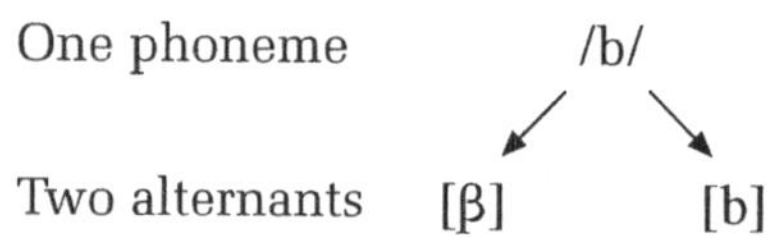

Figure 7.2 Two alternants derived from a single value

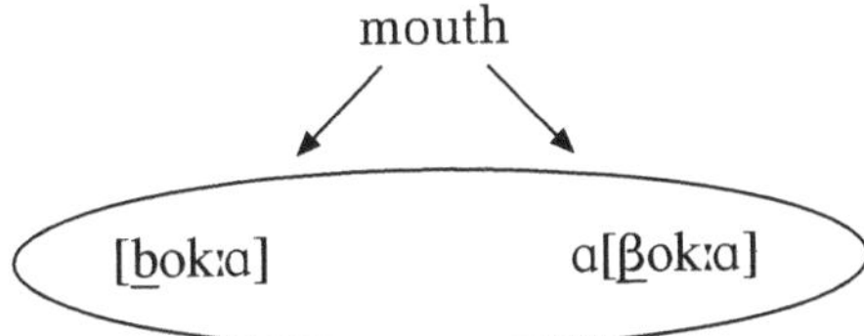

Figure 7.3 Two alternants whose functional identity is established due to their alternation

allophonic alternants with set notation: components of morphemes that alternate with each other emerge as functionally non-distinct. So recall an example from Corsican (see Figure 7.3).

In Corsican, there are (at least) two forms of the same word – [b̠ok:ɑ] and (ɑ)[β̠ok:ɑ]. As learners come to realize that these two forms have the same meaning, the phonetic differences between them are set into high relief against the stable phonetic background, and the functional non-distinctness between the two forms is established. Each allomorph – and so each allo*phone* – is as psychologically 'legitimate' or 'authentic' as the other, and so neither has a more privileged mental status. Learners *do not* conclude that the [b] and [β] are actually derived from the same underlying building block, that is /b/, simply because there is no evidence available that would prompt them to arrive at such a conclusion.

Revisiting elements of our discussion in Chapter Two, in this chapter I suggest that the phonemic approach to phonology can trace its origins to so-called 'alphabetism': because most linguists have been trained in an alphabetic orthography, their intuitions tell them that phonology is organized in accordance with alphabetic/phonemic principles. As will be shown, the uncontroversial mismatch between 'phonemism' and the actual phonetic content of the speech signal has required the 'phonemists' to posit a multi-levelled phonology. One level, the 'underlying level' is phonemic in organization, while an additional level captures the superficial aspects of speech production. The phonemists focus their energies on uncovering the psychological route from the underlying string of phonemes to the superficial content of the speech signal.

In this chapter I suggest that, because of its multi-levelled characterization of phonology, the phonemic approach often demands a conflation of synchrony and diachrony, and also a conflation of phonetics and cognition. It further requires positing a dichotomy between speakers' *intentions* and speakers' *performance*. I reject this position in its entirety.

I conclude by reiterating that phonology is best characterized as a self-organized system of substantive social conventions which evolves passively over generations of speakers. The regularities we observe in phonological systems are due to a complex interaction of phonetic and cognitive pressures acting over generations and generations of language use, and can be understood only when considering the communicative function of language itself. Hence, *parlo ergo es* 'I speak, therefore you are'.

Ease of perception

At least since the nineteenth century, linguists have entertained the proposal that phonological patterns may be influenced by a 'struggle' between two opposing forces, *ease of perception* and *ease of production*. Indeed, variants of this view have persisted in some theoretical circles up to the present day, and into the pages of this book. Regarding ease of perception, I have been providing evidence all along that the acoustic dispersion of contrastive sounds, and the acoustic quality of the transition from one articulatory posture to the next, are slowly and passively influenced by phonetic and functional pressures on speech variants that render communication *successful*. In a related way, allophonic alternations may be seen as the passive, long-term result of these same sorts of selectional pressures. The result is that linguistic signals are quite easy to perceive, but this is not due to the *intentions*, conscious or otherwise, of individual speakers.

Are speakers 'altruistic'?

Although few would deny that phonological systems are inherently easy to perceive by their possessors, the *origin* or *locus* of this inherent property is not fully agreed upon. While I have been providing evidence for a *diachronic* origin and an inherently *social* locus of this property of language, at least some researchers have placed the locus elsewhere: square in the lap of individual speakers. Consider an example case. In a paper from 2002, the linguist John Kingston discussed a well-known property of contrastively nasalized low vowels (for example, [ɑ̃]): these vowels tend to have *more* nasalization (in the form of a more significantly lowered soft palate) than do mid or high nasalized vowels. The greater degree of nasalization here is probably related to the fact that *most* low vowels have some degree of soft palate lowering, even those that are not contrastively nasalized. Although not fully understood, this soft palate lowering may be an automatic articulatory concomitant of implementing a low vowel: soft palate lowering correlates positively with the jaw lowering necessary to implement a low vowel. Consequently, if a language is to possess a *contrast* in nasality on its low vowels (such as [ɑ]–[ɑ̃]), then the nasalized form needs to be *especially* nasalized, in the form of *increased* soft palate lowering, so that it is rendered distinct from its oral counterpart.

Readers of Chapters Five and Six know that all the components – speech variation, exemplar theory, probability matching – are in place to understand the diachronic origins of this pattern. Kingston, however, places the locus of this mechanism elsewhere: '[S]peakers exert themselves to convey contrasts in ways that are entirely unexpected if they couldn't optimize their pronunciations to ensure that contrasts are maintained.' He concludes that 'Speakers must be altruists.'

This approach raises several questions. First, should we assume that speakers are being specifically *altruistic*? As noted in our discussion of the Lombard Effect, any 'exertion' on the part of speakers to render speech in a perspicuous fashion may just as readily be interpreted as *selfish* in origin, and not altruistic. Speakers may find that *not* exerting themselves while speaking does not get them what they want. Consequently, they may exert themselves to speak clearly in order to satisfy their own needs. Of course, this interpretation of the facts of speech is just as suspect as an altruistic one, but it does point to the arbitrary nature of Kingston's proposal. Perhaps, under the deepest genetic reading of the term, speakers may be regarded as altruistic in some sense, since linguistic evolution has *passively* resulted in a system of communication that is beneficial to listeners, much as genuine natural selection may have imbued the proper genetic material to produce certain altruistic behaviours in animals. However, in the synchronic sense suggested by Kingston – who, recall, suggests that speakers 'exert themselves' – speakers are far from altruistic. They are simply reproducing what they perceive.

But Kingston's synchronic, speaker-based locus of his proposed mechanism begs more fundamental questions. First, if one does not consider the *evolution* of such patterns, the extra soft palate lowering on low nasalized vowels is indeed 'entirely unexpected' unless speakers 'ensure' their speech is easier for listeners to interpret clearly. But it's not clear why a pattern that has *diachronically* evolved to a particular state should be accounted for in *synchronic* terms. When diachrony is taken into account, the pattern isn't 'entirely unexpected' at all. In fact, it makes perfect, natural sense.

Second, once speakers are – by any reasonable description of the facts – *faithfully reproducing* the speech patterns they encounter, why would they need to apply an overlay of altruistic intent to 'optimize their pronunciations so that contrasts are maintained'? Each speaker is *not* determining anew the articulatory configuration that might assist a listener (a listener who may have just been 'assisting' this very speaker, by the way!) in recovering the contrastive sounds of the language. Rather, all speakers who *implement* their low nasalized vowels with a greater degree of soft palate lowering have always *heard* these nasalized vowels with a greater degree of soft palate lowering. So again, speakers are simply reproducing what they hear.

Third, if we assume that certain aspects of phonological systems have their origins in an altruistic intent on the part of speakers, we must further assume a non-altruistic component of phonology as well, that is, a component of speech that is not a result of speakers' 'exerting themselves' to speak more clearly. But since speakers *copy* the very speech patterns that they hear, and they do so remarkably accurately, where would the evidence lie – both for the speaker and for the linguist – that speech patterns are indeed divisible along altruistic and non-altruistic lines?

As I remarked in Chapter Three, and have elaborated upon in subsequent discussion, present-day phonological patterns result from a dizzyingly complex and long-term interaction of articulatory, acoustic, auditory, aerodynamic, perceptual, functional and social forces, and it's facile to assume that the explanation for present-day phonetic and phonological patterns reduces to present-day factors. By failing to consider the evolution-like selectional pressures that give rise to speech patterns, and instead placing a synchronic altruistic burden on individual speakers, Kingston is playing an unwinnable guessing game about speakers' mental states. Hermann Paul, considering this sort of proposal in 1880, wrote, '[T]here is no such thing as a conscious effort made to prevent a sound change. For those who are affected by the change have no suspicion that there is anything to guard against, and they habitually pass their lives in the belief that they speak today as they spoke years ago, and that they will continue to the end to speak in the same way.' If we replace the word 'conscious' with 'unconscious' (which is no doubt the psychological level at which Kingston intends his 'altruism' to be operating), Paul's remark serves as a befitting rejoinder to Kingston's proposals of over a century later.

In sum, phonological systems are indeed organized such that they are easy to perceive by their possessors, but speakers, to put it starkly, are no more altruistic than are foraging rats and ducks.

Ease of production

In addition to phonological systems being organized such that they are easy to perceive, many linguists have also argued that phonological systems are organized such that they are *easy to produce*. In her 2001 book, the linguist Joan Bybee makes use of this notion when she observes a link between the *frequency of usage* and the *tendency to simplify speech patterns*. As in the present approach, Bybee argues that linguistic categories emerge as a consequence of patterns' use and re-use. According to Bybee, if sound changes are the result of phonetic processes that apply as a consequence of actual language use, then those words that are used more frequently are more likely to undergo phonetic simplifications. She provides many case studies – mostly from English and Spanish – illustrating how sound changes that simplify speech patterns may begin with words and phrases of the highest frequency, and then may gradually come to influence the pronunciation of other, less frequently employed items. For example, frequent words like 'camera' and 'every' have lost their second vowels ([ˈk^{h}æmɹə], [ˈɛvɹi]), whereas less common words with comparable structure retain these vowels: 'mammary', 'homily' ([ˈmæmə̲ɹi], [ˈhɑmə̲li]).

Bybee's research has its origins in the proposals of the nineteenth-century scholar Hugo Schuchardt. In his monograph of 1885, Schuchardt considered a number of examples of articulatory simplification in frequent words such as titles and greetings. For example, Hungarian *alazatos szolgája* (a greeting like 'your servant') has become *alá szolgáj*, Spanish *vuestra merced* has become *usted* ('you'), and German *guten Morgen* is often *g'Morgen* ('good morning'). He offered the following account of such simplifications:

> The change of a sound, its progress in a certain direction ... consists of the sum of microscopic displacements. It is therefore dependent upon the number of repetitions. If *x* requires 10,000 repetitions to become *x'*, these repetitions are to be counted within individual words, nevertheless. An *x* spoken one time each in 10,000 different words would not become *x'*. I will not deny that a word that has been spoken 10,000 times can favor the development of the sound *x* to *x'* in a word spoken only 8000 times, etc. The greater or lesser frequency in the use of individual words ... is ... of great importance for their phonetic transformation ... Rarely-used words drag behind; very frequently used ones hurry ahead ... They have been compared to small coins that, as they pass from hand to hand rapidly, are soon worn thin.

In other words, frequent words may lead the way in a simplifying sound change, and due to their lead, increasingly less frequent words may be recruited in this simplification as well. Indeed, in our discussion of Trique in Chapter Five, we considered how passive pressures toward homophone avoidance may trigger individual words to undergo pioneering changes, and may, in turn, induce other words to follow.

I should note, however, that 'ease of production' is not the same as 'simplicity of production'. With repetitive use, the words 'mountain' and 'Trenton' may *simplify* from [ˈmæ̃ᶷnˌtʰɨn] and [ˈtɹ̥ɛ̃nˌtʰɨn] to [ˈmæ̃ᶷʔn̩] and [ˈtɹ̥ɛ̃ʔn̩]. But these latter pronunciations might not be *easier* to produce; just ask a non-native speaker of English to pronounce both variants, and see what happens!

At a presentation in 2002, the linguist Mark Hale criticized, or more properly, *parodied* the Schuchardt/Bybee approach to the relationship between frequency and simplification with the expression 'practice makes imperfect': while piano players, for example, get *better and better* at their chosen task as they repeat and repeat the proper movements, language users, according to the parody, actually get *worse and worse*, since, according to Hale's characterization of the Schuchardt/Bybee approach, they become less and less adept at implementing all the necessary speech sounds. Hence, practice makes imperfect.

However, Hale does not consider the possibility that *exactly because* certain words are frequently encountered in the speech stream, they are more *predictably* present. For example, English has sequences like 'have to' and 'going to', which, because the meanings that underlie these constructions are needed quite often when expressing one's thoughts, are used over and over again. Because of their constant repetition and their consequent predictability, those particular spontaneous variants that are slightly simplified may yet effectively convey the intended meaning to listeners. Due to probability matching, in time these simplifications may become conventionalized, subject to further simplification, and 'have to' ([ˈhæːv̥ ˌtʰu]) and 'going to' ([ˈɡ̊owɪŋ ˌtʰu]) eventually become 'hafta' ([ˈhæftə]), and 'gonna' ([ˈɡ̊ʌnə]). Other constructions of increasingly less similar structure may consequently follow suit, depending on their frequency. So, by the year 1981, Joe Ely was able to release an album called 'Musta Notta Gotta Lotta' (as in 'I musta notta gotta lotta sleep last night') and all speakers of American English can understand exactly what he means. Consequently, even with less phonetic information, the intended message may be effectively communicated to the listener: frequent simplified productions may be correctly interpreted by listeners, and might come to be used more often by speakers as a consequence of probability matching. By contrast, less frequent items are *less* predictable, and so require *more* phonetic information in order to be unambiguously communicated to listeners. These will be more resistant to simplification, because those variants that are indeed simplified may not be successfully communicated, and so non-simplified variants are more likely to be pooled with those tokens over which probabilities are matched.

Hale's parody is based on the supposition that individual speakers are somehow constantly getting it *wrong*, that the locus of phonological simplification resides in speakers' incorrectly implementing what they are *trying* to say, and doing so over and over again. But, in fact, the typically *slow-acting* nature of phonological change – due in part to speakers' demonstrated talent for probability matching – shows that speakers are constantly getting it remarkably *right*, and that the locus of Schuchardt's and Bybee's observed simplifications lies not in *speakers' supposedly unreliable production of speech*, but instead in *listeners' demonstrably reliable perception of meaning*.

Most fundamentally, Hale's 'practice makes imperfect' parody suggests a marked disconnect between language function and language structure. Piano players practice and practice in order to faithfully and accurately copy what is written in black and white in a music score. In piano playing, copying the immutable score is the be-all and end-all of the process (apart from the interpretative component that separates the artist from the hack). The 'practice makes imperfect' parody assumes that there is indeed an immutable black and white 'linguistic score' – with a string of phonemes taking the role of a string of musical notes – that speakers are striving to reproduce. But, as demonstrated in this book, language users are not attempting to read an immutable 'linguistic score' the way a pianist does a musical one. Rather, speakers are intending to communicate *meaning* to listeners, and the speech signal is simply the *medium* by which this information is transmitted from speaker to listener. So, while it's true that speakers are remarkably adept at faithfully copying the perceived speech signal – variation and all – this copying is clearly mediated by the accuracy with which listeners recover the *meaning* which underlies the acoustic content of the speech signal. Under those circumstances where meaning is recoverable *despite* variation in speech (as in Schuchardt's and Bybee's simplifications) or *because of* variation in speech (as discussed in Chapters Five and Six), then certain variants – even simplified variants – effectively serve their linguistic function, and may consequently become conventionalized.

Ultimately, Hale's parody suggests a solipsistic view of language. Just like those researchers who might believe that the Lombard Effect is a consequence of a wholly internal feedback loop by which speakers modify their voice level solely as a consequence of self-monitoring, Hale too seems to assume that the social milieu plays no significant role in how language comes to be cognitively organized, and that language structure is largely independent of language use, language experience and language function. In truth, *language use, language experience and language function influence language structure, and any attempt to deny this fact will not advance our understanding of the organizing principles of language.*

Are speakers 'selfish'?

A number of phonologists have recently taken a very bold position on the matter of ease-of-production in phonology. They propose that ease-of-production is not (or not *only*) a slow-going, *passive physical constraint* on phonology, but, rather, is an *active mental constraint* that is part of an abstract system of phonological knowledge that every speaker automatically brings to the task of language learning; learners get the constraints 'for free'. The constraints may be of different strengths in different languages, but nonetheless they are assumed to be provided to us automatically as a simple consequence of our being Homo sapiens. For these phonologists, the task of the language learner is to determine the strength of one constraint relative to others (the constraints themselves, recall, come 'for free', although their strengths vary on a language-specific basis); the task of the linguist is to discover the constraints, and like the learner, to determine their relative strengths for any given language. The particular family of abstract constraints relating to 'effort minimization' have been termed 'lazy' by one of the most enthusiastic proponents of this approach, the linguist Robert Kirchner. 'Lazy' constraints are in conflict with 'faithfulness' constraints, which place a premium on keeping speech as similar as possible to hypothesized *non*-lazy or *pre*-lazy mental representations of speech sounds; this is the level of the 'alphabetic score', the phonemic level. In a paper from 2004, Kirchner writes that every possible phonetic realization of every phonological structure is matched against a mental calculation of its 'effort cost, the biomechanical energy required for [its] articulatory production.' A linguistic form which abides by the abstract constraint, then, is one which does not exceed the calculated effort cost allotted by the mental calculation, while remaining as faithful to the underlying value as the faithfulness constraints demand. It is these forms – out of a potentially infinite set of candidate forms – that actually earn the privilege of coming out of our mouths.

As with Kingston's 'altruism', if 'laziness' is part and parcel of the linguistic system, listeners must somehow be able to partition the incoming speech signal into at least two distinct components: that component which is a consequence of speakers' laziness, and the remainder, the component of the speech signal that is 'faithful' to the 'pre-lazy' phonemic level. These phonemic linguistic representations are neither *spoken* by speakers nor *heard* by listeners, but language users, because of the constraint system that they inherit, come to figure out they do indeed exist.

Let's briefly consider an example of how this works. As discussed at length in Chapter Six, many languages have an alternation between voiced stops and voiced fricatives, such that the fricative is found between vowels. For Kirchner, the stop and fricative alternants are phonologically the same entity, in that the stop is realized as a fricative due to the active laziness constraints; unlike the analysis presented in Chapter Six, Kirchner assumes that it is indeed more natural to produce an intervocalic fricative as opposed to an intervocalic stop, and so spirantization is a 'lazy' realization of the stop. So at the most abstract, phonemic, or 'underlying' level, the fricative is mentally represented as a stop, but, due to the laziness constraints, it is realized as a fricative when it finds itself between vowels.

Kirchner is actually making two conflations in his approach to the phonological role of ease of production. He is conflating the phonetic with the cognitive, and, like Kingston, he is conflating the diachronic with the synchronic. Let's consider each of these conflations in turn.

First, Kirchner's boldest assertion is essentially that *purely physical, phonetic* pressures on linguistic sound systems – a supposedly quantifiable measure of 'articulatory effort' – should be expressed in *purely abstract, psychological* terms. He writes in 2004 (using the common term *lenition* to refer to spirantization and certain other processes), 'I proceed from the intuition that lenition is driven by an imperative to minimize articulatory effort. Unlike standard approaches, however, I argue that lenition patterns arise directly from this effort minimization constraint (which I style LAZY).' For Kirchner then, demonstrable phonetic tendencies are fully 'psychologized', one might say; they are incorporated into a wholly abstract, psychological system of knowledge that every speaker possesses. The system of phonetically-rooted abstract constraints, then, is a synchronically active component of our linguistic knowledge.

This conflation of the phonetic and the cognitive is in stark contrast to the proposals espoused herein. Indeed, as Mikołaj Kruszewski wrote in 1881 (and as I have taken as the jumping-off point for this book),

> Language occupies a completely isolated place in the realm of nature: it is a combination of physiological and acoustic phenomena governed by physical laws, and of unconscious and psychical phenomena governed by laws of an entirely different kind. This fact leads us to a most important question: what is the relation ... between the physical principle and the unconscious and psychical principle?

Kirchner's answer to this question is that *phonetic* tendencies that might slowly play themselves out diachronically are recapitulated in (and conflated with) the synchronic *psychological* system that speakers are claimed to possess. However, it is difficult to see the advantage – or even the motivation – for this conflation of the *physical* – shaped by one set of laws and principles – and the *cognitive* – shaped by a wholly unrelated set of laws and principles. My misgivings here stem less from concerns about *parsimony* as such – indeed, most natural systems suffer from a harrowing degree of complexity – but rather from concerns about *plausibility*: proponents of this general approach unfortunately eschew the obvious (and obviously unanswerable) question of *how and why* creeping, slow-going phonetic tendencies have, over the course of human evolution, been transformed into all-at-once mental constraints on linguistic sound structure. Evolutionarily speaking, it would seem difficult to isolate the environmental and genetic factors that might have given rise to this remarkable saltation.

Regarding the conflation of the *diachronic* and the *synchronic*, again, Kirchner's approach contrasts with the present one, which argues that sounds in alternation in the present have evolved in the absence of the users who come to possess them, that present-day alternations have no present-day causes; they only have present-day effects. Once again, I bow to Hermann Paul, who wrote in 1880:

> One of the commonest errors is the supposition that a change which has arisen in a long period by numerous small displacements is to be referred to a single act resulting from a desire for convenience ... The truth is that ... the motory sensation developed by tradition ... belong[s] to a period perhaps long and gone. It is equally mistaken to refer the appearance of a sound change in each case to some particular manifestation of laziness, weariness, or neglect, and to ascribe its non-appearance in other cases to some special care and observation.

In short, while there may be ample textual, comparative, and/or internal reconstructive evidence to conclude that certain fricative alternants *historically* derive from stops, there is no evidence to conclude that such fricatives *psychologically* derive from stops.

'Alphabetism' and 'phonemism': whence and whither

> It is fascinating to read her scrupulous analysis of stage technique, where she notes that the name Fang is funny because it ends abruptly with a hard consonant ...
>
> Jane and Michael Stern, reviewing Phyllis Diller's memoir, *My Life in Comedy*. *New York Times Book Review*, March 13, 2005

How far has alphabetism led innocent language users down the garden path? Consider the quote above, and contemplate its multi-faceted mistakenness. New York Times reviewers Jane and Michael Stern find it fascinating that American comedienne Phyllis Diller apparently thought the name 'Fang' (her loosely fictional no-good rotten husband) was funny 'because it ends abruptly with a hard consonant'. The 'hard consonant' in question is presumably 'g', since that is the last letter in 'Fang'. But you and I know that this is merely an orthographic convention; what we write in English as 'ng' actually represents the tongue-body nasal, [ŋ]: [fæ̃ŋ]. This nasal is actually one of the 'softest' consonants you're likely to encounter, since, if you recall from Chapter Two, it is very vowel-like in its acoustic characteristics. So Diller is wrong on that count. The Sterns got it wrong as well, since they find Diller's 'scrupulous analysis' of the word 'Fang' so 'fascinating'. If 'Fang' really is funny, it certainly has nothing to do with the quality of its final consonant, at least according to the criteria that Diller establishes and that the Sterns buy into.

The wonderful comedian Buddy Hackett seemed to know better. He loved his name, because it had so many sounds that you could 'hook on to', that is, it had so many stops. Neil Simon got it right too, when, in *The Sunshine Boys*, the ex-Vaudevillian Willie Clark intones, 'I'm in this business 57 years. I know what's funny. Words with a "k" in it are funny. Alka-Seltzer is funny. Chicken is funny. Pickle is funny. All with a "k". "L"s are not funny. "M"s are not funny.' Nor, might I suggest, are [ŋ]s.

Remember, I called Diller (and the Sterns) 'innocent' language users. I can't expect them to know any better. But linguists have no excuse. Even in the face of phonetic and cognitive experimental evidence to the contrary, why have the phonemists been so steadfast in their assertion that phonology is organized along phonemic lines? The answer, I suggest, is that phonemism is rooted in alphabetism. Indeed, many linguists have suggested that there really *is* a /g/ phoneme at the end of 'fang' and other [ŋ]-final words in English, except that they are not pronounced!

What then, is the route from alphabetism to phonemism? I turn to this question now. Alphabetic writing has its origins in northern Semitic orthography, one which represents consonants but not vowels. Between 2800 and 2700 years ago, the Greeks adapted and modified the Semitic system by introducing vowel symbols. This Greek innovation may seem like an obvious improvement over the vocalically impoverished Semitic system (since all languages have both consonants and vowels), but its obviousness actually lies not in facts about phonetics, but rather in facts about morphology. The morphology of Semitic languages (among them the present-day Amharic spoken in Ethiopia, the Arabic spoken on the Arabian peninsula and adjacent lands, and the Hebrew spoken in Israel) is that root morphemes may be analysed as consisting of consonantal structure, while the inflectional system – tense, person, etc. – consists largely of vowel sounds that intervene between the root-based consonants. In Hebrew, for example, the three consonants ל [l], מ [m] and ד [d], when embedded in various contexts, all relate in some way to studying. Table 7.1 provides a few examples of both verbs and nouns. (Hebrew is written right to left.)

In isolation, many of these written words are what we might term 'orthographically neutralized': they are spelled identically. But in the context of written text, the intended word is quite clear to readers. Indeed, given the linear adjacency enjoyed by the root consonants in most forms, the specific root emerges quite effortlessly. Other consonantal roots, when embedded in these same contexts, produce words with the same inflectional properties, and are just as easy to read by anyone literate in Hebrew.

Due to the different morphological origins of consonants and vowels in Semitic, it becomes clear that the absence of vowels in the orthography is not a *shortcoming* of the system, but is instead an *innovation*: since vowel qualities are largely predictable by the grammatical context in which a given root is found, then representing them in the written code would be largely redundant. The northern Semites, then, devised a remarkably *efficient* orthographic system.

When the Greeks devised their own alphabet based on the Semitic model, they found the Semitic system wanting, because the vowel sounds of Greek morphology are not exclusively inflectional in origin, but instead are part of the root morphemes themselves. Consequently, the Greeks modified the nature of the Semitic system to include vowel symbols as well as consonant symbols; a useful innovation to be sure, but one that was naturally necessitated by the Greek morphological system. The Latin, Cyrillic and Sanskrit alphabets – used for Indo-European languages with morphological systems broadly akin to Greek's – all use vowel symbols as well.

Consider now orthographic systems that represent entire syllables, rather than individual consonants and vowels. These are known as *syllabaries*. Native Japanese orthography, for example, is syllable-based. Each symbol represents a particular combination of a vowel and a preceding consonant, if one, that is, an entire syllable. A Japanese syllabary is shown in Table 7.2.

Is a syllabary a less sophisticated orthographic system than an alphabetic one? Not at all; it is remarkably appropriate for the needs of its users. Japanese has a very limited number of syllable shapes.

Table 7.1 A partial list of Hebrew words with the root ל-מ-ד

למדתי	lamadət^{h}i	I studied	למדנו	lamadnu	We studied
למדת	lamadət^{h}a	You studied (m)	למדתם	ləmadət^{h}ɛm	You studied (pl, m)
למדת	lamadet	You studied (f)	למדתן	ləmadət^{h}ɛn	You studied (pl, f)
למד	lamad	He studied	למדו	lamdu	They studied (m)
למדה	lamda	She studied	למדו	lamdu	They studied (f)
יילמד	jilmad	I will study	נלמד	nilmad	We will study
תלמד	t^{h}ilmad	You will study (m)	תלמדו	t^{h}ilmədu	You will study (pl, m)
תלמדי	t^{h}ilmədi	You will study (f)	תלמדו	t^{h}ilmədu	You will study (pl, f)
יילמד	jilmad	He will study	ילמדו	jilmədu	They will study (m)
תלמד	t^{h}ilmad	She will study	יילמדו	jilmədu	They will study (f)
לומד	lomed	He studies	לומדים	lomdim	They study (m)
לומדת	lomɛdɛt	She studies	לומדות	lomdot	They study (f)
למד	ləmad	Study! (m)	למדו	limdu	Study! (pl, m)
למדי	limdi	Study! (f)	למדו	limdu	Study! (pl, f)
ללמדוד	lilmod	To study	למידה	lemida	Studying (noun)
תלמיד	t^{h}almid	Student (m)	תלמידה	t^{h}almida	Student (f)
למודיה	limudija	Studio	למוד	limud	Study (noun)
תלמוד	t^{h}almud	Book of (Jewish) law	למדן	lamdan	Researcher
למודי	limudi	Didactic	לומד	lumad	He was taught

Table 7.2 A native Japanese syllabary. The component parts of each syllable are not indicated, apart from the marker for obstruent voicing. See if you can find it.

あ a	い i	う u	え e	お o
か ka	き ki	く ku	け ke	こ ko
さ sa	し shi	す su	せ se	そ so
た ta	ち chi	つ tsu	て te	と to
な na	に ni	ぬ nu	ね ne	の no
は ha	ひ hi	ふ fu	へ he	ほ ho
ま ma	み mi	む mu	め me	も mo
や ja		ゆ ju		よ jo
ら ɾa	り ɾi	る ɾu	れ ɾe	ろ ɾo
わ wa	ゐ wi		ゑ we	を wo
				ん ũ
が ga	ぎ gi	ぐ gu	げ ge	ご go
ざ za	じ ji	ず zu	ぜ ze	ぞ zo
だ da	ぢ ji	づ zu	で de	ど do
ば ba	び bi	ぶ bu	べ be	ぼ bo
ぱ pa	ぴ pi	ぷ pu	ぺ pe	ぽ po

Consequently, a syllabary is a very efficient way to orthographically represent Japanese, although due to foreign influence – historically Chinese, and more recently American – Japanese has long used several different writing systems at once!

Finally, let's consider Chinese. As we discussed in Chapter One, each Chinese symbol, or character, represents a whole morpheme, and, like syllabaries, contains no information about the individual consonants and vowels that combine to form the phonetic quality of the morpheme. Surely, *this* is an inefficient and inappropriate writing system, right? Well, yes and no. It is very inefficient in terms of promoting literacy, but really, it's a very natural development, given the uniquely centralist socio-cultural heritage of China. 'Chinese' is actually a collection of five different languages – each of which possesses a myriad of dialects, many of which are mutually unintelligible – that nonetheless are spoken by an ethnic group that has always been culturally, politically and religiously homogenous. Although word-order is reasonably consistent across Chinese languages, the sound systems differ significantly from region to region. Consequently, a character-based writing system is the most appropriate means of making the written word accessible to speakers of all Chinese languages and dialects.

In general, then, other than those all-too-common cases when orthography has been imposed from the outside by a religious or cultural imperial power, writing systems are appropriate to the linguistic and cultural system for which they have been developed.

So why has alphabetism been elevated to pre-eminence, among lay people and – especially for our purposes – as the type of writing system that (mis)informs so many linguists' intuitions about phonological structure? I suspect the answer has its origins in a further fact: there is a strong correlation between orthography and religion. Indeed, orthographic systems are often thought to be of divine origin. Jewish languages are written with Hebrew letters, the script used in the torah. The Kabbalists believe that mere exposure to the Hebrew letters on the written page may enhance one's spiritual energy. Regarding the Devanagari script used for Sanskrit – the holy language of Hinduism – even its very name derives from the Sanskrit word for 'divine', *deva*. Arabic orthography – the system employed in the Koran – was brought to conquered lands when Islam was spread from the Arabian peninsula. Latin script – the orthographic system employed in the Christian scriptures – played a similar role in lands conquered by Christians. The Cyrillic alphabet – established by St Cyril and St Methodius about 1300 years ago for Old Bulgarian – is used by Orthodox Christians. So whereas Orthodox Christian Serbs use Cyrillic script, Roman Catholic Croats – who speak the same language as the Serbs – use Latin script. In a very recent example, the Pahauh Hmong script was invented for the Hmong language of Southeast Asia in 1959 by Shong Lue Yang. Both Shong and his followers believed that he was a messenger from God to help the Hmong people.

This is surely not to say that modern-day phonemists believe in the divinity of the Christian-based Latin script – the script through which the worlds' most influential linguists achieved literacy. Rather, these linguists are simply the inheritors of a system with an inherent Christocentric orientation, and so their wholly secular intuitions – intuitions that, for example, Classical Chinese linguists did *not* have – are nonetheless similarly tainted: the alphabetists of yesterday have become the phonemists of today.

As we discussed at length in Chapter Two, technological advances in the field of phonetics have demonstrated that the speech stream cannot be segmented into 'letter'- or phoneme-sized chunks, and that the transitions between any steady-state components of the speech stream are the most informationally rich. Moreover, psychological experiments have shown that speakers who are not trained in an alphabetic orthography have no notion of the segment-sized chunks that you, I and the phonemists take for granted. But even in the face of these uncontroversial findings, the phonemists have remained steadfast in their assertion that phonology is organized – at least at deep abstract levels – along phonemic lines. Why? Because they are relying on their *intuitions* about phonological structure. But these intuitions are directly traceable to their training in an alphabetic orthography, and so do not open any sort of window into the genuine structural properties of language. In short, the phonemists believe that alphabetic writing is the most insightful orthographic system because it reveals the phonemic organization of phonological structure. But in fact, they get it exactly backwards: phonemists believe that phonological structure is built out of phonemes because they have been trained in an alphabetic orthography. The phoneme is not a psychological reality. Rather, it is a cultural construct.

By embracing a mental entity for which there is no overt evidence – neither for the learner nor the linguist – the phonemists are forced to posit a multi-layered phonological system: the abstract level of the phoneme (the alphabetic level), the level of transformation (rules or constraints), and the output level (phonetic implementation), where the actual details that are present in speech are superimposed. As discussed in the previous sections, both 'altruistic' and 'selfish' approaches to phonology rely on the assumption that there exists a speaker-controlled component that is in some sense 'overlaid' on the more 'authentic', 'underlying' or 'phonemic' phonological level.

So, when the phonemists observe the extra nasalization on a contrastively nasalized low vowel, they might attribute this to an altruistic linguistic level that is overlaid on the phonemic one, because, after all, the *phonemic* nasality of contrastively nasalized vowels is a pure, discrete, categorical phonological value, and hence is identical regardless of the vowel quality with which it is phonologically affiliated: at the phonological level, nasality is nasality is nasality. Consequently, when the phonemists observe different degrees of nasality on contrastively nasal vowels that differ in their oral qualities (for example, more on [ɑ̃], less on other vowels), these differing degrees of nasality are 'entirely unexpected', and so must originate from another domain that is not phonemic in origin.

And when they observe stops alternating with fricatives in intervocalic position, they might invoke 'laziness' to account for their observations. According to the phonemists, despite their phonetic differences, the fricative and the stop are phonemically identical. The superficial phonetic fricative in Corsican (ɑ)[β̞okːɑ] is an underlying phonological stop (/b/), based on 'linguistic evidence' in the form of [bokːɑ].

When they observe the vowel nasalization that inevitably precedes a nasal consonant, they assign a different status to *this* nasalization as opposed to the nasalization that is co-extensive with the consonant itself. Recall that vowels have more nasality when an immediately following nasal consonant is made further back in the mouth, and have less nasality when an immediately following nasal is made further front in the mouth: the vowel in 'ding' [d̥ĩŋ] is more nasalized than the vowel in 'din' [d̥ĩn], as discussed in Chapter Two. But because this vocalic nasality does not fit into a letter- or phoneme-sized component of the speech stream (it is realized away from the nasal consonant itself, and might only partially overlap with a preceding vowel), these phonologists conclude that the nasalization is perhaps 'merely' phonetic, or at least of a different phonological status than the nasal consonant, which is the 'true' underlying phonological value. They propose this psychological distinction despite the fact that the vowel nasalization co-varies with the other cues to the oral component of the nasal consonant. That is, they propose this psychological distinction despite that fact that the vocalic nasality is functionally non-distinct from the nasal consonant itself – the complex is an integrated *Gestalt*.

When they observe the high component of rising tones being realized on a following vowel, as is found in Comaltepec Chinantec and many other languages (as discussed in Chapter Five), again they often regard such effects as a mere phonetic consequence: the underlying phonological affiliation – the 'target' – of the high pitch is on the preceding vowel, but speakers are continually *missing* this target at the level of phonetic implementation. They are missing their target despite the fact that they have always produced their rising tones in the way they have always *heard* them. So, according to the phonemists, speakers are continually *mentally undoing* aspects of the phonetic patterns that they hear, and then *physically reinstating* these patterns in their own speech! All this for the sake of maintaining the tenets of phonemism.

When they observe certain vowels in vowel harmony languages behaving in a *dis*harmonic way – recall from Chapter Three that in Hungarian some roots with [i] take back vowel suffixes, because they historically derive from back vowels, for example [hiːd] ('the bridge') versus [hiːdtoːl] ('from the bridge'), with a back vowel suffix, was likely *hɯːd in Hungarian history ([ɯ] is the back counterpart of [i]) – the phonemists might treat this disharmonic *front* vowel as an underlying *back* vowel. In other words, Hungarian speakers today have the same abstract vowel system as did the Hungarian speakers of long ago! All that has changed is the phonological rule or constraint that transforms the underlying back vowel into a phonetic front vowel.

The aforementioned are not just a few, isolated examples, by the way. Since Chomsky and Halle's book of 1968, theorizing on the route between the proposed underlying forms and actual surface forms (and back again) has pervaded the phonemists' phonological analyses; phonemism, far and away, is the dominant paradigm, although it should be said that rarely have phonologists gone so far as to invoke 'altruism' or 'laziness' in their attempts to defend this approach. Discussing a complex set of vowel changes that have taken place over the history of English, Noam Chomsky and Morris Halle write in 1968:

> [A]n observed [sound] change can only have one source – a change in the grammar that underlies the observed utterances.
>
> A straightforward way of effecting changes in a grammar is to add new rules. The addition of a rule to the phonological component may be regarded as the most rudimentary type of sound change ... Many sound changes known in diachronic phonology are of this type. By and large the familiar 'sound laws' are, in fact, rules added to the phonological component ...
>
> ... The conception of a linguistic change as a change in the grammar is also implicit in the traditional view of sound change. One of the crucial facts that linguists have tried to explain is that speakers are by and large unaware of the changes that their language is undergoing. The reason for this, it has been claimed, is that changes affect only the phonetic actualization of particular sounds – and, moreover, in so slight a measure that the changes appear to be gradual ... Thus, vowels may be articulated somewhat farther back than before, or consonants may be actualized in some environment with aspiration of degree 4 whereas earlier they were actualized in that environment with degree 2. While there is no logical reason to reject this view of sound change, there is certainly no reason to give it special status. With the exception of the fact that speakers are unaware of an ongoing change – a fact which is easily explainable on the ground that speakers are, in general, unaware of the contents of their grammar – there is very little factual data to bear out this view .... This lack of evidence, however, has not prevented scholars from continuing to espouse the gradual view of sound change.

Sanford Schane, in his 1973 textbook on the Chomsky and Halle theory (called 'generative phonology'), hints at some supposed 'evidence' for phonemism, and circularly reasons the following:

> Although the speech signal may be physically *continuous*, we seem to perceive it as a sequence of *discrete* entities.
>
> That utterances can be represented as a sequence of discrete units is one of the basic theoretical assumptions of phonology ... There is evidence that speakers also conceive of utterances as

> composed of discrete entities ... [*C*]*at* is composed of three sounds. You might say that speakers are influenced by the written language, in which *cat* is spelled with three letters. But alphabetic writing can in fact be used as one argument in favor of the segmental view of speech, since with such writing systems there is a correlation between a sequence of graphic symbols and a purported sequence of speech sounds.

Larry M. Hyman, in his generative phonology textbook of two years later, asserts – as do Chomsky and Halle – that some phonetic components of the speech stream are redundant and predictable. According to Hyman, these supposedly redundant components of speech are not phonemic, but are instead merely phonetic. The phonemes themselves are not predictable, because any single combination of phonemes that makes up a morpheme or word is in some sense arbitrary: another combination of phonemes might have just as effectively been employed for a particular word. However, due to the particular combination of phonemes, certain supposedly *predictable* phonetic consequences may follow, albeit usually on a language-specific basis. For example, according to phonemists like Hyman, it is *arbitrary* – hence phonological – that the English word 'pin' starts with a labial stop ('/p/'), but it is *predictable* that this labial stop will be aspirated in English ([pʰ]). To reconcile the dichotomy between the proposed phonemes and the proposed redundancies, Hyman needs to further propose a multi-levelled phonology.

> In order to characterize the relationship between the phonemes of a language and its inventory of phonetic segments, two levels of representation are distinguished, a *phonological level* and a *phonetic level*. Phonological representations consist of sequences of phonemes, transcribed between slashes (/.../); phonetic representations consist of sequences of phones, transcribed between square brackets ([...]). Thus the phonological representation of the word *pin* will be /pɪn/, while its phonetic representation will be [pʰɪn].
>
> Since the phonological level represents the distinctive sound units of a language and not redundant phonetic information (such as the aspiration of the initial [pʰ] of English /pɪn/), it is appropriate to think of it as an approximation of the *mental* representation speakers have of the sounds of words in their language.

It appears to be immaterial to Hyman that both listeners and linguists are more likely to predict the presence of a [p] based on the particular formant transitions that take place during the [ʰ] itself, rather than predict the aspiration based on the presence of the [p] closure. Clearly, the 'phonemic' status of the 'p' and the 'non-phonemic' status of the [^{h}] is a simple consequence of alphabetism – conveniently, we *spell* the word P-I-N, not P-H-I-N. Indeed, we might characterize the absence of an 'h' in the word 'pin' as an orthographic innovation, since *writing* this 'h' may be viewed as redundant; the 'p' symbol is sufficient to represent all the relevant contrastive phonetic components. But orthography is a *tool* that is put to a specific *use*, and is not representative of any psychological state. The criteria that Hyman uses to separate the redundant information from the phonemic content, then, is wholly arbitrary, and so, like Schane before him, Hyman lapses into circularity when trying to distinguish phonological from predictable content in the speech stream: he is driven by alphabetism.

Michael Kenstowicz and Charles Kisseberth draw a similar spurious distinction in *their* phonology text of 1979:

> [A]ll of the idiosyncratic features of the pronunciation of a morpheme are to be listed in the lexical representation of that morpheme in the lexicon of the grammar. On the other hand, features which are instances of systematic regularities will be assigned by phonological rules in the phonological component of the grammar. Correspondingly, we will make a distinction between two levels of representation of the phonological structure of a morpheme, word, phrase, or sentence: the *underlying representation* (UR), which will contain all the idiosyncratic information about the pronunciation of the constituent morphemes of the utterance, and the *phonetic representation* (PR), which contains the idiosyncratic information plus the predictable information about the pronunciation of the utterance.

Perhaps most boldly – in part because they state that a multi-levelled phonology is the *only* possible way to establish functional relationships among allomorphs – Carlos Gussenhoven and Haike Jacobs, in a textbook published in 1998, write:

> Why do phonologists assume that there are two levels of representation, an underlying one and a surface one? Three arguments can be advanced.
>
> 1. One argument is economy. Why supply allophonic information in the lexical entries if it can be stated in a set of allophonic rules that are valid for all morphemes of the lexicon? ...
> 2. [W]ith a single level it would not be possible to express the phonological relatedness of morpheme alternants ...
> 3. Many generalizations are only valid at a level other than the surface level ...
>
> ... The recognition of two levels of representation, a surface representation and a more underlying abstract representation, is the cornerstone of phonological theory.

Gussenhoven and Jacobs seem to be saying that phonologists *need* phonemes and the multi-levelled phonology that they demand in order to make their jobs easier, and they freely impart this *tool of the phonologist* a separate but equal *mental reality for the language user*.

René Kager, in his textbook of 1999, writes the following about vowel nasalization in English:

> Consider a language that has no lexical contrast of oral and nasal vowels. In this language oral and nasal vowels are *allophones*, variants of one another which are fully predictable from the phonological contexts. For example, vowels are generally oral when they directly precede a tautosyllabic [= 'belonging to the same syllable' -D.S.] nasal stop. This allophonic pattern occurs in many dialects of English.
>
> | | | | |
> |---|---|---|---|
> | cat | [kæt] | can't | [kæ̃nt] |
> | sad | [sæd] | sand | [sæ̃nd] |
> | met | [mɛt] | meant | [mɛ̃nt] |
> | lick | [lɪk] | link | [lɪ̃ŋk] |
>
> When we say that English lacks a contrast of oral and nasal vowels, we do not imply that English completely lacks either kind of vowels [*sic*], but only that no word pairs occur that are distinguished by orality/nasality of their vowels. Whatever variation there is between oral and nasal vowels is totally conditioned by the context and does not reflect lexical specification. Vowels are nasal when they precede a tautosyllabic nasal, and are oral in all other contexts. This complementary distribution, and the corresponding lack of word pairs that differ only in the specification of some feature, is what defines an allophonic pattern.

Kager asserts, in standard fashion, that English vowel nasalization is fully predictable because it is only found when a nasal consonant immediately follows within the same syllable. But is this sort of co-occurrence (between the nasal consonant and the vowel nasalization) really a solid diagnostic for concluding that the two components have differing phonological status? No, it isn't. When a [p] is found between vowels as in 'apart', for example, we can easily predict the general pattern of the [p]-to-vowel formant transitions based on the pattern of the vowel-to-[p] formant transitions (or vice versa): there will be a lowering of F2 (and the other formants) into the oral occlusion, and so there will be a raising of F2 (and the other formants) out of the oral occlusion. So would Kager claim that one set of formant transitions is phonological, and the other predictable? Of course not. Why? Because of alphabetism: because we have one orthographic symbol ('p') that – wholly arbitrarily – represents *both* of these phonetic elements, whereas our orthographic symbols for nasal consonants – equally arbitrarily – do not represent the nasality on a preceding vowel.

Kager, by the way, makes a further mistake when he says that vowel nasalization is found only when a tautosyllabic nasal follows. *Many* English speakers pronounce words like 'can't', for example, [kʰæ̝̃ə̯̃t] or [kʰæ̝̃ə̯̃ʔ]. In English then, we *do* find vowel nasalization even in the absence of a following nasal, at least when a voiceless stop follows.

Assertions like those quoted above typically come in the first few pages of phonology texts, and in the first few lectures in courses on phonology. Although axiomatic in nature, they are presented to neophytes as the established *facts* on which all subsequent discussion is based. Indeed, the phonemists are quick to impose their (pre)conception of phonological structure on their own language, and also on any other language that they analyse. And on those rare occasions when a pattern cannot be forced into the phonemic straightjacket, such as when its gradience or token-to-token variation is evident even to a phonetically untrained ear, the phonemists might regard the pattern as 'a sound change in progress', one that will ultimately be 'phonologized' as one phonemic pattern or another. But of course, there is no such thing as 'phonologization': at the proper level of description, *all* phonological patterns are sound changes in progress, as they are *all* gradiently and variably implemented, and they are *all* ever-changing. They are at once sufficiently stable to fulfil their communicative function and sufficiently variable to be under constant modification: gradience and variation are the very stuff of phonology and sound change – listeners perceive it, speakers produce it and listeners perceive it.

In sum, phonemism, which has its roots in alphabetism, requires phonologists to assume a multi-levelled phonology, an underlying level with the phonemes, and another level of derivation or transformation in which all the supposedly predictable (non-phonemic, non-alphabetic) phonetic content is added. And because phonemes are, by axiom, genetically-endowed 'building blocks' of linguistic structure, learners are pre-equipped with the linguistic faculties to figure all this out: despite the gradient and continuous nature of the speech stream, despite the inordinately complex way in which certain collections of phonetic properties might pattern together – co-vary – as a consequence of alternation (or might *not* pattern together due to an absence of alternation), learners can mentally undo all this complexity and arrive at a nice, neat system of a few stable elements that combine and re-combine. Then, as these listeners become speakers, they simply re-instate all the phonetic complexity that they have just mentally undone. All this for the sake of maintaining the tenets of phonemism.

Because of its derivational nature, phonemism typically involves a conflation of phonetics and cognition, and a conflation of diachrony and synchrony. Phonemism further forces a dichotomy between speakers' supposed *mental intentions* and the actual *physical facts* of their speech: because the phonemists maintain the phonemic principle, they are forced into guessing games about speakers' intentions. But indeed, the only intentions we may be confident that speakers possess are those that underlie speech acts themselves: speakers *intend* to speak, since they might just as readily choose to keep silent.

There are other ways the phoneme has been operationalized, however. In a landmark work published in 1939, the linguist Nikolai Trubetskoy discussed a conception of the phoneme that comes much closer to the present approach. He defined the phoneme in purely functional terms, rejecting both the *phonetic* and *psychological* approaches that have long outlived Trubetskoy himself:

> Reference to psychology must be avoided in defining the phoneme since the latter is a linguistic and not a psychological concept. Any reference to 'linguistic consciousness' must be avoided in defining the phoneme, 'linguistic consciousness' being either a metaphorical designation of the system of language or a rather vague concept, which itself must be defined and possibly cannot even be defined ... The phoneme is, above all, a functional concept that must be defined with respect to its function. Such a definition cannot be carried out with psycholinguistic notions ... The phoneme can be defined satisfactorily neither on the basis of its psychological nature nor on the basis of its relation to the phonetic variants, but purely and solely on the basis of its function in the system of language ... [E]very language presupposes distinctive (phonological) oppositions. The phoneme is a member of such an opposition that cannot be analyzed into still smaller distinctive (phonological) units. There is nothing to be changed in this quite clear and unequivocal definition. Any change can only lead to unnecessary complications.

For our purposes, though, the phoneme is not an entity on any level – functional, phonetic, psychological or even metaphorical. Rather, at best, 'phoneme' is merely a terminological expedient that might capture the functional non-distinctness of any collection of phonetic properties that allomorphically alternate. And yet, despite its expedience, I choose to avoid the term altogether, because terminological expedients have a demonstrated tendency to become reified by their users.

Parlo ergo es

Let's now reiterate some of the major points of all the preceding discussion:

- Phonology is best characterized as a self-organizing and self-sustaining system of substantive social conventions that evolves passively over generations of speakers. It is self-organizing because its structural properties are a consequence of its use, requiring no outside monitor, guide or force to affect its organization. It is self-sustaining because, by its very use, it repairs and maintains itself.
- The regularities we observe in phonological systems are due to a complex interaction of phonetic and cognitive pressures acting over generations and generations of language use, and can be understood only when considering the communicative function of language itself.
- Present-day phonological patterns result from a dizzyingly complex and long-term interaction of articulatory, acoustic, auditory, aerodynamic, perceptual, functional and social forces, and it's facile to assume that the explanation for present-day phonetic and phonological patterns reduces to present-day factors.
- Our effortless mastery of sound substitutions derives from familiarity and experience with words themselves, and not from a mentally-compiled list of sound-sequential rules or constraints on what constitutes a 'good' word.
- There is no reason to assume that language users subdivide the words they learn into distinct sound-components unless there is evidence from alternation to do so. Linguists may subdivide the speech signal into a myriad of constituents, but the only constituents that exist for language users are those which emerge as a consequence of language use, due to the linguistic functions that underlie them.
- The consonant–vowel sequences that we think we observe are simply artefactual, and it is the transitions between them that are most relevant, since these are the most informationally rich and often the most auditorily prominent components of the speech signal.
- It is impossible to account for the state of a language at a particular point in time without also considering the historical forces that have given rise to this state: sounds in alternation in the present often reflect sounds that have gradually changed in the past.

- Language is a system of conventionalized patterns of usage that arise from the minor and limited variations in which speakers naturally engage. The communicative success of certain spontaneous innovations over others – especially in the face of potentially confusing, homophonous forms – may very slowly, almost imperceptibly, drive the linguistic system in new directions.
- Very minor phonetic tendencies, coupled with the ambiguities they might induce or eschew, may eventually have far-reaching consequences for the phonological system.
- Our excellent-though-imperfect ability to engage in probability matching both causes and inhibits variation in speech. And the phonetic separation and stabilization of categories is as much a *consequence* of effective communication as it is a *cause* of effective communication.
- The presence of ambiguous tokens may result in listeners overestimating the prevalence of more distinct tokens. This overestimation, in turn, may result in more distinct tokens being produced, and, eventually, the better separation of phonological categories.
- Passive pressures toward homophone avoidance may trigger individual words to undergo pioneering changes.
- Phonological patterns evolve in the absence of the users who ultimately come to possess them.
- Present-day alternations have no present-day causes; they only have present-day effects.
- Alternations in the present – even when phonetically unnatural and superficially counter-functional – are the long-term product of small, local, and perfectly natural processes that play themselves out over generations of speakers.
- As phonetic pressures may influence a particular change in one sound, functional pressures may seize upon certain variants of another sound of the language, sending otherwise chance variation on a specific trajectory of change.
- Due to the inherent variability of speech production, and selectional pressures acting upon this variation, phonological systems evolve in fulfilment of their communicative function. It is the adaptation of a contrastive value to its context, and its subsequent survival as a functionally beneficial component of the communicative system, which is responsible for allophonic patterns.
- The origins of phonological simplifications lie not in speakers' supposedly unreliable production of speech, but

instead in listeners' demonstrably reliable perception of meaning.

- Language use, language experience and language function influence language structure, and any attempt to deny this fact will not advance our understanding of the organizing principles of language.
- Any approach to phonological structure that makes reference to speakers' supposed *intentions* should be regarded with suspicion.
- There is often evidence that one alternant *historically* derives from another, but there is no evidence to conclude that one alternant *psychologically* derives from another.
- All phonological patterns are sound changes in progress, as they are all gradiently and variably implemented, and they are all ever-changing. They are at once sufficiently stable to fulfil their communicative function and sufficiently variable to be under constant modification: gradience and variation are the very stuff of phonology and sound change – speakers produce it and listeners perceive it.

Homo sapiens possesses a predisposition for language. This endowed trait emerged by adapting to (and evolving along with) traits that evolution had already provided to our evolutionary ancestors: the hearing mechanism, cognitive capabilities such as probability matching and pattern generalization, and our vocal tract – sound, mind and body. But it is our predisposition toward socialization that truly sowed the seeds for this remarkable, quintessentially human adaptation: our species has evolved as a social one, and language is the culminating expression of this socialization.

As it is extremely unlikely that language is directly encoded in our genes, but is instead the emergent result of *other* genetically encoded traits, it is doubtful that language is directly susceptible to genetic mutation. Rather, language is a *fixed* and *immutable* characteristic of our species: if language were to change its fundamental characteristics, we would no longer be Homo sapiens.

Yet one of the most remarkable fixed and immutable properties of language is its built-in mechanism of *adaptation* and *change*. Due to the nature in which sound, mind and body interact, languages themselves *evolve*: the communicative success or failure of certain spontaneous innovations over others may slowly drive the linguistic system in new directions.

Consequently, our fixed and immutable predisposition for language does not require us to posit fixed and immutable structural elements of language: we don't need to assume the pre-determined existence of phonemes or other phonological features, or a fixed system of phonological rules or constraints that we inherit as a consequence of our being Homo sapiens. We observe comparable patterns in language after language, and in era after era, not because of any fixed and immutable elements of the linguistic system, but because the same physical and cognitive pressures and tendencies are continually acting and interacting in comparable ways. Collections of phonetic properties that *change* meaning, *eliminate* meaning distinctions, or *maintain* meaning distinctions might emerge and change as a consequence of their use, re-use and disuse.

Indeed, virtually every characteristic of phonological systems that we have discussed in this book is amenable to *external* explanation – explainable in terms of systems that demonstrably serve *another* function. Only as a very last resort should we posit domain-specific content to language, or to any other natural system, for that matter: simple, general and broadly applicable hypotheses are a hallmark of compelling scientific investigations. As of this writing, I have encountered no reason to breach the gates of this last resort in our attempts to explain phonological patterning. Both language itself and its structural characteristics are emergent consequences of our evolved status as social beings: *I speak, therefore you are.*

Mutatis mutandis, this quote from Charles Darwin's *The Origin of Species* serves as a fitting conclusion to all preceding discussion:

> Although I am fully convinced of the truth of the views given in this volume under the form of an abstract, I by no means expect to convince experienced naturalists whose minds are stocked with a multitude of facts all viewed, during a long course of years, from a point of view directly opposite to mine. It is so easy to hide our ignorance under such expressions as the 'plan of creation', 'unity of design', &c., and to think that we give an explanation when we only restate a fact. Anyone whose disposition leads him to attach more weight to unexplained difficulties than to the explanation of a certain number of facts will certainly reject my theory. A few naturalists, endowed with much flexibility of mind, and who have already begun to doubt on the immutability of species, may be influenced by this volume: but I look with confidence to the future, to young and rising naturalists, who will be able to view both sides of the question with impartiality. Whoever is led to believe that species are mutable will do good service by conscientiously expressing his conviction: for only thus can the load of prejudice by which this subject is overwhelmed be removed.

Further reading

On the Lombard Effect:

Lombard, Etienne (1911). 'Le signe de l'élévation de la voix', *Annales Des Maladies de l'Oreille et Du Larynx* 37: 101–19.

Lane, Harlan and Tranel, Bernard (1971). 'The Lombard Sign and the role of hearing in speech', *Journal of Speech and Hearing Research* 14: 677–709.

On altruism in phonology:

Kingston, John (2002). 'Keeping and losing contrasts', in Julie Larson and Mary Paster (eds), *Proceedings of the 28th Annual Meeting of the Berkeley Linguistics Society*. Berkeley: Berkeley Linguistics Society.

Kingston, John and Diehl, Randy L. (1994). 'Phonetic knowledge', *Language* 70: 419–54.

The Paul quotes ('*[T]here is no such thing* . . .', '*One of the commonest errors* . . .'):

Paul, Hermann (1880 [1970]). *Principles of the History of Language*. College Park, MD: McGrath, pp. 47–8.

On word frequency and sound change:

Bybee, Joan (2001). *Phonology and Language Use*. Cambridge: Cambridge University Press.

Hale, Mark (2003). 'The "diachronic filter" and phonological theory', paper presented at the 11th Manchester Conference on Phonology, Manchester, UK.

The Schuchardt quote ('*The change of a sound* . . .'):

Schuchardt, Hugo (1885 [1972]). 'On sound laws: against the Neogrammarians', in Theo Vennemann and Terence H. Wilbur, *Schuchardt, The Neogrammarians and the Transformational Theory of Phonological Change*. Frankfurt: Athenäum, pp. 57–8.

On 'laziness' in phonology:

Kirchner, Robert (2004). 'Consonant lenition', in Bruce Hayes, Robert Kirchner and Donca Steriade (eds), *Phonetically Based Phonology*. Cambridge: Cambridge University Press, pp. 313–45.

The Kruszewski quote ('*Language occupies* . . .'):

Kruszewski, Mikołaj (1881 [1995]). 'On sound alternation', in Konrad Koerner (ed.), *Writings in General Linguistics* (Amsterdam Classics in Linguistics 11). Amsterdam: John Benjamins, pp. 8–9.

On writing systems:

Coulmas, Florian (1996). *Encyclopedia of Writing Systems*. Oxford: Blackwell Publishers.

Smalley, William A., Chia Koua Vang and Gnia Yee Yang (1990). *Mother of Writing: The Origin and Development of a Hmong Messianic Script*. Chicago: The University of Chicago Press.

The Chomsky and Halle quote ('*[A]n observed [sound] change* . . .'):

Chomsky, Noam and Halle, Morris (1968). *The Sound Pattern of English*. New York: Harper and Row, pp. 249–50.

The Schane quote ('Although the speech signal may be physically continuous ...'):

Schane, Sanford A. (1973). *Generative Phonology.* Englewood Cliffs, NJ: Prentice-Hall, pp. 3–4.

The Hyman quote ('In order to characterize ...'):

Hyman, Larry M. (1975). *Phonology: Theory and Analysis.* New York: Holt, Rinehart and Winston, pp. 8–9.

The Kenstowicz and Kisseberth quote ('[A]ll of the idiosyncratic features ...'):

Kenstowicz, Michael and Kisseberth, Charles (1979). *Generative Phonology.* San Diego: Academic Press, p. 32.

The Gussenhoven and Jacobs quotes ('Why do phonologists assume ...', 'The recognition of two levels of representation ...'):

Gussenhoven, Carlos and Jacobs, Haike (1998). *Understanding Phonology.* London: Arnold, pp. 57–9 and 62.

The Kager quote ('Consider a language ...'):

Kager, René (1999). *Optimality Theory.* Cambridge: Cambridge University Press, pp. 27–8.

The Trubetskoy quote ('Reference to psychology ...'):

Trubetskoy, Nikolai S. (1939 [1969]). *Principles of Phonology.* Berkeley/Los Angeles: University of California Press, pp. 38, 39, 41.

Other applications of evolutionary theory to linguistic theory:

Blevins, Juliette (2004). *Evolutionary Phonology: The Emergence of Sound Patterns.* Cambridge: Cambridge University Press.

Croft, William (2000). *Explaining Language Change: An Evolutionary Approach.* Harlow, Essex: Longman.

Keller, Rudi (1990 [1994]). *On Language Change: The Invisible Hand in Language.* London: Routledge.

Schleicher, August (1850 [1983]). *Die Sprachen Europas in Systematischer Übersicht: Linguistische Untersuchungen.* Philadelphia: John Benjamins.

The Darwin quote:

Darwin, Charles (1859). *The Origin of Species by Means of Natural Selection.* London: John Murray.

Appendix
Primer of phonetic rudiments

Recall from Chapter One that phonology explores the *functional* aspects of spoken language, whereas phonetics explores its *physical* aspects. Both disciplines thus explore speech patterns, but to rather different – if highly interdependent – ends.

Broadly speaking, we may impose a bipartite division on the study of phonetics: *articulatory phonetics* and *acoustic phonetics*. Acoustic phonetics, which primarily investigates the physical properties of sound waves, may further include the investigation of *aerodynamics* and, perhaps, study of the *peripheral auditory system*. Properly speaking, *psychoacoustics* – the study of the cortical processing of sound – does not fall under the rubric of phonetics, as it involves higher-order cognitive functioning which does not – or at least does not *yet* – lend itself to a purely physical characterization.

I have intentionally titled this appendix to call your attention to its preliminary nature. This primer is not intended as a stand-alone introduction to phonetics, as any phonetician who reads it will be quick to tell you. Instead, I am providing it to help you through some of the phonetic questions that might be raised as you read the body of the book, especially the rather complicated discussions of Chapter Two, for which this appendix might be considered a supplement. At best, this primer should serve to whet your appetite: a jumping-off point for a more thorough and serious exploration of this vast and complex subject of study.

Rudiments of articulatory phonetics

The standard way of presenting consonants is to begin at the front end of the vocal tract (at the lips), and proceed down to the beginning of the vocal tract (at the larynx). As you scan the main IPA (International Phonetic Alphabet) consonant chart left to right (Figure A.2), you see that it follows this convention. Also, as you scan *down* the chart, you'll observe that the list proceeds from those consonants with the greatest oral constriction (stops or *plosives*, and nasals) to the least (the *approximants*).

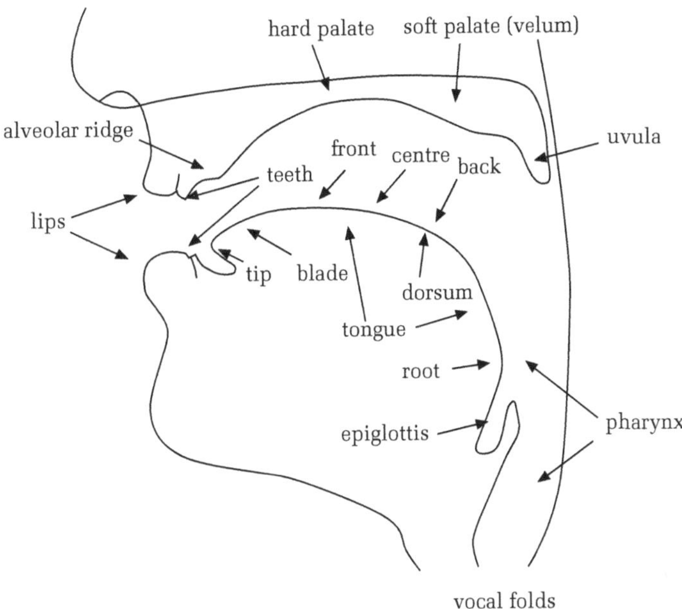

Figure A.1 The speech organs

Throughout this presentation, I am purposely avoiding the use of IPA symbols in my descriptions of sounds' articulatory make-up. If you want to see the symbol (and I hope you do), you must search it out in the accompanying IPA chart. This will get you actively involved in using the chart, and will help you to appreciate the articulatory relationship that one sound bears to others.

I provide Figure A.1 – a mid-sagittal view of the vocal tract – without further comment, to acquaint you with the names and locations of the speech organs.

Pulmonic *consonants*

Consonants are made with significant constriction (or constrictions) somewhere in the vocal tract, above the vocal folds. *Pulmonic consonants* are made by sending air up from the lungs, across the vocal folds and into – and ultimately out of – the vocal tract. Most consonants are of this type. When the vocal folds are set into vibration, these consonants are *voiced*. Symbols representing voiced sounds are placed to the right of their voiceless counterparts.

By convention, sounds are characterized by (1) their laryngeal state, (2) their place of articulation and (3) their degree of oral

CONSONANTS (PULMONIC)

	Bilabial	Labiodental	Dental	Alveolar	Postalveolar	Retroflex	Palatal	Velar	Uvular	Pharyngeal	Glottal
Plosive	p b			t d		ʈ ɖ	c ɟ	k g	q ɢ		ʔ
Nasal	m	ɱ		n		ɳ	ɲ	ŋ	ɴ		
Trill	ʙ			r					ʀ		
Tap or Flap				ɾ		ɽ					
Fricative	ɸ β	f v	θ ð	s z	ʃ ʒ	ʂ ʐ	ç ʝ	x ɣ	χ ʁ	ħ ʕ	h ɦ
Lateral fricative				ɬ ɮ							
Approximant		ʋ		ɹ		ɻ	j	ɰ			
Lateral approximant				l		ɭ	ʎ	ʟ			

Where symbols appear in pairs, the one to the right represents a voiced consonant. Shaded areas denote articulations judged impossible.

Figure A.2 IPA pulmonic consonant chart

constriction, in that order. For example, see if you can locate the voiceless bilabial stop, the voiced retroflex fricative and the voiceless pharyngeal fricative.

We'll begin with *place of articulation*, and then move on to consider the degree of oral constriction, or *manner of articulation*.

Place of articulation

The labial consonants

Bilabials involve the upper and lower lips. The lower lip is the *active articulator*, since this is the organ that engages in movement toward the stable or *passive articulator* (in this case, the upper lip).

Labiodentals involve the lower lip as the active articulator, and the upper teeth as the passive articulator.

The tongue-tip and tongue-blade consonants

Consonants made with the front portion of the tongue can be *apical* or *laminal*. Apical articulations are made with the tip of the tongue, laminal ones with the blade of the tongue.

Dentals are made with the tongue tip or blade placed against the upper teeth. Some languages have *interdentals*, in which the tongue is placed between the upper and lower teeth. These sounds are quite rare, English being one of the relatively few languages which possesses them. *Alveolars* involve the tongue tip or blade placed just behind the upper teeth, on the alveolar ridge. *Post-alveolars* are made with the tongue tip or blade placed slightly farther back along the alveolar ridge.

Finally, *retroflex* consonants are made by curling the tip of the tongue up and back so that its underside may approach or touch the back part of the alveolar ridge. Retroflex consonants are especially common among the languages of India.

The tongue-body consonants

Palatals are made with the front of the body of the tongue approaching or touching the hard palate.

The most common type of tongue-body consonants, the *velars*, involve the tongue body (known as the *dorsum*) moving up and back toward the soft palate, or *velum*.

Uvulars are made by moving the tongue body back toward the uvula, the 'punching bag' that hangs down in the back of the mouth. Quechua and Hebrew are two languages which have uvulars.

The throat consonants

Pharyngeal consonants are made by pulling the root of the tongue towards the back wall of the pharynx. These sounds are comparatively rare, though they are prevalent in the Caucasus, the Middle East and southwestern Canada.

The glottals

The *glottals*, or *laryngeals*, are not technically consonants, since they do not require any constriction above the vocal folds. In the American tradition, they are set off from both consonants and vowels as an independent class of sounds. The IPA chart groups them with the consonants, however. These sounds involve changing the aperture of the glottis (the space between the vocal folds), opening it to generate noise or shutting it completely.

Manner of articulation

Stops are made by temporarily stopping air from flowing through the mouth. Stops may be oral or nasal. Oral stops or *plosives* involve the full cessation of airflow through the mouth and nose. The nasal consonants are stops as well, since there is no airflow through the mouth, though they involve the free flow of air through the nose due to the lowering of the soft palate. Oral stops are usually just called stops, and nasal stops are usually just called nasals.

Trills are made with part of the tongue making brief repeated contacts with the alveolar ridge or farther back along the roof of the mouth. The tongue tip is set in motion by the current of air sent up from the lungs. English largely lacks trills, but they are common in a number of European languages. Spanish has an alveolar trill; many dialects of French have a uvular trill. There is actually a bilabial trill on record as well, in the African language Kele. This trill obviously lacks the involvement of the tongue.

Taps/flaps are made with one quick movement of the tongue tip, like a very rapid stop. For taps, the tongue tip moves in two directions – up to make a brief contact with the roof of the mouth, and then back down. For flaps, only one direction of movement is involved, with the tongue making a brief contact with the roof of the mouth while on its way to another destination. For example, when the tongue de-curls from a retroflexed position, it may flap against the roof of the mouth. American English and Korean are two of the many languages that have taps.

Fricatives, also called *spirants*, can be made using two different kinds of turbulent airflow: air rushing through a narrow channel (as in the labiodental fricatives), and air hitting an obstacle like the teeth, possibly also involving a narrow channel (as in the alveolar fricatives). Turbulence produced in these two ways differs acoustically. The fricatives using a channel turbulence are called *non-sibilant* fricatives and are quieter; fricatives produced against an obstacle are called *sibilant* fricatives (alveolars and post-alveolars) and are noisier.

For *lateral fricatives*, the tongue tip or blade makes contact with the alveolar ridge, but the sides of the tongue are lowered. These side openings are sufficiently critical that noise is generated as the air passes by.

Fricatives, along with oral stops (and *affricates*, which begin as a stop and end as a fricative; for example, the first sound in 'chimney') form the class of *obstruents*. In articulatory terms, obstruents are consonants that have a constriction somewhere above the glottis which inhibits airflow to the extent that turbulence or complete air stoppage is induced.

Approximants involve the nearing of two articulators without producing a turbulent airstream. They include the *liquids* – the lateral approximants and the *rhotics* (r-like sounds) – and the *glides*, which include the palatal approximant and the labio-velar approximant, among others.

The nasals, laterals and approximants form the class of *resonants*. In articulatory terms, resonants are those sounds in which airflow is not inhibited sufficiently that air turbulence or air stoppage is induced. Trills and taps are usually grouped with the resonants as well, although they indeed stop airflow, however briefly. In part for this reason, the resonants and these additional sounds are often grouped together in the class of *sonorants*. Resonants are usually *voiced*.

CONSONANTS (NON-PULMONIC)

Clicks		Voiced implosives		Ejectives	
ʘ	Bilabial	ɓ	Bilabial	ʼ	Examples:
ǀ	Dental	ɗ	Dental/alveolar	pʼ	Bilabial
!	(Post)alveolar	ʄ	Palatal	tʼ	Dental/Alveolar
ǂ	Palatoalveolar	ɠ	Velar	kʼ	Velar
ǁ	Alveolar lateral	ʛ	Uvular	sʼ	Alveolar fricative

Figure A.3 IPA non-pulmonic consonant chart

Non-pulmonic *consonants*

See Figure A.3.

Non-pulmonic consonants are less common than pulmonic ones. This class contains sounds for which the source of airflow is not the lungs, but is instead either the larynx or the velum. While all pulmonic sounds are *egressive*, that is, involving air flowing from farther down to farther up the vocal tract, non-pulmonic sounds may be either egressive or *ingressive*, involving air flowing from farther up to farther down the vocal tract.

Clicks are *velaric ingressive* sounds. They are made by first forming two seals in the mouth, one at the soft palate, and one further forward. As both seals are implemented, the tongue slides backward along the soft palate with the seals being maintained. This tongue-sliding gesture serves to increase the size of the sealed chamber created by the two constrictions, thus lowering the air pressure in this small 'pocket'. Now the front seal is released, and air comes streaming back into the pocket from the front end of the mouth, producing a click-like sound. The 'tsk tsk tsk' what-a-pity sound is a dental click. The horse-calling sound is a lateral click. In some languages spoken in Africa, these and other clicks are free to combine with other sounds, and thus play a fully contrastive role in the sound system.

Implosives are usually *voiced glottalic ingressive stops*. A closure is made somewhere in the mouth, but, also, the glottis is mostly shut down as well; the vocal folds are usually vibrating, which produces voicing. Now the larynx is pulled farther down in the throat, thus increasing the size of the chamber made by the seal in the mouth and the near-seal at the larynx. This often lowers the pressure in this chamber, and so, upon release of the oral seal, air may be sucked inward, producing a slightly thuddish sound. Vietnamese is a language with implosive stops, and quite a few African languages have them as well.

Ejectives are *voiceless glottalic egressives*. Like implosives, most ejectives involve a full oral seal, but unlike implosives' *near*-glottal seal, there is a *complete* glottal seal. Instead of lowering the larynx, in ejectives the larynx is raised, thus shrinking the cavity created by the two seals, and so air pressure within this cavity is increased. Upon release of the oral seal, air shoots out of the mouth quite rapidly, giving ejectives their characteristic 'pop'. Quechua and Amharic are two languages that have ejectives. The fricative ejective does not necessarily involve a full glottal seal at all, since the glottis should be open to allow strong airflow so that noise can be generated at the upper constriction site; ejective fricatives are extremely rare.

Vowels

Of all sound classes, vowels allow the freest flow of air, even freer than the resonant consonants. A rather different system of classification is used for vowel sounds, as shown in the IPA vowel chart (Figure A.4).

Vowel classification requires at least three degrees of height (usually implemented by opening or raising the jaw), and three degrees of backness. The terms *height* and *backness* may refer to the location of the tongue body in the formation of vowel sounds. (*Open* or *low* vowels involve a moderate-to-pronounced pharyngeal constriction.)

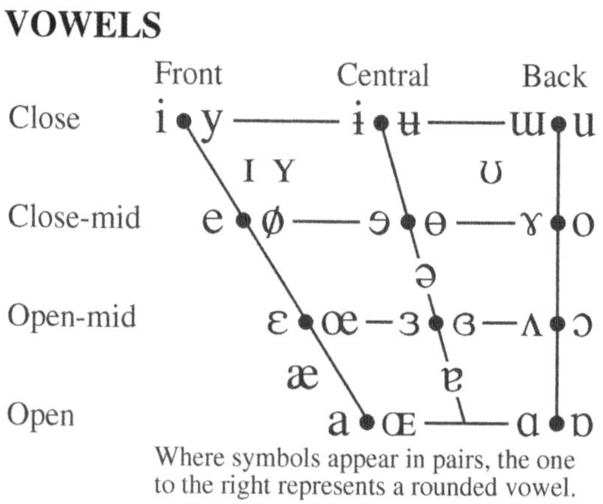

VOWELS

	Front		Central		Back
Close	i • y		ɨ • ʉ		ɯ • u
		ɪ ʏ		ʊ	
Close-mid	e • ø		ɘ • ɵ		ɤ • o
			ə		
Open-mid	ɛ • œ		ɜ • ɞ		ʌ • ɔ
	æ		ɐ		
Open	a • ɶ				ɑ • ɒ

Where symbols appear in pairs, the one to the right represents a rounded vowel.

Figure A.4 IPA vowel chart

Additionally, vowels may be rounded or unrounded, which refers to the posture of the lips. The three vowel qualities situated off the main gridlines of the chart (between the *close* and the *close-mid* sets) are sometimes characterized as the *lax* counterparts to the *tense* close vowels; they are somewhat lower, and somewhat more central. A similar tense–lax distinction is often used to distinguish the *open-mid* from the *close-mid* vowels. The cross-classification of tense–lax, height, front–back, and round–unround should produce at least thirty-six (2 × 3 × 3 × 2) major vowel qualities among the world's languages. This turns out to be a fairly good approximation, although there are fewer low (open) vowels than expected. The reason for the smaller number of lower vowels is related to the fewer opportunities for rendering vowels acoustically distinct in this region, in comparison to vowels implemented with a higher tongue height. This is suggested by the irregular shape of the vowel space as shown in the IPA vowel chart.

Schwa, the so-called featureless vowel, is in the middle of the chart; the other qualities, likes spokes on a wheel, splay outwards from this centre region. Simply place your tongue and lips in the positions that the chart indicates, and before long you'll master any and all of the major vowel qualities.

Diacritics

The IPA has a rich system of diacritics which may be used to modify the standard symbol set (shown in Figure A.5). These diacritics may be used to convey subtle articulatory departures from the main symbols. Linguists who claim that 'the IPA doesn't have a symbol for that sound!' (a protest that I've heard on occasion) do not appreciate the flexibility that the system of diacritics affords. The whole point of the IPA is to establish a set of flexible and universally recognizable symbols of phonetic transcription, so that scholars can easily and accurately convey phonetic information to their readers. Due especially to the system of diacritics, the IPA succeeds remarkably well at this task. When scholars do not use the IPA, they are doing both the field and themselves a disservice. Of course, once in a while, a linguist might discover a truly new sound. Under these circumstances, the IPA may be modified by agreement of the board of the International Phonetic Association (also IPA). For example, a linguo-labial sound was documented on the island of Vanuatu in 1989. A linguo-labial involves the tongue tip reaching out of the mouth to make contact with the upper lip! The IPA board was able to verify the existence of the sound, and devised a new diacritic for the chart.

DIACRITICS Diacritics may be placed above a symbol with a descender, e. g. ŋ̊

◌̥	Voiceless	n̥ d̥	◌̤	Breathy voiced	b̤ a̤	◌̪	Dental	t̪ d̪
◌̬	Voiced	s̬ t̬	◌̰	Creaky voiced	b̰ a̰	◌̺	Apical	t̺ d̺
ʰ	Aspirated	tʰ dʰ	◌̼	Linguolabial	t̼ d̼	◌̻	Laminal	t̻ d̻
◌̹	More rounded	ɔ̹	ʷ	Labialized	tʷ dʷ	◌̃	Nasalized	ẽ
◌̜	Less rounded	ɔ̜	ʲ	Palatalized	tʲ dʲ	ⁿ	Nasal release	dⁿ
◌̟	Advanced	u̟	ˠ	Velarized	tˠ dˠ	ˡ	Lateral release	dˡ
◌̠	Retracted	e̠	ˤ	Pharyngealized	tˤ dˤ	◌̚	No audible release	d̚
◌̈	Centralized	ë	◌̴	Velarized or Pharyngealized ɫ				
◌̽	Mid-centralized	e̽	◌̝	Raised	e̝ (ɹ̝ = voiced alveolar fricative)			
◌̩	Syllabic	n̩	◌̞	Lowered	e̞ (β̞ = voiced bilabial approximant)			
◌̯	Non-syllabic	e̯	◌̘	Advanced Tongue Root	e̘			
˞	Rhoticity	ɚ a˞	◌̙	Retracted Tongue Root	e̙			

Figure A.5 IPA diacritic chart

Labial diacritics

Vowels and consonants may be *more rounded* than normally expected or *less rounded* than normally expected (where 'normally expected' should be interpreted as 'typically found for that particular sound'). Sounds may also be *secondarily labialized*, for example a tongue-tip stop with a rounding gesture superimposed on the stop's release, as in the word 'twelve'.

Tongue-tip diacritics

As already mentioned, tongue-tip consonants may be *dental* (with the tongue tip or blade approaching or contacting the upper teeth), which in turn may be *apical* (made with the tongue tip) or *laminal* (made with the tongue blade). Some languages in South Asia, for example Malayalam, have contrasts between apical and laminal stops. We have already discussed how to make a linguo-labial. I include this sound among the tongue-tip diacritics instead of the labial diacritics because the tongue tip is the active articulator. *Rhoticity* typically involves a retroflexion of the tongue.

Tongue-body diacritics

On the front–back dimension, the tongue body might be more *retracted*, more *centralized* or more *advanced* than normally expected. On the high–low dimension, the tongue body might be slightly raised or slightly lowered. Also, the tongue may be both more centralized and in a more medium height posture than normally expected. When high vowels are slightly raised, turbulence may be created at the constriction site; when fricatives are slightly lowered, they may lose their characteristic turbulence. Sounds might also be *secondarily palatalized*, in which a tongue-raising gesture is superimposed on a consonant, the way a Londoner pronounces the alveolar stop of 'tube', for example. Sounds may also be *secondarily velarized*, involving the tongue moving towards the soft palate, or velum, as an American produces the lateral of 'pill'.

Tongue-root diacritics

Some sounds may possess a more *expanded pharynx* than expected, which involves an *advanced tongue root*, or they may possess a more *constricted pharynx* than expected, involving a *retracted tongue root*. A more significant backing of the tongue root might result in *pharyngealization*, in which the root of the tongue is sufficiently close to the back of the throat to generate fricative-like noise. For example, in animated or emphatic speech, the Korean low vowel may be pharyngealized to the extent that it spirantizes.

Laryngeal diacritics

The *voiceless* symbol indicates a sound that is normally expected to be voiced, but is instead implemented as wholly or partially devoiced. For example, Burmese is a language with *voiceless nasals*. Similarly, the *voicing* subscript indicates a sound that is normally expected to be voiceless, but is wholly or partially voiced. *Aspiration* involves a puff of air due to a wide open glottis, usually coordinated with the release of a stop. Rarely, we find pre-aspirated stops. The *breathy voiced* symbol is used when a sound possesses both some degree of voicing and some degree of aspiration. These sounds may be either consonants or vowels. The languages of South Asia often have both breathy vowels and breathy consonants. *Laryngealized* or *creaky voiced* sounds involve irregular vocal fold vibration due to the vocal folds being tensed and/or partially pressed together. Again, we find them among both consonants and vowels. Creaky vowels are found in southern Mexico, Southeast Asia, West Africa and elsewhere.

Release diacritics

Some South American languages have stops that are *nasally released*, while some Mexican languages (including loans into Mexican Spanish) have *laterally released* stops. Some English speakers might laterally-release the first stop in words like 'Atlantic'. Many languages of East Asia and elsewhere have *inaudibly released* stops (also somewhat inaccurately called *unreleased* stops), in which a stop closure is made but is not released in an audible fashion.

Syllabicity diacritics

Sometimes vowels are not long enough to act as the centre, or peak, of a syllable, and sometimes consonants are long enough that they do indeed play this role. The IPA has symbols for each of these situations, although it should be emphasized that there is no satisfactory articulatory definition of a syllable, and so these symbols impose a degree of abstraction on the IPA that is perhaps somewhat unwarranted.

Nasalization diacritic

Nasalization involves lowering the soft palate from its raised position, thus opening the *velo-pharyngeal port*, and so air flows through the nose as well as the mouth.

Suprasegmentals

Suprasegmentals are listed in Figure A.6.

Suprasegmentals refer to those components of the speech stream that involve a temporal span greater than (or sometimes less than) that which a single main IPA symbol represents.

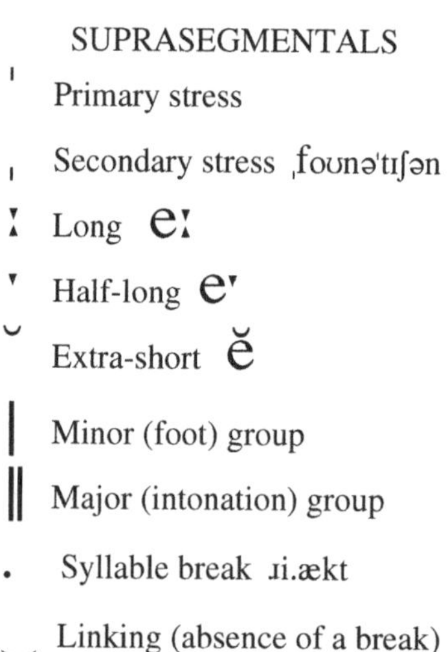

Figure A.6 IPA suprasegmentals chart

Virtually all languages have words with a main or *primary stress*, and many languages, like English, have words with *secondary stress* as well.

Vowels may be of varying lengths. A vowel without a diacritic is assumed to be of more or less normal length, but vowels may be *half-long* or fully *long* as well; vowels might also be *extra short*.

As stated, there is no reliable phonetic evidence for syllables and syllable divisions. Nonetheless, the IPA makes allowances for those phoneticians and phonologists who prefer to express some patterns in terms of syllable structure. There are diacritics for an unexpected *syllable break*, and an unexpected absence of a syllable break, or *link*. Some phoneticians and most phonologists assume that pairs of syllables are grouped into *feet*, which are the domains over which the alternating stress patterns of many languages are manifested (such as strong–weak, or weak–strong). Feet, in turn, may be grouped into *intonational phrases*.

Tones and word accents

See Figure A.7 for tones and word accents.

Tones and *word accents* are suprasegmental in nature as well. They make specific reference to relative *pitch*. *Tone* refers to a linguistic usage of relative pitch for words; a majority of the world's languages use different pitches to serve a distinctive function such that individual words might be distinguished solely in terms of their relative pitch value. In so-called *tone languages* every syllable

TONES AND WORD ACCENTS

LEVEL		CONTOUR	
e̋ or ˥	Extra high	ě or ˩˥	Rising
é ˦	High	ê ˥˩	Falling
ē ˧	Mid	e᷄ ˦˥	High rising
è ˨	Low	e᷅ ˩˨	Low rising
ȅ ˩	Extra low	e᷈ ˧˦˧	Rising-falling
ꜜ	Downstep	↗	Global rise
ꜛ	Upstep	↘	Global fall

Figure A.7 IPA tones and word accents chart

of every word is usually specified for relative pitch. Chinese, Zulu and Navaho are examples of tone languages. *Word accent* is also a pitch-based distinction. In so-called word accent or *pitch accent languages*, only certain syllables in some words are specified for a relative pitch value. Japanese, Lithuanian and Swedish are examples of pitch accent languages.

There are two ways of indicating tone in the IPA: with diacritics placed above the vowel symbols, and with adscripts, in which the *pitch contour* is expressed by a non-vertical line, and the potential *pitch range* is expressed by a rightward vertical line. This latter system is very flexible; it may be easily modified to indicate any and all pitch patterns one might encounter. Thus the symbols in the chart are merely a small subset of possible tone marks.

Some languages, such as many languages of Africa, have *upstep* or *downstep*, in which the overall pitch is incrementally affected at some point in an utterance. *Global rises* and *global falls* in pitch may be indicated as well.

Other symbols

Several other symbols are found in the IPA chart (see Figure A.8), most of which represent quite rare sounds, but at least one of which is very common (the voiced labial-velar approximant).

With enough practice, a phonetician can readily transcribe anyone's speech, in any language. Here are a few *caricatures* of well-known English accents that you can have fun with.

> [ˈwiə̯ ðə ˈbʌɪ̯ʔɬ̩z̥ frɜm ˈlɪvəˌpʰɛɣ̯]
> [ˈmɑɪ̯ ˈmʌðəz̻ ə ˈd̻ˢɑːk̻tsɨʊ̥ n̩ ˈmɑɪ̯ ˈfɑðəz̻ ə ɬɔːjəʊ̥ ɔ̞ᵊn ði ɔ̞ɬɨnd̻ˢ]
> [ɑz b̥ɔ̃ːn‿ɹeɪ̯z̥ n̩ dɪksɪ̥]

OTHER SYMBOLS

ʍ	Voiceless labial-velar fricative	ɕ ʑ	Alveolo-palatal fricatives
w	Voiced labial-velar approximant	ɺ	Alveolar lateral flap
ɥ	Voiced labial-palatal approximant	ɧ	Simultaneous ʃ and x
ʜ	Voiceless epiglottal fricative		
ʢ	Voiced epiglottal fricative		Affricates and double articulations can be represented by two symbols joined by a tie bar if necessary.
ʡ	Epiglottal plosive		

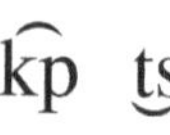

Figure A.8 IPA chart of other symbols

Rudiments of acoustic phonetics

Waves and waveforms

When you strike an object, this object is set into vibration. Depending on their bulk and their flexibility, different objects vibrate in different ways. Vibrations cause disruptions to the distribution of air molecules in the surrounding environment. The disruptions propagate in *waves* outward from the source, and often consist of regular or *periodic compressions* and *rarefactions* of the air molecules which eventually impinge on the ear of a listener, ultimately culminating in a sound percept. It's important to emphasize that it's the *disruptions* that propagate outward, not the air molecules themselves. So as a wave propagates outward toward a listener, the air molecules that ultimately impinge on the ear of a listener have not travelled from the sound source itself. Instead, these molecules were already in the general vicinity of the ear, and have simply been set into back-and-forth motion due to the energy that emanates in waves from the source. It's much like a piece of wood floating on the ocean. The water itself is quite stable in terms of its *horizontal* movement. Rather, the water is *vertically* displaced by the passing waves. So waves traverse the water, but the piece of wood simply rides up and down with the wave, and does not travel much along with the wave itself.

In fact, though, a single object vibrates at a number of different rates simultaneously, the *slowest* rate of vibration normally the most pronounced. If the object vibrates at a rate to which the human auditory system is sensitive, the slowest of these vibrations normally corresponds to the perceived pitch of the resulting sound.

Regarding this slowest vibratory pattern, it has *sine wave* characteristics; the pressure compressions and rarefactions are spaced at regular intervals over time, resulting in a regular and repeating cycle propagating from the source. For example, if an object vibrates regularly 100 times per second, then the sine wave that corresponds to this vibration will repeat itself 100 times per second, or 100 'cycles per second' (cps). We usually express cps in Hertz (Hz), after the nineteenth-century physicist Heinrich Hertz. Thus, the wave we are discussing is a 100Hz wave. The faster the rate of vibration (i.e. the greater the *frequency*), the *higher* the perceived pitch; the greater the displacement of the air molecules from the atmospheric norm (i.e. the greater the *amplitude*), the *louder* the perceived sound. As the wave propagates outward from the source, it steadily loses energy, which means that its amplitude steadily declines.

However, we have only been discussing the sine wave characteristics of the slowest of the cycles which result from striking some object. As stated, for most objects the actual vibratory pattern is more complicated. Most objects, in fact, vibrate at many frequencies. The frequencies of these additional vibrations are multiples of the lowest or *fundamental* frequency. These additional frequencies are collectively referred to as a wave's *harmonic* or *overtone* series. For our 100Hz example, there are harmonics at 200Hz, 300Hz, 400Hz, etc. Now, each of these additional vibratory patterns, taken individually, has the same sine wave characteristics as the slowest pattern. That is, they repeat at regular intervals, except, of course, that their rate of repetition is faster (and faster still as we multiply the fundamental). Also, all else being equal, the faster the rate of repetition, the lower the amplitude of the harmonic. In the schematic display of a 100Hz wave and its first two overtones in Figure A.9, the x-axis indicates relative amplitude and the y-axis indicates time.

The vibrations result in *complex waves* that are a consequence of the combination of the fundamental frequency with its harmonic series. While a complex wave may indeed be viewed as a pattern that repeats over time, the harmonic series serves to obscure the sine wave characteristics of its components. Since the entire harmonic series is completely overlaid in time, the complex waveform has the appearance (when transduced into a visual display) of a great jumble (an actual wave would be far more complex than our simple example). Joseph Fourier first documented this analysis of complex waves in the early nineteenth century.

A *power spectrum* is a far more visually perspicuous display of a complex wave, in comparison to the visual display of the wave itself. A power spectrum plots frequency on its x-axis, with each harmonic being plotted left to right. The y-axis shows amplitude. Thus each harmonic is shown as a line extending up to its amplitude level (Figure A.10). Power spectra do not indicate changes over time; they merely isolate a very brief window of time.

In speech, the objects that are set into vibratory motion are the vocal folds. Their vibration is a consequence of air from the subglottal chamber (the lungs) being forced through them. Depending on their posture, the folds repeatedly open and close at near-regular intervals. As the vocal folds are flexible and may readily be adjusted in terms of their stiffness, thickness, etc., they are able to vibrate in a surprising number of different ways, which gives rise to pitch, amplitude and other differences.

The opening and closing pattern of the vocal folds is a consequence of the Bernoulli Effect (after Daniel Bernoulli). Briefly, when the vocal folds are appropriately postured, and in full contact (the glottis is shut), and, also, when air is being pushed up from the lungs, the subglottal

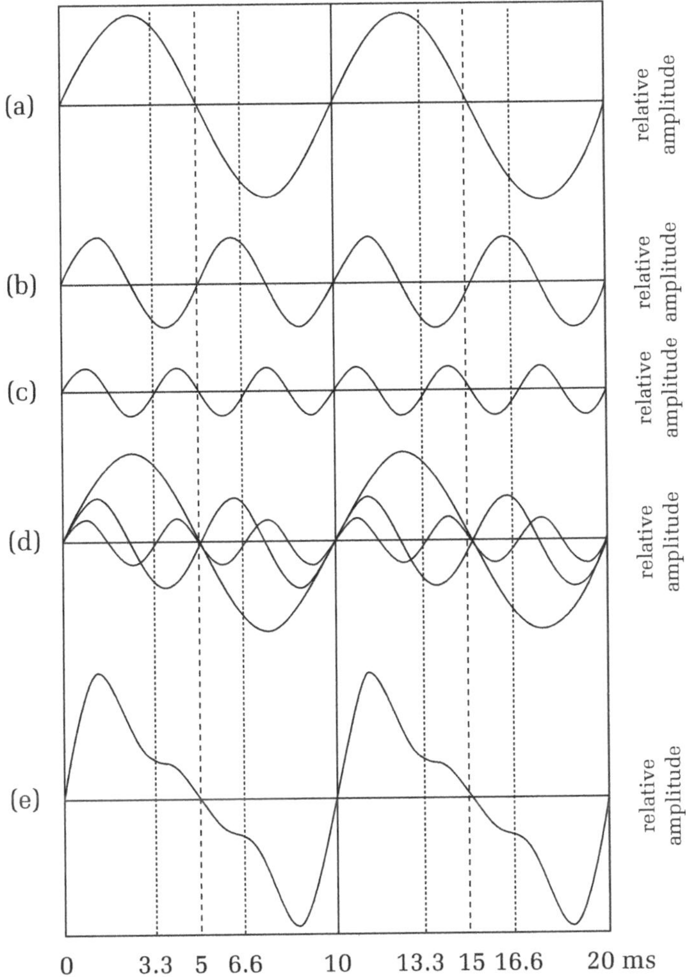

Figure A.9 Two cycles of a 100Hz sine wave (a), four cycles of a 200Hz sine wave (b), six cycles of a 300Hz sine wave (c). For a complex wave, as the sine waves get higher in frequency, they get lower in amplitude. The three waves may be superimposed on each other (d), thus showing the components that are additively combined into a complex wave (e). Since one complete cycle of the slowest wave takes 10 ms (milliseconds), this complex wave repeats 100 times per second; it is a 100Hz complex wave.

pressure will become sufficiently great that the folds are blown apart, with air rushing through into the vocal tract. However, it is the very rushing of the air across the now-open glottis, in combination with the vocal folds' natural elasticity, that induces its shutting down: as

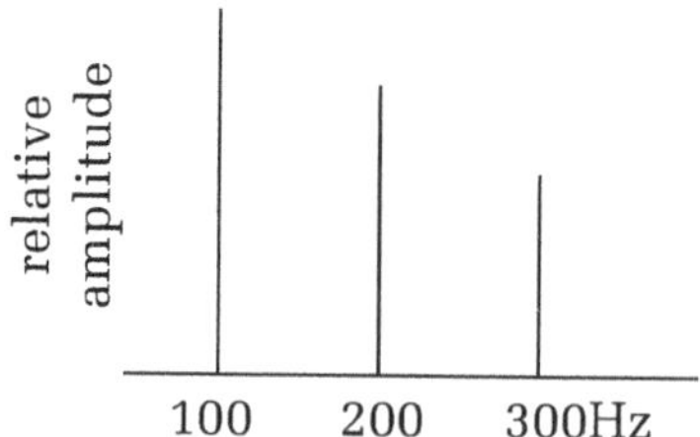

Figure A.10 A schematic power spectrum of the first three harmonics of our complex wave

air passes across the folds, pressure drops in the glottis, thus drawing the folds together and shutting down the opening (this is the Bernoulli Effect). Now, subglottal pressure builds again, and the cycle repeats until a sufficient change in conditions takes place. This is, then, the glottal cycle, which corresponds to the fundamental frequency in speech.

Resonant frequencies in the vocal tract

If you were to chop off your head, and expose your vibrating larynx to the elements (don't try this at home), then the resulting complex wave would look quite like our example schematics as drawn in Figure A.9. The fundamental frequency would be the loudest, and the harmonics would incrementally decrease in amplitude as they were multiplied in frequency (though they would extend far above 300Hz). Such a sound would probably approximate an annoying buzz. However, fortunately for us, we have heads, and in our heads is a system of *resonating chambers*, including the throat, the mouth and the nasal passages. These resonating chambers *filter* the complex wave emanating from the laryngeal *source*. Depending on the shape of these filters, the amplitude of different frequency ranges of the harmonic series is changed. These changes are crucial to speech production and perception due to their effect on sound quality. To understand how all this happens, let's begin with discussing the resonating properties of a simple tube.

A tube has characteristic *resonant frequencies*. Broadly, resonant frequencies refer to those frequencies which are increased in amplitude relative to the others that are present in the tube. More accurately, resonant frequencies are those that meet the proper *boundary conditions* for resonance. Boundary conditions refer to the amplitude properties of a given sinusoidal wave at the *ends* of the tube. These amplitude properties are a consequence of the *wavelength* (the distance required for the completion of one full wave, or one *cycle*) as it relates to tube length.

Consider a tube of 20cm that is closed at both ends, with one end providing a vibratory source, and the other end consisting of a solid wall. A 20cm tube is only a little longer than the average distance from the larynx to the lips of an adult male. For this sort of tube, the resonant frequencies are whole number multiples of a frequency with twice the wavelength of the length of the tube itself. Why should this be so? To answer this question we have to consider specific physical properties of the sound wave, and the reflective properties of the sealed tube.

As we now know, a periodic wave consists of regularly repeated pressure compressions and rarefactions of air which, respectively, crowd the air molecules closer together than average, and space them farther apart than average. The greater the deviations from the atmospheric norm, the greater the amplitude of the wave and, ultimately, the greater its perceived loudness.

As we have further learned, one sinusoidal wave can be added to another, and their amplitudes at a given point in space are summed. So, if the pressure increase induced by one wave is simultaneous with a pressure *decrease* induced by another wave, the two additively combine, resulting in a pressure level lower than the first component, but higher than the second (if the compression and the rarefaction are equal in amplitude, they add to zero, and pressure at this point in space is equivalent to atmospheric pressure). However, if *both* waves induce an increase (or decrease) in pressure at a particular point in space, their respective amplitudes will combine to produce a wave of greater (or lesser) amplitude.

In our tube, the resonant frequencies are those that are at peak amplitude at both ends of the tube. As such a wave propagates through the space of the tube from the source, it ultimately hits the solid end. Now the wave is reflected back toward the source. The resonant frequencies are thus those that achieve maximal amplitude as they return to the source just as a new wave is emitted from this source: the two waves are combined in a wholly additive fashion, thus maximally increasing the amplitude at the source. There is thus an obvious relationship between the length of the tube and its resonant frequencies: any frequency whose wavelength is such that these boundary conditions are met is a resonant frequency. The first such frequency has a wavelength twice the length of the tube, because the wave has gone through half its cycle as it hits the reflective boundary, and so it completes one full cycle just as it returns to the source.

In the 20cm tube in our example, what is the lowest frequency that meets these boundary conditions? This resonant frequency is determined by the speed of sound through the air (c, which is 34,400cm/sec), divided by the wavelength, which we now know is twice the tube length ($2L$; remember, L is 20cm in our example). Thus $f = c/2L$, or 34,400/40, or 860Hz.

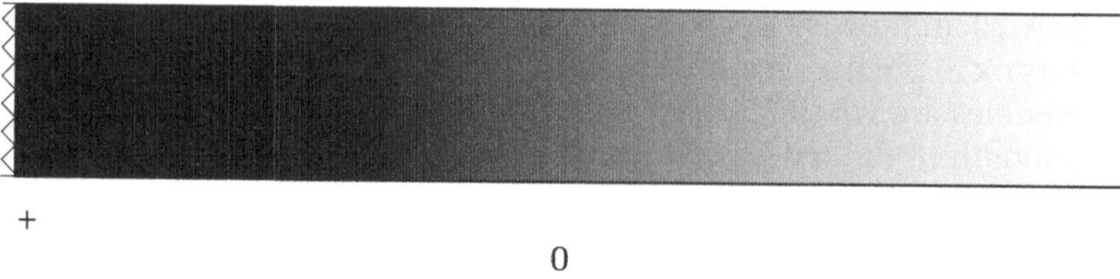

Figure A.11 Schematic snapshot of the first resonant frequency of a tube with a sound source at the left end and closed at the right end, which has a wavelength one-half of the tube length. As this tube is closed at both ends, boundary conditions for resonance are met by a wave whose length is half the tube length. The grey scale is suggestive of air particle density, where black indicates maximal density, grey atmospheric density and white minimal density; the labels '+', '0' and '–' refer to particle density as well, and are graphically arranged to convey the sinusoidal characteristics of the wave. This becomes more evident in Figure A.12.

This resonant frequency is not the only one meeting the boundary conditions, however. The second lowest frequency meeting these conditions consists of a wavelength that fits exactly one complete cycle in the tube. This frequency is rather obviously twice the first resonant frequency, or 1720Hz. The third resonant frequency is three times the first (3440Hz), and so on. See Figures A.11 and A.12.

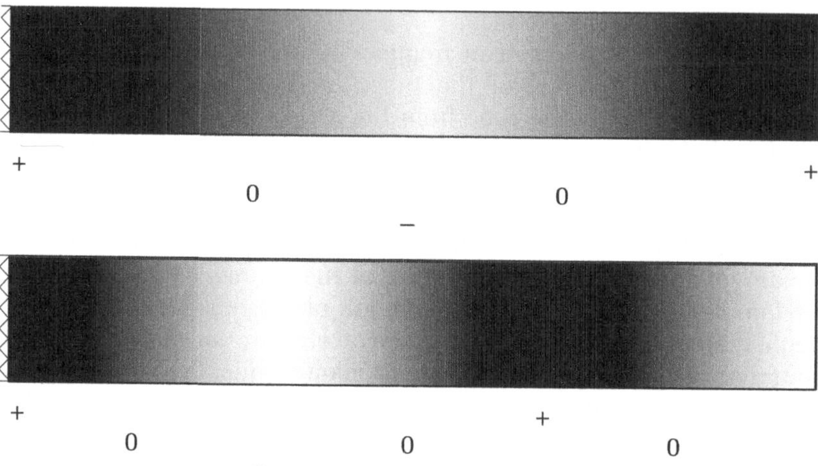

Figure A.12 Schematic snapshots of the second and third resonant frequencies of a tube closed at the right end. The second resonant frequency has half the wavelength of the first, and is thus twice the frequency of the first. One full cycle fits in the tube. The third resonant frequency is a wave with one-third the wavelength of the first resonant frequency, and three times the frequency of the first. One and a half cycles fit in the tube. The sine wave characteristics of the component frequencies become more apparent here.

Now, when we make vowel sounds, the vocal tract is tube-like as well, but qualitatively different from our model tube, because it is open at the mouth – the opposite end from the source (the vocal folds). It turns out that the reflective properties of open-ended and close-ended tubes are different. While a closed tube reflects a wave back to the source with the same sign (+ or −) at which it arrives at this boundary, an open tube reflects back to the source by *reversing* the sign at the reflection site (+ → −, − → +). So if a wave *peaks* at the open end, it is reflected back as a *trough*.

Given these different boundary conditions, the characteristics of the resonant frequencies in an open tube differ as well. The requirement that the amplitude be additive at the source is still in effect, but the wavelengths (relative to tube length) which meet these requirements are different, given the differing reflective properties here. Specifically, while the resonant frequencies for a closed tube possess maximal amplitudes at both ends, the resonant frequencies of an open tube possess amplitude *minima* or *nodes* at the open end.

The first frequency which meets this requirement possesses a wavelength four times the length of the tube, because such a wave possesses zero amplitude one-quarter of the way through its cycle (assuming the cycle begins at maximum amplitude at the source). The second resonant frequency fits three-quarters of its wavelength into the tube. The third resonant frequency fits five-quarter wavelengths into the tube, and so on.

Thus, in a 20cm tube open at one end, the first resonant frequency will be $c/4L$, or 34,400/80, or 430Hz. The second resonant frequency will be $c/1.33L$, or 34,400/26.66, or 1290Hz. The third resonant frequency will be $c/.8L$, or 34,400/16, or 2150Hz. Figure A.13 gives a schematic snapshot.

The source of sound in the vocal tract (the vocal folds) produces a complex wave, not a pure sinusoid as in our tube model. Since there are harmonics accompanying the fundamental frequency, many frequencies are present simultaneously, some of which will be resonant. Given that the average length of the adult male vocal tract (from the vocal folds to the lips) is approximately 17.5cm (not 20 cm as in our model), the first three resonant frequencies are approximately at 500Hz (34,400/70), 1500Hz (34,400/23.275), and 2500Hz (34,400/14). These values correspond to the amplitude prominences that are characteristic of schwa ([ə]), the vowel quality that is perceived when no significant constriction is made within the vocal tract. Though there is an infinite number of waveforms which will fit the tube in this fashion, the shortest three waveforms fitting the tube are of primary consideration here.

Figure A.13 Schematic snapshots of the first three resonant frequencies of a tube open at the right end

Our tube model can account reasonably well for the resonant frequency characteristics of schwa, that is, the vowel without any significant constrictions along the length of the vocal tract. But what happens when constrictions are implemented somewhere along the vocal tract length? Such tract postures arise whenever a sound other than schwa is implemented. For the time being, we will consider only vowel-like constrictions, although eventually we have to understand the acoustic characteristics of any and all sorts of constrictions – at different locations, of differing degrees – that are employed in speech production.

If we take our model tube again, and pinch it along its length such that we create two different chambers, we can loosely model the shape of the vocal tract during certain non-schwa vowels.

As a first approximation, consider a tube with a long narrow back tube opening into a shorter wider front tube. Here, both tubes have the same boundary conditions, since they both may be regarded as closed at their back ends, but open at their front ends. This configuration roughly models the vocal tract shape for [ɑ]. For [ɑ], the lowest resonant frequency is about 800Hz, deriving from the back cavity, or throat. The second lowest resonant frequency is about 1500Hz, which derives from the front cavity, or mouth. The third resonant frequency is three times the first, or about 2400Hz. This third resonant frequency is actually the *second* resonant frequency of the back cavity. We call the resonant frequencies of the vocal tract *formants*, and so [ɑ] has formants at about 800Hz (the first formant, or F1), 1500Hz (F2), 2400Hz (F3), etc.; it is the first two formants that are most important in the determination of vowel quality.

Now let's squeeze our tube at the other end, making a narrow channel at the 'mouth'. This approximates the configuration of [i]. For [i], the first formant is quite low, about 280Hz. With a short front cavity, the second formant is quite high. You may be wondering why F1 in high vowels is so very low. After all, F1 for a schwa, which involves a tube running from the vocal folds to the lips, has an F1 of about 500Hz. It turns out that the vocal tract configuration for high vowels (long wide back cavity and short narrow front cavity) actually sets up a different resonance condition (known as a Helmholtz resonator, after Hermann von Helmholtz, the nineteenth-century scientist who documented it). A Helmholtz resonator involves a body of contained air with an open hole or neck connecting to the outside. The frequency of a Helmholtz resonance is determined by the mass of air in the neck resonating in conjunction with the compliance of the air in the cavity.

Now, if instead of squeezing the tube at one end, as in the preceding examples, we create a narrow pinch in the middle of the tube, differing resonant conditions result. In this two-tube model, we may regard the back tube as closed at both ends – the vocal folds at one end, and the small port into the narrow constriction at the other end – while the front tube may be regarded as open at its far end – at the lips. Consequently, as we now know, the two tubes will have different boundary conditions, and according to their respective lengths, they will have different resonant frequencies. We still assume that the overall length of the two-tube complex is fixed at 17.5cm (again, the length of a typical adult male vocal tract), and thus the tubes' lengths are complementary – lengthening one of the tubes shortens the other, and vice versa, such that the overall length is always 17.5cm. This does not accurately reflect actual conditions, since it is possible to effect length changes in the vocal tract by lowering the larynx and protruding the lips, but these complications can be ignored for the present. Most other vowel qualities can be roughly modelled along these lines. Pinching the tube somewhere along its length will affect the resonating properties of the two chambers created by the pinch itself.

Broadly speaking, F1 fairly correlates with back cavity (pharynx) length: the shorter the back cavity, the higher the F1; the longer the back

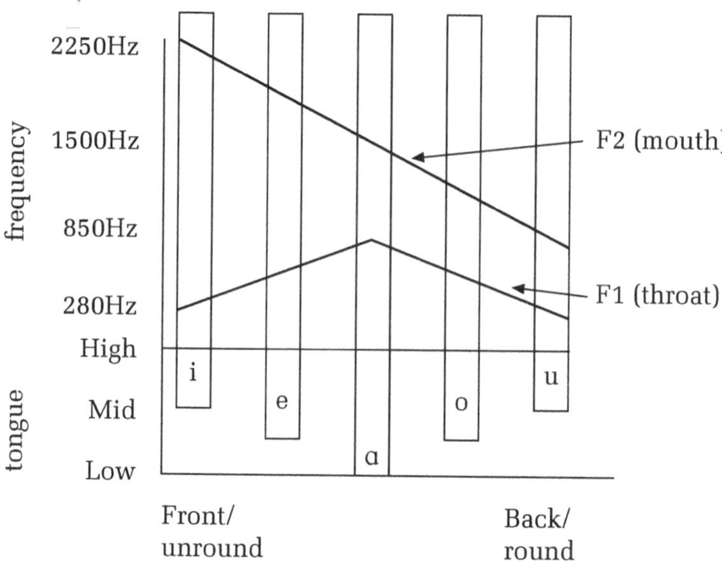

Figure A.14 Gross acoustic and articulatory properties of major vowels. The vertical 'bars' merely call attention to the formant properties of the given vowel quality.

cavity, the lower the F1. As back cavity size inversely correlates with tongue height, we can say that the higher the tongue, the lower the F1. So high vowels have a low F1, and low vowels have a high F1. Meanwhile, F2 fairly correlates with front cavity (mouth) length. Generally speaking, the shorter the front cavity, the higher the F2; the longer the front cavity, the lower the F2. As front cavity size correlates with tongue backing, the farther back the tongue, the lower the F2; the farther front the tongue, the higher the F2. So front vowels have a high F2, and back vowels have a low F2 (Figure A.14). These correlations are merely good rules of thumb; they should *not* be taken as good rules of aerodynamics, however.

In general, F1 and F2 contribute the most to the perception of different vowels. Thus, each vowel has a different spectral shape, meaning each vowel has different formant values.

A *spectrogram* is a graphic representation showing time information (on the x-axis), frequency (on the y-axis) and amplitude (indicated by the darkness of the display). We won't go into any details about how spectrograms are made; suffice it to say that the acoustic energy is transformed into a visual display. The spectrogram in Figure A.15 shows my production of the five vowels [i e ɑ o u]. I held each vowel quality for about one second, and glided from one vowel to the next. Above the spectrogram I have marked which vowel

I am producing with its IPA symbol, and I have drawn a vertical line straight down from each symbol, thus clarifying which component of the display corresponds to which vowel quality.

The display provides a wealth of information about the way I produce these sounds. I have chosen to display the energy that is present between 0Hz and 4000Hz. There is energy well above 4000Hz, but the energy below this cut-off is the most important for vowels. You can easily see the formant regions, indicated by those frequency ranges that are especially dark. F1 gets higher as the vowel quality gets lower, and F2 gets lower as the vowel quality moves further back. I have highlighted these patterns in schematic form, with white lines running through the spectrogram itself. The black vertical striations indicate the glottal pulses. Each striation correlates to a positive amplitude peak induced by a single slapping together of the vocal folds. An unwieldy method of determining the fundamental frequency of my voice would be to count how many striations are present for each second of speech (there are far easier methods, I assure you).

Now look at the circles that I superimposed on the spectrogram. I placed these at the intersections between the approximate centre frequency of each of the first two formants, and, roughly, at the temporal centre of each vowel quality. (There isn't a perfect match between the actual spectrographic display and the schematics, but this rough approximation is a good way to bring out the relevant patterns.)

The superimposed vertical lines serve an additional purpose. Follow them down through the spectrogram, and look at the pictures to which each is pointing. These pictures provide information about spectral energy at a particular point in time, as indicated by the vertical lines themselves. In these displays, frequency increases along the x-axis (again, from 0Hz up to 4000Hz), and relative amplitude is indicated along the y-axis. Unlike spectrograms, these displays do not have a time axis; the information here is taken from only an extremely brief time 'window', and so doesn't provide information about spectral changes over time (much like a power spectrum). If you have trouble relating these displays to the spectrograms, then just imagine slicing the spectrogram vertically along one of the white lines. You can readily envision spectral peaks and valleys emerging outward from the paper in the third dimension, in topographical form. Dark regions are mountains, lighter regions are valleys. Now imagine peering at the mountain range from the left edge of the spectrogram. It will look like a harsh cliff formed by the cut we have made, its elevation rising and falling as a consequence of the mountains and valleys that we have cut into. These latter displays thus provide us with this point of view at

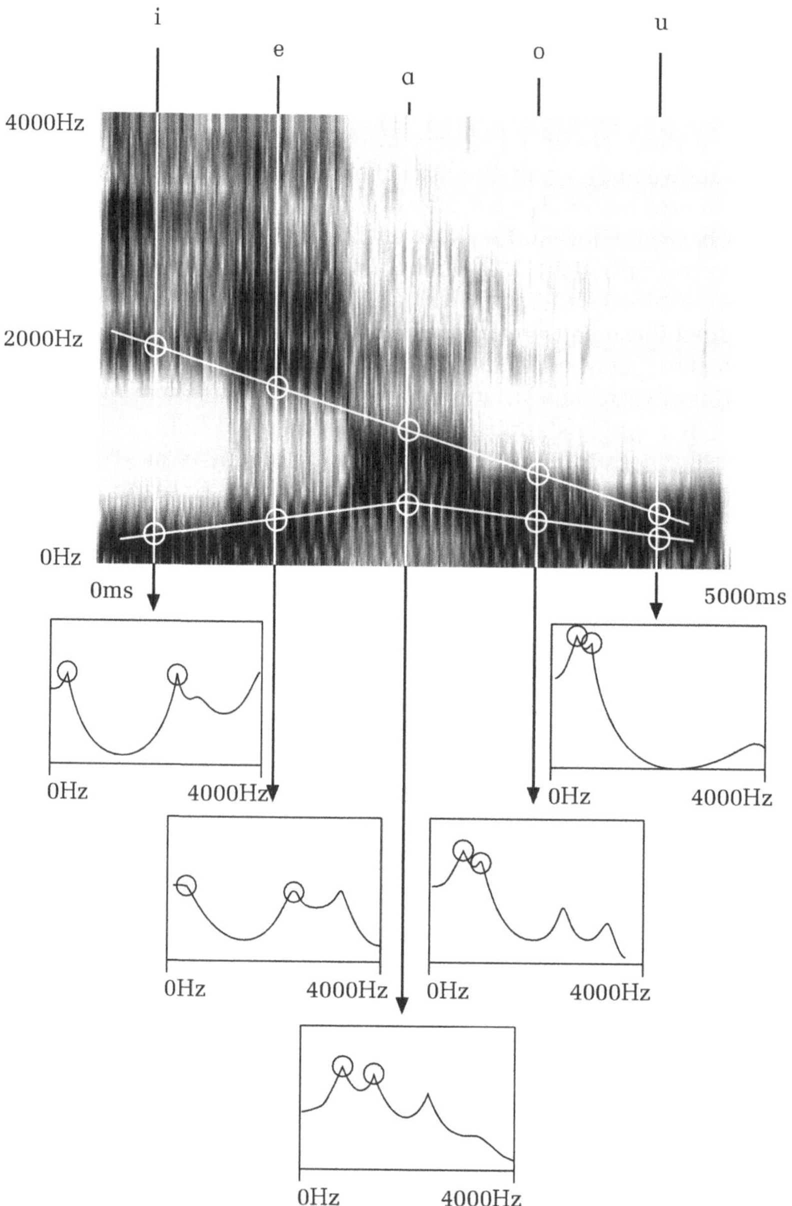

Figure A.15 A spectrogram and five spectral 'snapshots' of [i e ɑ o u], as spoken by me

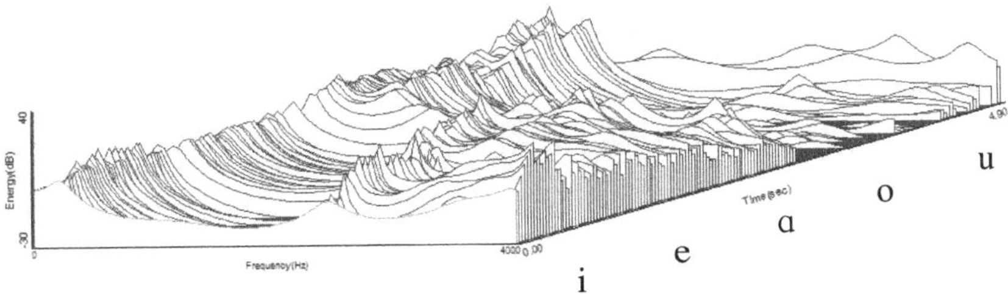

Figure A.16 Bird's-eye view of the three dimensions – energy, frequency and time – during my production of [i e ɑ o u]

five points of time, one each for the five vowel qualities. Again, I have circled the first two spectral peaks – the first two formants – which correspond to the circled regions of the spectrogram.

The next diagram (Figure A.16) provides a 'bird's-eye view' of a spectrogram-like display, which should help you to understand the five spectral 'snapshots' correlating with each of the five vowel qualities.

Fricatives

The constriction that accompanies most vowel qualities is, by definition, never sufficient to significantly obstruct airflow across the vocal folds or out of the mouth. But if such constrictions *are* significantly increased, the airflow is significantly altered in its aerodynamic characteristics. Specifically, when air is forced through a narrow opening, the flow becomes *turbulent*, characterized by the random quality of its motion. For fricatives, it is this turbulent air that is the primary sound source.

During the production of a fricative, air particles are shot through this narrow constriction. Since amplitude increases as particle velocity increases, then, all else held constant, the narrower the channel, the greater the particle velocity, hence the greater the amplitude of the consequent noise.

The noise of fricatives, like the harmonics of vowels, is shaped due to the resonant characteristics of the vocal tract. However, for fricatives, the chamber behind the constriction site does not significantly influence the acoustic signal, since, due to the pronounced constriction, very little energy may pass into the front chamber and out of the mouth. So it's the chamber in front of the constriction that shapes the noise: the shorter the front cavity, the higher the frequency of the amplified noise. [s], with its very short front cavity, has a prominence above 4000Hz. Lip protrusion and palatalization create a longer

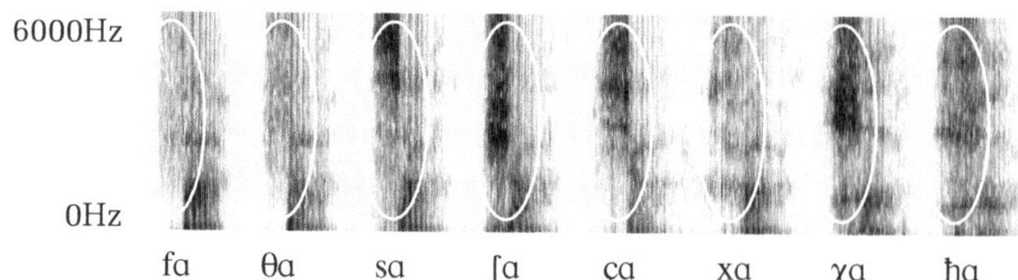

Figure A.17 Spectral properties of the noise associated with all major voiceless fricatives, along with the vowel [a], up to 6000Hz

cavity for [ʃ], and so the acoustic prominence is in a lower range, about 2500Hz and above. The front fricatives – the labials – possess virtually no shaping, because they lack a front cavity that might shape the sound. See Figure A.17.

There are two further *temporal* components that are important in the recognition of fricatives on the part of listeners. Fricatives are the longest segments among the obstruents, and thus the noise which is associated with them is sustained. Additionally, the *rise time* of fricative noise is gradual, not sudden. That is, the increase in energy at the onset of a fricative is comparatively gradual. This is an important cue to the distinction between fricatives and *affricates*, which have a very short rise time.

Formant transitions both into and especially out of fricatives also cue their place of articulation. We discuss formant transitions in the next section.

Stops

Stops require dynamic information about acoustic transitions in order to be properly characterized. Since stop closures possess extremely little energy – indeed, voiceless stop closures possess only silence – all that can be determined during this steady-state component is the *manner* of articulation, i.e. that a stop is being produced. However, information about *place of articulation* is fairly absent during such oral occlusions. It is only during the dynamic transitions into, and especially out of, a stop closure that place of articulation can be conveyed to listeners.

Air trapped behind the oral closure is suddenly shot out of the mouth as a stop is released. This increased airflow results in a high-amplitude *transient*, a 2–3 ms stop *burst*. Each place of articulation has a different characteristic *burst frequency* which is a consequence of the filtering characteristics of the front cavity: burst frequencies are similar to the corresponding acoustic prominences of fricatives. This becomes intuitive when considering the articulatory and aerodynamic characteristics of a stop release: like fricatives, the first portion of a stop release requires the articulators to be very closely approximated such that a brief period of turbulence is induced. Immediately thereafter however – and unlike fricatives – the articulators travel farther apart, and the conditions that induce this turbulence are lost. For labials, which have no front cavity, there is little shaping of the burst noise – it consists of noise across a broad frequency range. Dentals and alveolars have a high-frequency [s]-like burst, while velars have a lower-frequency burst due to the noise being shaped by the longer cavity in front of the release site.

Of extreme importance in the identification of stop place of articulation are the formant transitions into and especially out of the closure portion. After the burst, the articulators are of course set farther apart. The resonant properties of the back cavity – behind the constriction site – are now introduced into the acoustic signal, and so the acoustic signal now possesses a more vowel-like quality. Consequently, the transition from stop to vowel is reflected in the form of formant transitions. The formant transitions will be shaped according to the place of articulation of the stop and its adjacent vowel(s).

For bilabials, F2 and F3 typically lower as the constriction is made, and rise at release. For alveolars, F2 typically points to a *locus frequency* of about 1800Hz. Velars display the so-called 'velar pinch', in which F2 and F3 merge toward each other as the constriction is made, and move away from each other as the constriction is released.

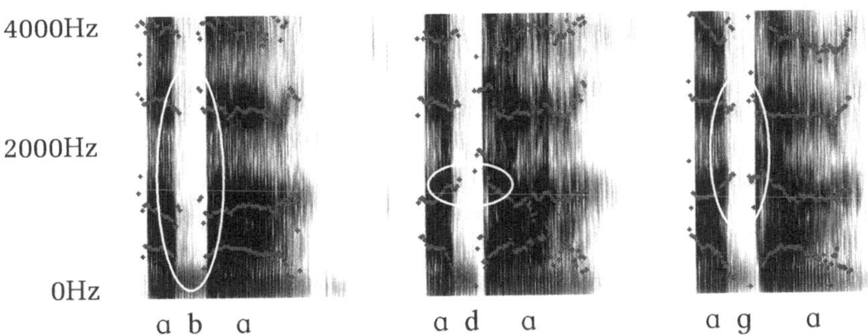

Figure A.18 Spectrogram of me saying [aba ada aga], along with 'formant tracks' which highlight the formants. Each consonant-to-vowel and vowel-to-consonant transition is unique to the particular vowel-consonant-vowel combination. Labials induce a drooping of all formants; alveolars induce F2 to veer toward 1800 Hz; velars usually involve a pinch – F2 and F3 moving toward each other; all circled

There are, broadly speaking, four laryngeal postures for stops, some of which may combine to increase the number of possible contrastive laryngeal states: plain (moderate laryngeal abduction), voiced (vocal fold vibration), aspirated (wide laryngeal abduction, usually at the release of the stop) and glottalized or creaked (laryngeal constriction, usually at the release of the stop). Voicing may occur with aspiration, resulting in breathy-voiced stops, and may also occur with the glottalized posture, typically resulting in imploded stops.

Nasals

Due to their (usually) voiced status, and the free flow of air through the nose, nasals have resonant properties much as vowels do. But since nasals involve a lowering of the velum, hence a *coupling* of the nasal cavity to the oral cavity, their acoustic characteristics are significantly more complex than either oral stops or vowels.

Consider first the uvular nasal. This is the simplest nasal stop to describe, since the oral cavity plays very little role in its acoustic characteristics: basically, a uvular nasal involves a single cavity starting at the larynx and continuing into the nose (Figure A.19); since the oral closure is made so far back, the mouth cavity has very little influence on its acoustic quality; in effect, the uvular closure seals off the mouth from the larynx-to-nose tube.

Given the tube characteristics here, we know the boundary conditions, and so all we need to know is the length of the tube to plug into our resonant frequency formula. The total distance from the vocal folds to the nostrils in a normal adult male is about 21.5 cm, and so our formula is:

$$F1 = c/4L = 35{,}000/4 \times 21.5 = 35{,}000/86 = 407\text{Hz}$$
$$F2 = 3c/4L = 1221\text{Hz}$$
$$F3 = 5c/4\ L = 2035\text{Hz}$$
$$F4 = 7c/4L = 2849\text{Hz, etc.}$$

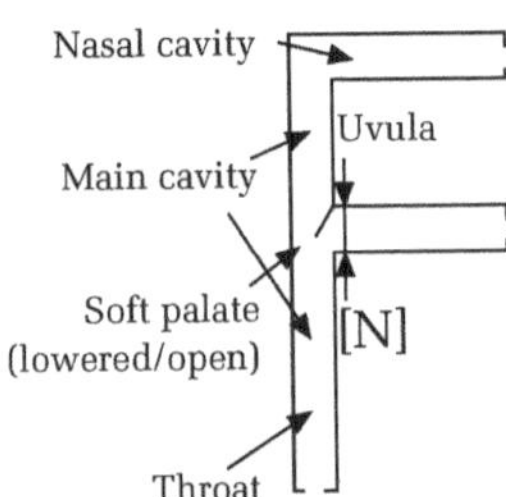

Figure A.19 Opening the soft palate and making an oral seal at the uvula basically creates one long tube from the larynx to the nostrils

These values are actually a little bit high (F1 for nasals is usually at about 300Hz). This is due to the simplification in our model of the actual properties of the oral/nasal tube complex. For now, however, they suffice. Due to the tube length here, nasal F1 is lower than vocalic F1 for all but high vowels (which have a Helmholtz resonance), and, also, nasal formants are spaced closer together than vowel formants, simply because the tube is longer, and so the resonant frequencies are lower and so spaced closer together in frequency.

When we consider non-uvular nasals, things get rather more complicated as a consequence of the side cavity, that is, the oral cavity, which connects to the main larynx-to-nose tube. For the labial, this side cavity is about 8 cm in length. This side branch shouldn't be expected to behave as a simple addition to this resonant system, since it does not open into the atmosphere, but rather its energy is largely dumped back into the main cavity, where most of it will be absorbed. So, the resonant frequencies of the oral cavity will cancel out the corresponding frequencies within the nasal cavity, resulting in an *anti-resonance, anti-formant* or *nasal zero*. For the labial nasal, the anti-formant is at about 1100Hz. For shorter oral cavities, obviously, the anti-formant(s) will be higher in frequency. For the alveolar nasal (with an oral cavity length of about 5.5cm) it is about 1600Hz, and for the very short side cavity that accompanies a velar nasal, it is over 3000Hz.

In addition to the place and manner cues that are present during the oral closure portion of a nasal, also called the *nasal murmur*, there are further cues which derive from the formant transitions into and out of the oral closure. Since we've discussed these already in the context of stops, we don't need to discuss them again.

Nasalized vowels

Velum lowering implemented during a vowel induces the appearance of a nasal formant at a low frequency level. The nasal formant is of a constant frequency regardless of the shape of the oral cavity. Perceptually, it tends to have the effect of raising low vowels and lowering high vowels. This becomes intuitive when considering the interaction of the nasal formant and oral F1. For high nasalized vowels, the nasal formant serves to upwardly expand the lower resonant frequencies, thus perhaps inducing the perception of a lower vowel: listeners hear an acoustic prominence that consists of both the orally- and nasally-derived energy, and cannot necessarily correctly partition this energy between the nasal and oral sources. Given the potential for perceptual confusion here, listeners might think that the higher frequency range derives both from the lower nasal formant (N1) *and* from a higher first oral formant (F1), that is, they pattern together to produce the perceptual effect. (Such confusions are rare – listeners usually faithfully reproduce what speakers are doing – and so these confusions might be merely the diachronic origin of the pattern.) High nasalized vowels do tend to be made with a lower tongue position than their oral counterparts. The opposite is true for low nasalized vowels: the nasal formant serves to downwardly expand F1, consequently inducing the perceptual effect of a higher vowel; these vowels tend to be made with a slightly higher tongue position than their oral counterparts. The F1 of mid nasalized vowels, however, is not significantly affected by nasalization. Indeed, when we investigate languages that have contrastively nasalized vowels, many lack nasalized counterparts to their mid oral vowels. Since superimposing nasality here does not significantly alter the perceived formant value, nasal mid vowels tend to maintain similar tongue-height properties to their oral mid vowels. Consequently, the contrast between oral mid vowels and nasal mid vowels lacks an important cue that helps signal their distinction. In the absence of this cue, the contrast is less likely to be maintained.

Due to the (diachronically-derived) lowering of nasalized high vowels, and the raising of nasalized low vowels, Figure A.20 shows the nasal vowel qualities slightly 'squooshed' together in terms of their tongue height, in comparison to their fully oral counterparts (shown in grey). This squooshing together is another reason why it is less likely that languages will possess three degrees of vowel height among their contrastively nasalized vowels: the acoustic distinction between high and low nasalized vowels may be insufficiently robust to allow a saliently distinct third degree of contrast on the height dimension.

Liquids

Liquids include the laterals and the rhotics. The lowest formant in laterals shows little difference regardless of which lateral is being produced. F2, by contrast, is lower for a velarized lateral with its longer front cavity, higher for the palatal lateral with its shorter front cavity. F3 is often obliterated due to a lateral zero present in this spectral range. However, the retroflex and palatal laterals may possess a relatively prominent F3. F4 varies with front cavity length.

Between F1 and F2, at about 1000Hz, is the first lateral zero (Z1). Finally, the second zero, which often overlaps with F3, displays only minimal variation across places of articulation.

With their often obliterated F3, their similar Z1, and their only minor variability in their other formants and Z2, laterals at distinct

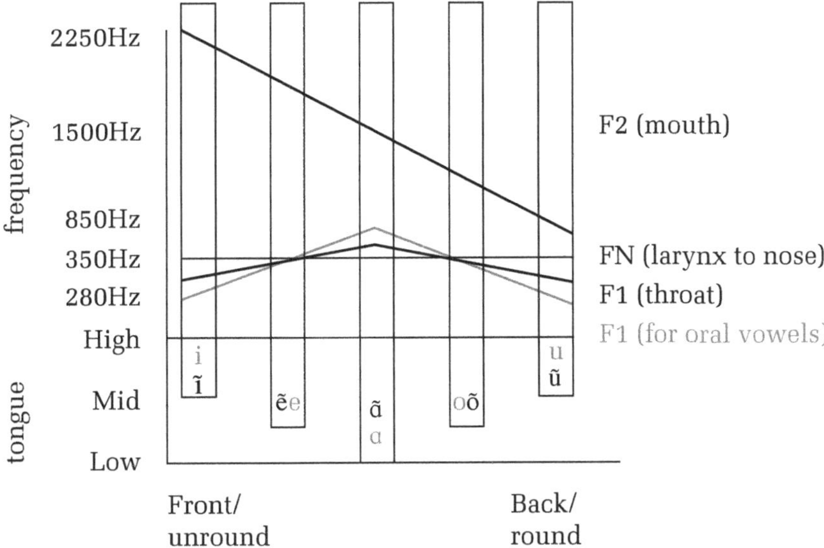

Figure A.20 F1, F2 and FN for five major nasal vowel qualities, along with F1 for the corresponding oral vowels (in grey). The superimposition of the nasal formant may eventually effect a slight articulatory lowering of high vowels and a slight articulatory raising of low vowels, due to the moderating influence this formant has on the spectral properties in this frequency range.

places, unlike other classes of constrictions, display comparatively minor acoustic distinctness. In part for this reason, languages very rarely exploit more than one lateral place of articulation.

The alveolar rhotic is most readily distinguishable from its lateral counterpart by an F3 that dips below 3000Hz.

Further reading

Borden, Gloria, Harris, Katherine and Raphael, Lawrence J. (1994). *Speech Science Primer*. Baltimore: Williams and Wilkins.

Catford, John C. (1977). *Fundamental Problems in Phonetics*. Edinburgh: Edinburgh University Press.

Catford, John C. (1988). *A Practical Introduction to Phonetics*. Oxford: Clarendon.

Denes, Peter B. and Pinson, Elliot N. (1993). *The Speech Chain: The Physics and Biology of Spoken Language*. New York: Freeman.

Fry, Dennis B. (1979). *The Physics of Speech*. Cambridge: Cambridge University Press.

Johnson, Keith (1997 [2003]). *Acoustic and Auditory Phonetics*. Oxford: Blackwell.

Kent, Ray D. and Read, Charles (1992). *The Acoustic Analysis of Speech*. San Diego: Singular.
Ladefoged, Peter (1971 [2001]). *A Course in Phonetics*. San Diego: Harcourt Brace.
Ladefoged, Peter (1971). *Preliminaries to Linguistic Phonetics*. Chicago: University of Chicago Press.
Ladefoged, Peter (2001). *Vowels and Consonants: An Introduction to the Sounds of Language*. Oxford: Blackwell.
Ladefoged, Peter and Maddieson, Ian (1996). *The Sounds of the World's Languages*. Oxford: Blackwell.
Laver, John (1994). *Principles of Phonetics*. Cambridge: Cambridge University Press.
Lieberman, Philip and Blumstein, Sheila E. (1988). *Speech Physiology, Speech Perception and Acoustic Phonetics*. Cambridge: Cambridge University Press.
Pickett, James M. (1999). *The Acoustics of Speech Communication*. Boston: Allyn and Bacon.
Pullum, Gregory K. and Ladusaw, William A. (1986). *Phonetic Symbol Guide*. Chicago: University of Chicago Press.
Rosen, Stuart and Howell, Peter (1991). *Signals and Systems for Speech and Hearing*. London: Academic Press.
Stevens, Kenneth N. (1999). *Acoustic Phonetics*. Cambridge, MA: MIT Press.

Glossary

Acoustics: the study of sound waves; the physical properties of sound waves

Aerodynamics: the study of the motion of gases (especially air) and its effects on solid bodies

Affix: a morpheme that attaches to a word

Affricate: a sound consisting of a stop–fricative sequence

Allomorphy: the phenomenon that a single morpheme has different realizations depending on its phonological context

Allophonic sound substitution: a sound replacement that maintains word meaning

Alternation: a non-contrastive sound substitution

Anisotropy: variation towards a particular phonetic direction; variation that is radially asymmetric

Anti-formant: a frequency range of reduced energy, often induced by a side cavity

Articulation: relating to the positioning of the organs of the vocal tract

Aspiration: a puff of air, a result of air flowing rapidly through an open glottis, and out of the mouth (or, rarely, the nose)

Assimilation: a process whereby one sound becomes more similar to another (usually neighbouring) sound

Audition: the study of hearing; hearing

Bernoulli Effect: pressure is lower in a moving fluid than in a stationary fluid

Bi-uniqueness: a non-existent linguistic state in which each sound sequence which makes up a word uniquely matches up with a single meaning, and each meaning uniquely matches up with a single sound sequence

Clear 'l': an 'l' sound made with the tongue tip and tongue body placed toward the front of the mouth

Comparative method: a method of linguistic reconstruction in which different, though obviously related, languages are compared. Based on their differences and similarities, we might reconstruct an earlier state of one or more of the languages

Complementary distribution: two (or more) sounds that allophonically alternate are said to be in complementary distribution; also two (or more) sounds that are never found in the same environment, but *don't* alternate

Consonant: a sound made with a closed or comparatively constricted vocal tract.

Contrastive sound substitution: a sound replacement that changes word meaning

Dark 'l': an 'l' sound made with the tongue body pulled toward the back of the mouth

Diachrony: across time; the history of a language
Diphthong: a vowel whose quality changes during its production
Disharmonic: in vowel harmony systems, vowels that do not harmonize, although they might be expected to do so
Exaptation: a feature that evolved for one function, but is functionally harnessed in service to another
Exemplar model: an approach to categorization in which categories emerge from experience with examples or tokens
Formant: a resonant frequency range within the vocal tract, usually associated with resonants
Formant transitions: the dynamic changes in formant frequencies that result from moving the speech organs from one posture to another
Frequency: the number of vibratory cycles per second in a sound wave
Fricative: an obstruent consonant in which the articulators are sufficiently close to produce a turbulent airflow
Function: related to the communication of meaning
Fundamental frequency: the lowest frequency of the vocal folds when they are in vibration; usually corresponds to perceived pitch
Gestalt: a configuration or pattern of elements that functions as a non-decomposable whole
Glottalization: a laryngeal state in which the vocal folds are tightened and pressed together, typically producing intermittent interruptions of glottal airflow
Glottis: the space between the vocal folds
Harmonics: multiples of the fundamental frequency: overtones
Hertz: cycles per second
Homophony: the product of neutralization: two (or more) morphemes or words which, due to alternation, sound the same. Also, any two (or more) words that sound the same
Inaudible release: a stop consonant in which the release of the closure cannot be heard
Internal reconstruction: a method of linguistic reconstruction whereby the sounds in a single language at a single point in time are analysed. Based on how the sounds phonologically interact with each other, we might reconstruct an earlier state of the language
Intervocalic: between vowels; flanked by vowels
Isotropy: variation toward no particular phonetic direction; variation that is radially symmetric
Larynx: the complex of muscle and cartilage that houses the vocal folds
Lateral: a sound made with the tongue tip or tongue body making contact with the roof of the mouth, with one or both sides down, allowing air to stream around the side(s) of the tongue
Lexicalization: diachronic process whereby a morphologically complex word starts to behave like a word composed of a single morpheme
Monophthong: a vowel composed of a single quality
Morpheme: the smallest component of a word that possesses independent meaning

Morphology: the study of word structure; the word-structural properties of a particular language
Nasal formant: a frequency range of increased energy, due to the resonating properties of the larynx-to-nose cavity
Nasals: sounds made with the soft palate lowered, thus connecting the nasal passages to the throat cavity
Nasal zero: an anti-formant due to the mouth cavity connecting to the larynx-to-nose cavity
Neutralizing sound substitution: a sound replacement that eliminates the phonetic distinction between (or among) words
Non-bi-uniqueness: the one-to-many and many-to-one relationship between sound and meaning that characterizes all languages
Obstruent: a consonant in which airflow fully ceases (a stop) or is sufficiently obstructed so that turbulence is generated at the constriction site (a fricative), or a sequenced combination of these (an affricate)
Oral occlusion: a seal in the oral cavity created by two articulators coming together, thus allowing no air to pass; a stop
Orthography: writing systems
Overtones: multiples of the fundamental frequency; harmonics
Palatalization: a synchronic and diachronic process in which a sound comes to involve the tongue body brought toward the hard palate
Palaeophonetics: the study of historical phonetics; how and why sounds change over time
Pattern generalization: the tendency for a pattern to be extended or applied to new cases
Phonetics: the study of the physical properties of linguistic sound systems; the physical properties of the sound system of a particular language
Phonology: the study of the functional properties of linguistic sound systems; the sound system of a particular language; the cognitive organization of a particular linguistic sound system
Pitch: the perceptual correlate of (usually) the fundamental frequency of a sound wave
Place of articulation: the location in the mouth and/or throat of the primary (and sometimes secondary) constriction of two articulators
Prefix: an affix that precedes a root
Probability matching: the phenomenon whereby the variation in a stimulus is proportionally matched in a behavioural response
Prototype model: an approach to categorization in which categories are defined in terms of stable, abstract targets
Reduplication: a morphological operation whereby all or part of a morpheme or word is copied
Relaxed constraints model: an approach to categorization in which constraints on category membership are not so strictly imposed
Resonant: a sound that possesses a harmonic series
Richness of the stimulus: the proposal that children learn the structural properties of language due in part to their vast listening experience
Root: the main morpheme of a word, to which affixes might attach

Sound merger: a historical development whereby the phonetic and phonological distinction between two (or more) sounds is completely eliminated, that is, their categorial distinction is eliminated
Sound substitution: the replacement of one sound with another
Speech community: a group of language users that share a common language
Spirantization: a synchronic alternation whereby a stop alternates with a fricative; a diachronic process whereby a stop evolves into a fricative
Stop: a consonant made with full oral closure, including oral stops (plosives) and nasals
Stress: the rhythmic structure of language, often manifested by alternating degrees of acoustic and/or perceptual prominence of a component (vowel or syllable) of a word
Suffix: an affix that follows the root
Synchrony: at the same time; a contemporary state of a language
Tense 'a': a raised and diphthongized low front vowel found in and around New York
Token: a single instance, a single utterance
Tone: lexically distinctive pitch; changing the tone changes the meaning of a word
Truncation: a morphological process whereby a word is shortened by deleting a portion or portions of the full form
Voiced: a sound made with the vocal folds vibrating
Voiceless: a sound made without the vocal folds vibrating
Vowel: a sound made with a generally open vocal tract
Vowel harmony: a synchronic and diachronic process affecting the words of a language whereby one vowel becomes more similar to another, usually neighbouring, vowel

Index

Akan 101–6, 111–12
allomorphy 24
allophony 9, 18–21, 28, 87–112, 193
'alphabetism' 193, 202–15
alphabets 31, 41, 48 *see also* 'alphabetism'
Altaic 73, 79
alternation 24–8, 50, 62, 68, 84, 104, 182–5
altruism 191, 192, 194–6, 200, 208
American English 159, 167–82, 198
Amharic 203
anisotropy (phonetic) 144, 148, 151, 158, 162–3, 168–70, 177
Arabic 204
audition 8–9, 46–7, 55, 79

Baudouin de Courtenay, Jan 24, 55, 61, 142, 153–4, 186–7
bi–uniqueness 9, 10, 18, 28
Bloch, Bernard 6, 13, 88
Bloomfield, Leonard 78, 186
Bybee, Joan 143, 197, 198, 199

Cantonese 76–7, 79
Caribbean Spanish 125
categorization 95–100
chain shifts 159, 166
Chinese 12, 72–4, 75–8, 93, 206–7 *see also* Cantonese, Mandarin, Taiwanese
Chinese characters 12, 206–7
Chomsky, Noam 192, 210
Chong 79–80
Christianity 207
'closed class' vocabulary 83–4
Comaltepec Chinantec 144–52, 158, 209
comparative method 105, 136, 149, 173, 202
complementary distribution 101–12, 185
consonants 31, 54–5, 72
contrastive sound substitution 5, 9, 10–13, 31–56
Corsican 111, 90–3, 159–67, 193
co–variation (of acoustic cues) 49, 68, 209
Croatian 207
Cyrillic 204, 207

Darwin, Charles 144, 186, 219
Devanagari 207
diachrony 69, 84, 120, 136–43, 177–82, 193, 194, 195, 201, 202, 215
dispersion/symmetry (acoustic) 126–35, 159, 166, 173, 194
Duanmu, San 77
Dutch 63, 68

ease of perception 194–6
ease of production 194, 196–200

English 88–90, 111, 127, 197 *see also* American English, New York English
evolution (of species) 66, 69, 73, 106, 121–2, 141, 186, 195, 196, 218
exaptation 138, 174
exemplar model 116–20, 123–6, 131, 138, 160, 174, 177–82, 195

Finnish 51–3, 80, 126
formants (and formant transitions) 38, 39, 42–8, 52, 62–6, 67, 68, 87, 88, 89, 92, 102, 114, 126, 127, 137, 171, 211, 213
French 78
frequency (of usage) 68, 100, 143, 176, 197–200
fundamental frequency 35, 36

generative phonology 210
German 197
Germanic 172, 173
Gestalts 25, 39, 49, 69, 105, 209
Gould, Stephen Jay 189
Greek 203, 204
Gurevich, Naomi 165
Gussenhoven, Carlos 212

Hale, Mark 198, 199
Halle, Morris 192, 210
hanyu pinyin 12
harmonics 34–8, 46
Hebrew 204, 207
Hinduism 207
Hockett, Charles 100, 185
Hovland, Carl 96, 99, 100, 111
Hungarian 80–4, 126, 197, 209
Hyman, Larry M. 211

Indo–European 172, 173, 204
intention (in spoken language) 73, 76–7, 80, 192, 193, 199, 215
internal reconstruction 105, 136, 149, 172, 180, 202
intuitions (linguistic) 6, 10–11, 13, 14, 28, 55, 89, 159, 193, 207, 208
irregular forms 100, 106
isotropy (phonetic) 144, 158, 163–7, 170–2

Jacobs, Haike 212
Japanese 204–6
Jenkins, Herbert 96, 99, 100, 111
Judaism 207

Kabbalah 207
Kager, René 213, 214
Kenstowicz, Michael 212

Kingston, John 194, 195, 196, 200, 201
Kirchner, Robert 200, 201, 202
Kisseberth, Charles 212
Koran 207
Korean 69–75, 79, 80
Kruszewski, Mikołaj 55, 117, 124, 201

Labov, William 62, 123–4, 126, 177
Ladefoged, Peter 33, 165
Latin 72, 204, 207
'laziness' 165, 200–2, 208
lexicalization 110
Lombard Effect 191, 192, 199
Lombard, Etienne 191

Mandarin 12, 76–7
Martinet, André 115
merger 76, 82, 178, 182
Middle English 107–8
misinterpretation (of strays) 129–32
Mongolian 73
Mon–Khmer 79–80

nasal assimilation 61–9
nasalized vowels 45, 47, 48, 125, 194, 208, 209, 213
Nasal consonants 41–50, 61–9
natural selection 128
Naturalness (in phonetics and phonology) 151, 152, 153, 162, 163, 166, 167, 167, 169, 172, 173, 174, 186, 201
neutralizing sound substitution 9, 13–18, 28, 26, 61–85, 131
New York English 106–11, 112, 184

Old Bulgarian 207
'open class' vocabulary 83–4
orthography 11, 203–15 *see also* alphabets
Otomanguean 135, 144

Pahauh Hmong 207
paleophonetics 103, 111, 147, 183
pattern generalization/regularization 68, 72, 106, 149, 151, 166, 169, 197
Paul, Hermann 55, 116–17, 118, 124, 196, 202,
phonemes 16, 192, 199, 200, 201 *see also* 'alphabetism', 'phonemism'
'phonemism' 193, 202–15
phonologization 214
pitch 36, 146
probability matching 120–35, 138–43 160, 167, 174, 177–82, 195, 198, 199
prototype model 116–20, 123–6

reduplication 103, 112
relaxed constraints model 116–20, 123–6
release (in stops) 19, 20, 31–3, 40, 51, 55, 69–76, 79–80, 91, 102, 122, 136–7, 146, 162, 168, 170, 171, 175, 181, 182
religion 207
Rensch, Calvin 149
'richness of the stimulus' hypothesis 23, 25, 26

Sanskrit 176, 204, 207
Sapir, Edward 15–18, 32, 192
Sarcee 15–18
Schane, Sanford 210
Schuchardt, Hugo 143, 197, 198, 199
selfishness 191, 200–2, 208
self–organization 29, 116–20, 132, 186, 194
Semitic 203, 204
Serbian 207
Shepard, Roger 96, 99, 100, 111
Shong Lue Yang 207
similarity (phonetic) 27, 29, 87–8, 92–3, 94, 95–100, 103, 111, 182, 183
simplification (of speech) 197–200
Sino–Korean 73–6
sound change 62, 65, 68, 99, 102, 104, 105, 124, 133, 141, 142, 153, 158, 210
Spanish 127, 129, 197
spirantization 164–7, 192, 201, 208
St. Cyril 207
St. Methodius 207
stops 31–41, 69–80, 123, 159–67, 167–82
stray tokens 129–35, 138, 142, 143, 178, 180, 183
stress 171–2, 175–6, 182
support (semantic) 177, 181
syllabary 204
synchrony 69, 78, 84, 149, 193, 195–6, 201, 202, 215

Taiwanese 93–5, 98, 100, 111
tense 'a' (in New York) 106–11
tone 15, 93–5, 142, 144–52, 209
Trager, George L. 6, 13, 88
Trique 135–43, 158
Trubetskoy, Nikolai 215
truncation 109–11, 112
Tungusic 73
Turkic 73
Twadell, William Freeman 16–17

variation (and gradience) 77–8, 114–54, 163, 182,
voice level 191, 199
voicing 36, 37, 42, 71, 90–3, 95, 107, 122–3, 159–82, 201
vowel harmony 50–3, 80–4, 136, 158, 209
vowels 31, 55, 72

Whitney, John 15, 16, 17, 18, 192

Yiddish 8, 104

Lightning Source UK Ltd.
Milton Keynes UK
UKOW07f0833100115

244286UK00003B/33/P